SHAI
BREATHWORK

"Linda Star Wolf has written a landmark book describing her incredible healing and transformational process. *Shamanic Breathwork* is a must for transpersonal therapists who truly desire to help people move through the middle toward higher consciousness, peace, and a healthy planet."

Wendyne Limber, author of *Imagine Recovery*
and creator of the Imagination Process

"*Shamanic Breathwork* provides readers with a powerful process that heals us both individually and collectively as citizens of Planet Earth. Linda Star Wolf is one of those rare transformers whose visions and words weave their way into the depths of our psyches and bring us out the other side empowered and deeply connected to our inner guidance and soul's path."

Judith Corvin-Blackburn, author of
Journey to Wholeness* and *Empowering the Spirit

"*Shamanic Breathwork* will help you use the power of the breath to access 'the shaman within' and activate your soul's purpose. I highly recommend this practical guide for turning the ideal into the real deal."

Steve Bhaerman, author of *Driving Your Own Karma*
and coauthor of *Spontaneous Evolution: Our*
Positive Future and How to Get There from Here

"The Shamanic Breathwork practice is the perfect way to journey beyond the limits of the self. I am very happy to see a book about breathwork from the shamanic perspective."

Leonard D. Orr, author of *Breaking the Death Habit:*
***The Science of Everlasting Life* and founder of**
Rebirthing Breathwork International

"Shamanic Breathwork is a Living Way to personal truth and freedom. We are not the 'self,' we are the one experiencing the 'self,' and *Shamanic Breathwork* brings that experience to the forefront of our consciousness. With love, light, and creativity, Linda Star Wolf offers others the power and grace of the Shamanic Breathwork practices."

Lee R. McCormick, author of
The Spirit Recovery Meditation Journal

"The Shamanic Breathwork process of personal and planetary transformation is Linda Star Wolf's gift to the generations to come. She honors the ancestors as she shares a new form of wholeness and healing with all who take this breath of life into their hearts.

Rev. Charla J. Hermann, author of
The Blue Star Portal of Transformation

"In *Shamanic Breathwork*, Linda Star Wolf shares the process that has helped so many to find the healing they were desperately seeking. I know from personal experience that the breathwork process is indeed life changing, and I endorse both the process and this wonderful book.

Cindy Henson, LCDC, ADCII, former co-owner and
program director of Shades of Hope Treatment Center

"In these times of fast-moving change, Linda Star Wolf teaches us how to connect with our internal guidance and inborn ability to heal, spiritually and psychologically. She brings traditional shamanic consciousness into the 21st century in a form accessible to anyone with the courage to explore self-awareness."

Karen Craft, author of *The Cosmic Purr:*
Inspiration for Animal Lovers

"*Shamanic Breathwork* reclaims and activates the Emotional Body, which is important because it is the seat of our power, the engine of manifestation.

Baba Dez Nichols, author of *Sacred Sexual Healing:*
The Shaman Method of Sex Magic

"*Shamanic Breathwork* will give you insight into the world of the shaman and help you connect with your own healing wisdom."

Lee Lipsenthal, M.D., ABIHM, founder of
Finding Balance in a Medical Life

"Linda Star Wolf brings great integrity, love, experience, wisdom, and, yes, even magic to her life's work. Her Shamanic Breathwork process brings you into right relationship with yourself and the world around you, shifting you into a new dimension of emotional, spiritual, and physical centeredness. I wholeheartedly recommend Shamanic Breathwork to anyone looking for lasting health and vitality in their life."

Molly M. Roberts, M.D., coauthor of
Blackwell Complementary and Alternative Medicine

*To: Ginger + Dirk
Thank you for breathing.
In love
Star Wolf*

SHAMANIC BREATHWORK

JOURNEYING BEYOND THE LIMITS OF THE SELF

LINDA STAR WOLF

Bear & Company
Rochester, Vermont • Toronto, Canada

Bear & Company
One Park Street
Rochester, Vermont 05767
www.BearandCompanyBooks.com

Bear & Company is a division of Inner Traditions International

Library of Congress Cataloging-in-Publication Data
Wolf, Linda Star.
  Shamanic breathwork : journeying beyond the limits of the self / Linda Star Wolf.
    p. cm.
  Includes bibliographical references and index.
  Summary: "Utilizing the healing power of breath to change consciousness"—Provided by publisher.
  ISBN 978-1-59143-106-0 (pbk.)
  1. Shamanism. 2. Breathing exercises. 3. Respiration—Religious aspects.
  4. Spiritual life. 5. Spiritual healing. I. Title.
  BF1621.W65 2009
  299'.93—dc22

                                                                    2009025922

Printed and bound in the United States by Lake Book Manufacturing

10   9   8   7   6   5   4   3   2   1

Text design and layout by Virginia Scott Bowman
This book was typeset in Garamond Premier Pro with Gill Sans as the display typeface

The poem "Change" is reprinted here with the kind permission of Ellen Bass.

The poem "Hieroglyphic Stairway" is reprinted here with the kind permission of Drew Dellinger, from his book *Love Letter to the Milky Way*.

"I Live My Life in Growing Orbits" by Rainer Maria Rilke reprinted from *Selected Poems of Rainer Maria Rilke*, Harper & Row Publishers, New York, 1981. Translation ©1981, Robert Bly. Used with his kind permission.

Photos for color plates 13–26 are reprinted here with the kind permission of Pat Cummins.

The tracks on the accompanying CD are used with the kind permission of SoulFood Music. See page 254 for more information.

*This book is dedicated to
the shaman within us all . . .
and to Casey, who embodies the spirit
of the Aquarian shaman.*

Contents

FOREWORD

I first met Linda Star Wolf over the Internet in 2002. I suppose it's fairly common to meet people over the Internet, however, when I initially contacted her, it was the first time I had reached out to someone electronically based on the strength of a newsletter. When I read her newsletter I thought: *I wish I had written that.* . . . It was like reading myself, and I wanted to know where that voice had come from.

Star Wolf had a center at that time in Fairfax, California, so I called to make a connection and see if I could teach there. She happened to be coming up to Oregon for an event in Portland, so I boldly invited her to stop in Eugene, where I lived, and spend the night. She and her husband, Brad Collins, took the chance and became enchanted; first with my garden, second with Normandi Ellis when I read to them a chapter from *Awakening Osiris* (Normandi's exquisite translation of *The Egyptian Book of the Dead),* and eventually, with me and my work. Star Wolf returned two weeks later to take the Egyptian Mysteries retreat seminar, Becoming An Oracle, with Normandi and me.

The rest, as they say, is history.

At our workshop, Star Wolf showed herself to be a true master of the cycles of shamanic death and rebirth; her oracle burst forth from the depths of her being in an intense and spontaneous rebirthing experience that remains engraved in the memory of her midwives and our garden. Although Star Wolf is a natural-born visionary, this experience prompted her to commit more fully than ever before to the supersensitive part of her being, that part that taps directly into her sublime divinity.

Thus the Star was born, again.

Shortly after we connected, Star Wolf moved her Venus Rising Institute for Shamanic Healing Arts to North Carolina and developed a conscious community. It was not long before I visited Venus Rising at Isis Cove and had the honor of participating in, and observing first-hand, the Shamanic Breathwork process. I was especially impressed with the integrity of the work, and the care that was taken with each and every individual who participated. This was very different from my first experiences with breathwork back in the days. . . .

It was in the early '70s, on stage at a Grateful Dead concert, that I first became aware of conscious breathing. The legendary Beat poet Allen Ginsburg was an honored guest, and I clearly remember him exhorting us to breathe with the music. I cannot remember his original intention, however, the power of the moment was indelible. (It was also one of the first instances I can remember of being turned on to a Tibetan Buddhist practice.)

Although conscious breathing as a spiritual practice has been employed throughout history in both the East and West, Star Wolf's Shamanic Breathwork process is primarily rooted in two important streams of previous research: Rebirthing and Holotropic Breathwork, both of which focus on the concentrated use of the breath to achieve healing and wholeness.

Leonard Orr is considered by many to be the father of the rebirthing movement; he attracted the attention of the world in the '70s and '80s as a result of his groundbreaking rebirthing research. Co-authored with Sondra Ray, *Rebirthing the New Age* was published in 1983 and remains a classic in the field.

In the 1980s I found myself studying rebirthing as part of a healing program. Although my path as a healer would ultimately take me in a different direction, the powerful experiences and lessons learned at that time are still with me. Co-journeying with another individual is part of rebirthing and most often a part of the Shamanic Breathwork process. As I delved into rebirthing, it became clear to me just how much responsibility was required to sit for another person and hold sacred space for them throughout the process, and how much trust it required to relinquish oneself completely while being held throughout a full rebirth session.

I can still remember the ether-like smell of the anesthesia that my mother took during my actual birth—it was released from my body during a particularly strong session. Upon completing a rebirthing session, I have always felt cleansed, purified, renewed, and exhilarated, with the keen sensitivities of a newborn.

A story that impressed me deeply was the profound experience related by a close friend whom I turned on to rebirthing: She went back in time beyond her birth, to her conception, and could even perceive details of the room where the conception happened. She recognized the room, however, this posed a problem for her. The room she saw in her vision was not the bedroom of her parents, but that of one of her father's best friends. (Whoops!) She was quite shaken by her experience, and eventually decided to tell her mother what she had visioned. After a rather lengthy pause, her mother quietly responded, "I recommend you keep on doing whatever it is that you are doing."

The second important stream of transpersonal/spiritual research that evolved independently around the same time was developed by Stanislav and Christina Grof. Stanislav Grof, M.D., Ph.D., had been at the forefront of psychedelic research for decades when he and Christina realized that conscious breathing could be a catalyst for deep psychotherapeutic healing without the risks inherent in the psychedelic experience. Their healing modality, known as Holotropic Breathwork, continues to generate worldwide interest because it enables people to safely explore non-ordinary states for inner healing and transformation.

Grof anticipated a natural evolution of breathwork and indeed, over the years various practitioners, including one of Star Wolf's main teachers Jacquelyn Small, a modern-day practical mystic and the founding director of the Eupsychia Institute, delved deeply and discovered powerful techniques, procedures, and adaptations that provide a strong link between Dr. Grof's work and the truly extraordinary Shamanic Breathwork process that Linda Star Wolf has created.

By articulating her work in the language and dimensions of shamanism, Star Wolf has taken breathwork to new realms of consciousness. Her personal journey as a "walker between the worlds" has prepared her to be the worthy midwife of this next-generational form. The book you have picked up and are about to read will give you much more than basic information about Shamanic Breathwork and the path Star Wolf took to become the spiritual teacher/leader that she is.

It also includes moving stories of transformation from those who have taken part in the Shamanic Breathwork process, and information about other programs offered by Star Wolf and her stellar staff at Venus Rising. For those who are unable to travel to attend her programs, there is a chapter of instruction on how to safely journey through a Shamanic Breathwork session. (Pay particular attention to what Star Wolf writes about music and its essential part in the process. Evocative music enhances the experience, and Star Wolf has exquisite taste in this department.)

Any kind of transpersonal work usually involves meeting one's shadow, and Shamanic Breathwork is no exception. Star Wolf has danced with the shadow for most of her life and is well qualified to prepare you to meet yours. The Thirty Shamanic Questions included in the book are designed to keep you awake and alert while accelerating your process of self-discovery and transformation.

Star Wolf is devoted to helping others reclaim their wholeness, and to overcoming addictions—whether they be to substances or to old habit patterns and characteristics that keep us from becoming whole and fulfilling our sacred purpose. Be prepared. You are about to meet and embrace the wholeness of you. I think you will delight in the experience.

NICKI SCULLY

Nicki Scully has been teaching healing and shamanic arts and the Egypitan Mysteries since 1983, when she began teaching "Egyptian Huna" as initially taught to her by Nadia Eagles. For the next twenty years she developed, practiced, researched, and taught alchemical healing before publishing her findings. She is a lineage holder in the Hermetic Tradition of Thoth and maintains the Lyceum of Shamanic Egypt. She is ordained as a priestess of Hathor by Lady Olivia Robertson, cofounder of the Fellowship of Isis. In the late 1980s, Nicki founded Shamanic Journeys, Ltd., and has been guiding inner journeys and spiritual pilgrimages to Egypt, Peru, Greece, and many other sacred sites. Nicki's most recently released work is a seven-CD set called *Becoming an Oracle, Connecting to the Divine Source for Information and Healing.* Her published books include *The Anubis Oracle* and *Shamanic Mysteries of Egypt,* both co-authored with Linda Star Wolf, *Alchemical Healing,* and *Power Animal Meditations.*

ACKNOWLEDGMENTS

. . . .

In some ways it would be so much easier to simply say thank you to all those who have supported me and my journey of birthing this book into being. I do not want to leave anyone out in these acknowledgments, since there have been many along the way whose incredible spirits have touched my spirit with their own.

I will make a humble attempt to express my gratitude to some of you by name and to others in a more general way, but know that I am deeply grateful to all those who have crossed my path in a shamanic way, "the light, the dark, no difference;" and that this book is born, at least in part, because of the shared space, time, energy, and experiences between us.

I want to begin my acknowledgments by expressing my deepest gratitude to Jacquelyn Small, my incredible breathwork, psychospiritual mentor and friend of many years at Eupsychia Institute: You pointed the way back home, Jacquie Sue. Gratitude to the peace elders who have gone before us and whose lives have been dedicated models for how to live in dignity and trust on this blessed planet. Thank you, Grandmother Twylah Nitsch, Mammy and Pappy Jones, Grandma and Grandpa Finley. Thank you to Daniel Giamario, Eric Botner, Jeremiah Abrams, Nita Gage, Lisa Gordon, Janet Cooper, Anyaa McAndrew, Eric Gonzales, the Good Luck Soul Group, and the Wood Acre Spirit House for being important influences in the birthing of Venus Rising Institute for Shamanic Healing Arts in the beginning years.

Thank you, Nita and Mary Lou Masko, for revisioning the Twelve Steps for Shamanic Transformation and supporting the birth of Isis

Cove. Thank you to the Portland "Love Dogs" and Jeff Berger for being the inspiration for the original SHIP program, and to all those intrepid shamanic souls who have passed through the Shamanic Breathwork portals of healing and training with Venus Rising.

Thank you, Barb Westover, for inspiring the birth of Shamanic Breathwork Reiki with your healing touch. Thank you to the Wild Wolf Women's breathwork group in Kentucky, and the Wild Women and Road Kill Group in Fairfax, California, for breathing into wholeness. More recently, my deepest gratitude goes to my incredible soul family, friends, and Venus Rising staff members who live in the magical Blue Mountains of western North Carolina at the Isis Cove Community and Retreat Center. Thank you, Ruby Falconer, Kathy Morrison, Windraven, Sarah Jane, and Judy Red Hawk for your heartfelt work and service to Venus Rising, and for loving me. Deep gratitude to our Venus Rising development team members, including Bonnie Rubenstein, Megan Beachler, and Peter Weiler.

Thanks to Paula Bravehart, Gary Stamper, Dennis and Judith Corvin-Blackburn, Thea Stacey, Chuck Willhide, Steve Irestone, Maria and Bunny, Bob Masach, Karen Smith, and Ryan Brooks for being wonderful community members. Thank you to the Aquarian Wise Wolf Women's Council founding members: Amai Myrna, Clarice Munchus, Judith Corvin-Blackburn, Reverend Charla Jo Hermann, Anyaa McAndrew, Bonnie Rubenstein, and Shari Starrfire Lowe. Thank you to my Blue Star Sisters for your never-ending love and support for me, each other, and the blue star energies, and many thanks to Sun Lion, Paul Henderson, and Thad Hollis.

Thank you, Laura Prana Wolf, for your amazing spirit and support as my personal assistant and PR manager. Thank you, Tirrell Magnuson, for being my special "medicine woman" and helping to amp up my energy level to meet all that is required of me during these high energy times. Thanks to all my favorite massage and body workers: Windraven, Sarah Jane, Barb Westover, Melanie Leithauser, and Andrea Ford, for the extra loving touch. Kelly Timco, thank you for assisting Brad and keeping his office on track.

Thanks to Lesley Fouche for introducing me to the exciting networking world of Facebook and creating the virtual shamanic community. Thank you, Judy Red Hawk, for the Shamanic Shakti Art Process. Thank you to all those ordained with the Shamanic Ministers Global Network, especially those who are becoming our first outreach congregations around the country: Deb Irestone, Sophia Savory, Barb Westover, Wendyne Limber, and Jeri Birdsall. Molly Roberts, thank you and Bruce for keeping the faith. Thank you to the board for the new Venus Rising University, especially Marla Frantum. Sara and Terry Curran, thank you for your support on many levels and for being co-visionaries in the future development of Dove Mountain.

Thank you to all the Soul Recovery Group and your valuable contributions to the chapter on soul recovery, and to Pat Cummins for your wonderful "eye" and gifted photography throughout this book.

Thanks to my wonderful family—to Mom and Dad Finley for "seeing me"; and to my son, Casey Piscitelli, for being such a huge support in the original first edits and for honest feedback. Thank you to my husband, Brad, for seeing me through three books in four years and for your endless support in every area of our life together—you are the absolute best; and to my beautiful grandchildren—Aidan, Cian, and Anthony—for being motivating forces in my life to bring the healing gift of Shamanic Breathwork to the world.

Nicki Scully, thank you for being a powerful catalyst in my life and for writing the foreword to this book. I am grateful for all I have learned from you and our cocreations with other projects.

Thank you to all the highly skilled and wonderful staff at Inner Traditions • Bear & Company, especially Jon Graham for your encouragement early on by saying "this book has feet" and most especially to the best editor in the whole world, Anne Dillon, for your tireless, patient faith in me and constant excitement and support for the birth of this Shamanic Breathwork manuscript.

IN LOVING SERVICE TO THE ONE SOURCE,

LINDA STAR WOLF

Hieroglyphic Stairway

it's 3:23 in the morning
and I'm awake
because my great-great-grandchildren
won't let me sleep
my great-great-grandchildren
ask me in dreams
what did you do while the planet was plundered?
what did you do when the earth was unraveling?

surely you did something
when the seasons started failing

as the mammals, reptiles, birds were all dying

did you fill the streets with protest
when democracy was stolen?

what did you do
once
you
knew?

I'm riding home on the Colma train
I've got the voice of the Milky Way in my dreams

I have teams of scientists
feeding me data daily
and pleading I immediately
turn it into poetry

I want just this consciousness reached
by people in range of secret frequencies
contained in my speech

I am the desirous earth
equidistant to the underworld
and the flesh of the stars

I am everything already lost

the moment the universe turns transparent
and all the light shoots through the cosmos

I use words to instigate silence

I'm a hieroglyphic stairway
in a buried Mayan city
suddenly exposed by a hurricane

a satellite circling earth
finding dinosaur bones
in the Gobi desert
I am telescopes that see back in time

I am the precession of the equinoxes,
the magnetism of the spiraling sea

I'm riding home on the Colma train
with the voice of the Milky Way in my dreams

I am myths where violets blossom from blood
like dying and rising gods

I'm the boundary of time
soul encountering soul
and tongues of fire

it's 3:23 in the morning
and I can't sleep
because my great-great-grandchildren
ask me in dreams
what did you do while the earth was unraveling?

I want just this consciousness reached
by people in range of secret frequencies
contained in my speech

DREW DELLINGER

Introduction

By picking up and reading this book you have opened a shamanic portal, which will offer you the amazing opportunity to deepen your soul's journey. If you can believe that none of us are here on earth by accident, then we can only suppose that we must be here on purpose. The divine appointment for each soul's awakening is encoded within the matrix of our spiritual essence. Each of us has a wise one within who remembers the way back to wholeness and our life's sacred purpose. This wholeness is who we really are and is right beneath our very own nose!

Shamanic Breathwork is a highly experiential process that leads us onto the path of direct experience. On the path we encounter and recover lost soul parts, while also restoring our true spiritual essence of higher love, wisdom, and power. Shamanic Breathwork creates an opening through a magical inner doorway into the innate, perennial wisdom lying dormant within our DNA. I often refer to this inner healer and wisdom-keeper as "the shaman within." When we awaken the shaman within, we begin to walk and act in empowered ways in the world.

Through the healing power of the breath, our ego finds its appropriate place in our psyches, and the inner voice of spirit returns and reclaims its rightful reign in our daily lives. I have personally experienced (and witnessed in countless others) the shift and transformation from ego agenda to spiritual essence through the Shamanic Breathwork journey.

We are all here on a soul mission, but few of us, it seems, are aware of that mission. This book is an introduction to Shamanic Breathwork, which is the integration of other forms of breathwork with universal shamanic principles and psychospiritual teachings. It is written with the intention of assisting in the reawakening of the essential self, which is at the very core of our true being. It is said that we are spiritual beings having a human experience. Our true soul powers lie hidden from our egoic states of consciousness, waiting to be retrieved and embodied so that we may offer them as gifts—not only to ourselves but also to the world around us as an integral part of our soul purpose during this earth walk.

If you are seeking a more fulfilling way to be on this planet and longing for a soulful path of living, the Shamanic Breathwork process can guide you there. By using your breath in a powerful and transformative way, you will be able to move beyond the ego long enough to reach your core self and engage in a highly intuitive connection to your inner teacher, or higher self, also known as your wisdom keeper.

This inner place of wisdom has all the solutions, guidance, and answers that cannot be found anywhere else but within your own inner world. There are numerous wonderful methods and pathways that will enable you to encounter higher states of being; however, the Shamanic Breathwork process is unique. In my many years of working as an agent of change for both myself and others, I have not encountered anything as informative, magical, and transformational as the Shamanic Breathwork process.

If you have been searching without finding answers, perhaps Shamanic Breathwork will become an ally and useful tool for transformation in your life. In our programs and workshops at the Venus Rising Institute for Shamanic Healing Arts, we often see people who have exhausted all sorts of traditional therapies and alternative methods of healing. They are frequently frustrated, disillusioned, and disappointed at their prior attempts to transform old addictive patterns of dysfunction and disease. We also attract many spiritually minded seekers who have followed one or more spiritual paths, yet still feel a kind of emptiness and longing to connect on a deeper level with the sacredness of their lives, personal relationships, and sacred soul purpose.

I have spent more than thirty years assisting others in the process of change, and throughout this time I have learned that there is a sacred formula for healing and transforming one's life. The sacred formula consists of engaging the *whole* person rather than just certain limited aspects. The disciplines of spirituality and psychology have both been remiss in addressing only fragments of the person seeking help. I have found that the key to authentic healing and lasting transformation at a deep core level requires one to enter into a more soulful journey that includes and unifies the physical body, mind, heart, soul, and spirit.

I have coined the phrase "shamanic-psychospiritual experience" to signify the sacred union between all parts of our many selves. By doing shamanic-psychospiritual work, which integrates all of our parts in all realms, we are able to move forward and become practical shamans, or mystics, in our everyday lives. In this way we are both grounded in the earth and uplifted into the cosmic realms of spirit. This unification of the whole person results in an embodiment that gives us the strength and courage to fulfill our capacity as wise beings. Finally we have the felt sense and real knowing that our inner and outer worlds are beginning to match up with each other. In other words, we are walking our talk and becoming the change we have sought outside of ourselves in the world around us. How empowering to learn (or, perhaps, remember) that we hold the key to our own personal healing and spiritual seeking.

We live in shamanic times; therefore, we need shamanic answers. Shamanic times are times of extreme and rapid change. I refer to these cycles of change as symbolic death and rebirth experiences that create dramatic shifts in the world around us. At this very moment in history we are all witnessing the end of an old paradigm and the birth of a new way of being. There is a spiritual maxim: "As within, so without; as above, so below." We need to understand that our outer world is only a manifestation of the inner visions and processes we are experiencing.

The Shamanic Breathwork process is a powerful shamanic-psychospiritual tool that greatly assists in changing the inner landscape. In this work, shamanic counselors and facilitators lovingly assist people (as midwives do) through sequences of symbolic death and rebirth that result in major life transformations. We utilize psychological, physical, and spiritual portals to create an alchemical opening and shift in the body, psyche, and spirit. If you are doing only spiritual work without dealing with the psychological and human parts of yourself, you may find yourself using your higher self to disassociate and bypass your humanity. In some circles this is referred to as being in spiritual bypass.* The shamanic being within you instinctively knows how to walk between the very different worlds of your ego, soul, and spirit.

Within the Shamanic Breathwork process lives a map of alchemical transformation and shamanic consciousness that is comprised of the Five Cycles of Shamanic Consciousness. This alchemical map of transformation provides a practical guide for change, both in and out of the actual breathwork experience itself. The five cycles show us how to move from ego agenda to soul purpose in a grounded way. Today, many of us are called to enter the world of shamanic consciousness. We are seeking a consciousness born of integrity, love, and introspection, and we have a burning desire for healing and integration to occur among all cultures and races. When we are truly awake, our actions begin to emanate from our soul's purpose, rather than from our ego's purpose. Our souls inherently know the path to the best and highest good for all involved, while our egos often seek only safety.

The ego is protective of the little self and is neither interested in, nor capable of, seeing the whole of our inner and outer landscapes. The soul, however, sees and knows the whole. Shamanic Breathwork is not only about the spiritual paths and psychological teachings of the past, but also about the new consciousness toward which we are moving. The

---

*Spiritual bypass is a concept developed and coined by John Welwood, a California psychologist.

well-known medical symbol, the caduceus of two intertwined snakes, is a powerful shamanic representation of these two psychospiritual realms—the energy from above informing us of spiritual purpose, and our human selves opening to receive the higher energies pouring into physical form.

As with all alchemical processes, one must have a strong container, or vessel, in which to transform. In alchemy, the first thing required is the pot, the cauldron, or the vessel. This container begins with an open heart and mind, sitting within an open and grounded body. The heart womb is an ancient symbol of an alchemical vessel for transformation. In order for the heart to be that vessel, it must be capable of receiving the outpouring of uplifting energies from above through the upper chakras, and grounding energies through the lower chakras. One must first build the solid form, or human temple, in order to become an embodied spirit.

Authentic spirituality is fluid, always evolving to the next level; it is not written in stone or dogmatic in nature. There are numerous paths to transformation, enlightenment, and healing. The way of the shamanic warrior means learning how to stalk ourselves by developing the ongoing ability to observe our thoughts and actions from an objective perspective, and to make the necessary shifts in consciousness. This allows us to continually attune to our divine mission—what we came here to be and to experience.

By engaging in conscious dialogue with others and with ourselves, and communing with the Divine, we raise planetary consciousness, as well as our own. Rather than merely complain about, or ignore, the social, political, and spiritual landscapes of the world, it is essential to engage in rigorous self-inquiry. Love and wisdom are at the core of our essence, and there is more than enough to heal ourselves along with the world. When the Beatles sang, "All you need is love," they were correct (with the proviso that we consider "love" as a verb). Love, in this case, equals consciousness and the healing of our own wounds. We cannot take others to where we ourselves have been unwilling to go.

The shaman, a quintessential figure in numerous cultures, is often viewed as the medicine man or woman and wisdom keeper of the tribe. In the past (and in some remote areas of the world still), the shaman was sought out much as a physician, counselor, or minister is today. In ancient shamanic traditions, healers (shamans) attempted to restore balance to others by performing sacred rites or ceremonies that usually included prayers, songs, chants, and rituals. They invoked power animals, spirit guides, and allies for assistance in journeying to other realms in search of healing and wisdom for those in need.

The shaman has long been the archetypal image of one who knows how to use higher love and wisdom to navigate between the worlds of matter and spirit. Shamans are shape-shifters who know how to open to bigger energies in the cosmos, find larger answers to problems and challenges, and bring healing to themselves and their communities.

In traditional shamanism, the shaman is sometimes referred to as the wounded healer—one who has survived a number of trials and initiations (sometimes even near-death experiences) and returned to share the teaching, healing, and wisdom gained from those experiences. Intimately connected to the elements, the cycles of change, the spirit world, and the earth, the shaman knows that we are all multidimensional beings living simultaneously on many planes of existence.

Chanting, praying, dancing, singing, smudging, and playing musical instruments, such as drums and rattles, help to create a ceremonial setting and an altered state of consciousness in shamanic ritual. In these highly charged states of non-ordinary consciousness, healing takes place beyond the brain, beyond ordinary consciousness as we know it. In these altered states of consciousness, the waking and observing ego steps aside to allow deeper spirit to come forth and heal us, those around us, and planetary consciousness.

Sometimes a shaman is called a "spirit lawyer"—one who negotiates with the spirit guides of another for the return of parts of a soul. At other times the shaman may need to perform a soul extraction to assist an individual in releasing some form of trapped negative energy.

For many tribes the shaman is traditionally the guide who assists others in discovering their wholeness and healing. Knowing that all healing has its origins in the spiritual realms, and that without Divine intervention true healing does not occur, shamanic healers feel compelled to heal and to help others to heal as well, whether on the physical, mental, emotional, or spiritual plane.

They were, and are, essential spiritual guides who teach tribe members how to die consciously and rebirth themselves into a greater reality. The shaman innately understands that we continuously move between cycles of death and rebirth. More than just physically dying, we continually die to old ways of being that no longer serve the path of love and wisdom, and are born into new ways of spirit and consciousness. The ancient shamanic symbol of the serpent is a perfect visual representation of the shamanic alchemical process of learning to shed our skin, die to our smaller selves, and be born into a greater self. It's also similar to the caterpillar that wraps itself in a cocoon, dissolving its own body and emerging as a new butterfly.

Human beings could learn much about proactive transformational processes from the ancient and modern shamanic traditions. It is my spiritual belief that we need to learn how to consciously cocreate our shamanic death and rebirth experiences. Taking cues from our inner shaman we would, much like the caterpillar, volunteer to dissolve and grow wings when the time is right. We are all on some level seeking this depth of awareness and transformation.

The processes I describe in this book provide an opportunity to understand and access the part of ourselves that knows, remembers, and can tap into universal truth, love, and wisdom. The Shamanic Breathwork process allows us to dialogue and connect with the archetypes that are the psychic blueprints of creation. They exist in a pure state as an ideal. While we may not be able to reach that state of perfection in this physical form, we can certainly progress toward that end. We are learning to align our human will with these higher energies. Just as we are connected to the natural world, from a shamanic perspective, we are also connected to the supernatural spirit world that is beyond the physical.

Tragedy is evident around us all the time. Rather than feel so overwhelmed that we become apathetic and dissociate from the dark aspects of society, tragedies might instead serve as a catalyst to help raise the consciousness of our planet. If we believe we can make a difference, it will be so. The answer lies in discovering our unique roles. Here on earth we do not have to do anyone else's part, or live up to others' expectations. Our true spiritual path is to awaken the shaman within, who will guide us to our sacred purpose.

The Shamanic Breathwork process differs from many New Age and modern-day shamanic processes in that it does not focus on journeying out of body; or even, necessarily, on discovering our spiritual allies and animal totems. This awareness can, and does, occur in breathwork journeys, but is not the specific purpose. One of the primary purposes of the Shamanic Breathwork process is to enliven the journeyer's awareness and ability to remove waking-life obstacles and embrace her soulful and sacred purpose.

Venus Rising is committed to bringing the Shamanic Breathwork process and other shamanic-psychospiritual teaching and healing modalities to the world. It is Aquarian in nature, which essentially means we believe that although teachers, shamans, healers, and gurus may be wonderful guides along the path to spiritual awareness, true healing is found through one's own direct soul experience. The Piscean Age (age of the disciple) is ending as the age of Aquarius (embodiment of spirit) is being born.

The Shamanic Breathwork process can be done in a group or alone. Both of these options are addressed in this volume, and at the end of the book are abundant follow-up suggestions for continuing to embody shamanic consciousness in everyday life. We are all being called to embody the shamanic spirit within ourselves. Our own transformations can be a powerful catalyst for others to take the journey to wholeness as well. The healing changes that we wish to see in the world around us will magnify and take quantum leaps if those of us who feel called to transform will commit to doing our parts.

More than twenty-six years ago, when I was a counselor working in the field of mental health, I realized that I was addicted to numerous self-defeating patterns hidden even to myself. My addiction to alcohol had brought me to my knees, and I had hit what Alcoholics Anonymous refers to as an "emotional bottom" of despair and hopelessness. Although I considered myself a spiritually aware person and was professionally trained to help others heal their mental health problems, in many ways I was naive in the ways of true healing. I was functioning at a low level of awareness in disembodied consciousness, even though my ego had me—and others—fooled into believing that I was functioning just fine.

I am one of the fortunate ones who broke out of denial and found a loving connection to a higher power. I was led out of the darkness and into the light of rebirth, which gave me a profound respect and gratitude for both the hard-won lessons of the dark and the nurturing spirit of light that replenished my soul and set me free. This symbolic death and rebirth (which I later understood as a shamanic initiation and near-death experience) led me into an even deeper longing for my lost soul parts and higher consciousness.

Over the years my spiritual longing and thirst took me to many incredible places, spiritual teachers, and direct healing experiences of my own. During this journey I also taught what I had learned; I had found in my earlier recovery and discovery journey that I embody best what I have learned if I can share it with other kindred spirits who show up on my path. My soul path eventually prepared me to become a vessel for the birth of a new kind of breathwork process. The Shamanic Breathwork process and the Five Cycles of Shamanic Consciousness were cooked in the vessel of my own life experiences. They alchemically emerged from my personal and professional experiences within the fields of addiction, mental health, bodywork, various spiritual teachings, experiences with shamanic healers, and training in other forms of breathwork.

I am very passionate and excited about the potency of Shamanic Breathwork and its seemingly magical ability to accelerate needed life shifts. Shamanic Breathwork is not only for wounded healers, but also for all those truly seeking, and ready for, healing life changes in both their inner and outer worlds.

Wolf Clan Seneca Nation Grandmother Twylah Nitsch once said, "Don't worry too much about the world. The world will be here long after humans are gone. The waters can heal themselves over time, the earth's surface and air will heal over time, but we may not be here to see it." To truly heal the planet, we must also heal the hearts and minds of human beings.

I often end my monthly newsletter with these words: "If you have heard the inner howl of the wolf reminding you that it is time to wake up and remember that the shaman is within, then welcome to the Shamanic Breathwork process, and welcome home."

I Live My Life in Growing Orbits

I live my life in growing orbits,
which move out over the things of the world.
Perhaps I can never achieve the last,
but that will be my attempt.
I am circling around God,
around the ancient tower,
and I have been circling for a thousand years.
And I still don't know if I am a falcon
*or a storm or a great song.**

RAINER MARIA RILKE

---

*Selected Poems of Rainer Maria Rilke, translated by Robert Bly

1
AWAKENING THE
SHAMAN WITHIN

. . . .

Have you recently had a wake-up call in your personal life? Do you recognize that, on a planetary level, there are signs all around that we need to heal ourselves and change the outer conditions of our world?

Amidst continuing violations of civil rights, accelerating conflicts among nations, and severe economic issues, humanity is experiencing a collective time of crisis. All cultures are struggling to find ways to communicate with each other, to respect differences of opinion and belief, and to treat each other with integrity, dignity, and respect. Many countries have shut down communication with each other, and we see this mirrored in some of our own important relationships. We need to learn, at the deepest level, the concept of *power with* versus *power over*. *Power with* emanates from a place of love and connection, whereas *power over* emanates from a place of control and disconnection. We also need to recognize that when we are in conflict or on opposite sides of an issue, it is counterproductive to shut down the communication process. In fact, this is often an important time to get serious and push through, while opening ourselves to higher wisdom.

This will allow answers to emerge from a deeper place within ourselves, where opposites naturally reconcile. It has been my experience that conflict resolved often breeds true intimacy and trust, whereas conflict avoided or unresolved breeds only alienation and discontent. Imagine for a moment the great spiritual masters who have visited humanity's consciousness: Buddha, Krishna, Christ, Kuan Yin, and Isis, to name a few. Each of these energetic beings emanated love, wisdom, and connection *with* others, not *over* others. However, none of them avoided the outer world of conflict when it presented itself. We are creatures of both light and dark, and we often learn life's greatest lessons from dealing with both wisdom and woe.

Never on our planet have we needed to awaken our consciousness more than now. Many healers and teachers are awakening to the healing power of shamanic consciousness and are discovering ways to synthesize the timeless wisdom of the ancients, as well as more contemporary philosophies. The Shamanic Breathwork process merges the older Scorpio mysteries of death and rebirth with newer downloads from the Aquarian energies of peace, love, and inner wisdom. We are now being called to embrace and unite these two paradigms, incorporating both of their gifts into our present-day lives. This approach of both/and, rather than either/or, honors ancient traditions, yet also honors the path of direct experience that is governed by the heart's wisdom. We are becoming cocreators in the now and, as present-day shamanic beings, helping to envision and invent the future, rather than becoming a passive byproduct of it.

Many religious and spiritual traditions have suggested that healing and enlightenment are entirely the responsibility of religious/spiritual leaders and deities. However, shamanic consciousness calls upon all of our inner energies and wisdom, as well as those of the collective consciousness, archetypal forces, power animals, spiritual guides, and God/Goddess to illuminate the highest path. In the Shamanic Breathwork process we consciously create the alchemical sacred space to allow an individual's soul to resonate with his core truth. From this place of soul resonance, the person is able to follow that inner truth, blending it with higher energies and forces, in the quest to connect to the natural and spirit worlds.

The time to heal is now, the time to remember who we really are is now, and the time to take our creative healing vision back to our communities is now. The motivation for awakening the shaman within is to bring more depth and richness into our lives, and to be able to shift from outer authority to the inner wisdom of the individual soul's journey. The impetus to awaken the inner shaman is to discover who we really are and to explore the bigger questions in life, such as, "What are we here to do?" My personal answer to this question is that we are here to live a much bigger story than the one we have been unconsciously playing out in the past.

To live a bigger story from a spiritual perspective requires not only a call, but a willingness to awaken to the bigger picture of who we really are. Sometimes there is a vague sense that there is something larger—a longing for connection and remembering our deeper purpose. This is our first phase of awakening and often occurs in response to a trauma or disappointment, such as addiction, divorce, illness, loss of a career, or a mental or spiritual crisis.

Sometimes we are more proactive in our spiritual search to discover who we are beyond ego, but in my experience, it's rare. In this age of consumerism it has become our nature to stay distracted and hide out in our comfort zone. Most of us become proactive in our need for change only after turbulent times awaken our longing for something more. Having to deal with critical issues pushes us to awaken to the deeper aspects of the soul's true path.

Traditional psychotherapy serves a specific purpose and is sometimes an important aspect of our journey, but it is definitely not the *whole* journey. Often it puts us back in the box, a process somewhat akin to trying to put a baby back in the womb. For many of us, staying rooted in traditional therapy is just a postponement of facing and embracing our deeper spiritual issues. On some level it feels safer and more comfortable to stay asleep and disconnected by being a couch potato, compulsively watching TV, engaging in addictive behavior, losing ourselves in relationships, or otherwise engaging in activities that dull the mind and numb consciousness.

When asked if he was a god, Buddha replied that he was not. When asked if he was a saint, the Buddha replied that he was not.

"Then what are you?" he was asked.

"I am awake," Buddha replied.

In order to awaken our inner shaman, we need a crack in our outer armor and a willingness to step outside the box. We need to know that there is something going on beneath everything. We need to resonate with that deep wellspring of knowledge that flows within us. If we can consider this possibiity, then we are ready for the amazing discovery of our true nature.

When this happens, we send a spiritual message to the universe saying, "I am ready to surrender to something beyond my human ego. I am open to divine assistance from God, Goddess, a Higher Power, or whatever we envision as being sacred and capable of transforming our lives." When we communicate this willingness and readiness to the Great Mystery and what we hold as sacred, we are saying that we are willing to transform and be receptive to something bigger than our smaller, everyday personas. We are calling in the collective, eternal wisdom of the Divine and moving from *I* to *we*.

This opening is often referred to as a sacred marriage between the human and the Divine that creates an embodiment between the two. The transformative mystery of experiencing the union of our humanity with spirit is the basis of many spiritual traditions. It is also the solid foundation for the first three steps of all the 12-step recovery programs that in synopsis say, "I can't—Higher Power can—I'll surrender to Higher Power."

When we surrender in this way, we find that synchronistic things begin to happen in our lives according to divine providence. We can trust that we are experiencing energetic attunements with the universe when we begin to see coincidental resonances—in books, on TV, and in conversations, for instance—in our everyday lives. These synchronistic events hold within them the visible reassurance that our inner shaman has heard our call.

A question often asked is, "How long will it take to awaken the shaman within?" The answer is that this is a path of ongoing discovery and enlightenment. If we step onto a path of awakening, there is a continuing sense of expansion and growth. We see this all the time in the natural world around us. The tree that is already fifteen-feet high does not necessarily stop growing. It continues to reach toward the sun while simultaneously putting down deeper roots.

This shamanic awakening can happen in our dreams. It can happen as a spiritual experience—through meditation, prayer, or retreat. It can happen while we are working with a therapist, minister, or elder; while we are walking in the woods; at the birth of our children or the death of our parents. Your calling is to stay awake to the synchronistic events that are happening all around you, because when you are truly ready to awaken the shaman within, the way will magically open before you.

2

THE CREATION OF THE SHAMANIC BREATHWORK PROCESS

. . . .

When I was nineteen and a student at the University of Kentucky, I hit a very stressful period in my life that resulted in severe anxiety attacks. At the time I had no idea what was happening to me; all I knew was that I felt a sense of dread and suffocation. I also had the sensation that I was out of my body and dying. After a trip one evening to the local emergency room, the doctor on call reassured me that I was not dying, nor was I suffering from lack of air. In fact, I was hyperventilating and having a panic attack.

He offered me Valium (it was, after all, the early '70s) and told me I needed to calm down. He insisted that I breathe into a small brown paper bag (the kind I used to take my lunch to school in, when I was a kid) and count inward and outward breaths very slowly to the count of ten. I thought he was crazy and insisted that I needed oxygen immediately. However, since I was desperate, I reluctantly placed the paper bag over my mouth and nose and followed his instructions. Within a few minutes my breathing had completely returned to normal, and the tingling in my hands and limbs had ceased. I no longer felt as if I might die from lack of oxygen and, in fact, I felt rather calm and peaceful. I left the ER confused and embarrassed, clutching my magical paper bag.

It took some time before I was able to fully understand what had actually triggered those uneasy feelings and the rapid breathing that had resulted in panic and an inability to function in the normal world. In the meantime, for the better part of a year, I never went anywhere without making sure my paper bag was neatly folded and tucked securely in the back pocket of my blue jeans.

It was during this time that I became increasingly interested in studying Eastern philosophy, meditation, yoga, and other spiritual subjects. This was nothing new. My parents had introduced me to reading at an early age, and my father, in particular, had shared his interest in books about Native Americans and a very famous local psychic, Edgar Cayce, who lived nearby in Hopkinsville—thirty minutes from where I was born. In my teen years I consumed these books with a passion. I found myself relating profoundly to these stories in ways that were a mystery to me. Since I, too, had many psychic tendencies and experiences, I found Edgar Cayce's journey comforting. It gave me a sense of being normal.

Many of the books that I was drawn to during this period talked at great length about the importance of using the breath to enter into an altered state, thereby reaching a higher level of consciousness and access to higher selves and spirit guides. The breath was often mentioned as an important vehicle for a variety of healing processes. This fascinated me, especially since I continued to suffer from occasional unexplained bouts of rapid breathing that resulted in feelings of unreality and suffocation. I could somehow sense that these experiences were related to a healing crisis in my inner self, but I was uncertain of how to connect the dots.

I became very interested in not only studying, but also participating in my own personal healing through therapy and counseling. I found that I always resonated more closely with anything I could find on alternative healing therapies, especially those that involved bodywork and the breath. Over time some of the panic subsided and I was able to go back to work.

When I was twenty-one, I returned from college to my small hometown in rural western Kentucky and took my first professional social work job at a mental health center. The year was 1972 and there was a big push to transplant the mentally ill from confinement in mental institutions, or *asylums* as they were called, into mainstream society. Although this sounded like a great idea at the time, it was fraught with many problems and a dearth of responsible planning. This deinstitutionalization project often left these individuals heavily medicated, chain-smoking, and sitting in front of a TV twenty-four hours a day, either in nursing homes or back with their families. Many other folks, throughout this country, ended up on the streets and became homeless.

In my first job at the mental health center I was a day treatment case manager, assisting in operating a program for the chronically mentally ill. I assisted these individuals in their daily struggle to maintain a tenuous connection with the world and with other human beings. My main qualifications for the job were two years studying social work, a near-death experience brought on by a bad drug episode while in college, and an ensuing year of intense panic attacks. The requirements for working with the mentally ill were much more lax than they are now and, in fact, the administration was happy to hire me for the job.

Many of the individuals I dealt with on a daily basis were still actively hallucinating, even while on medication, and several were on suicide watch. I spent four or five days a week working from 9 AM until 4 PM with these individuals. They were amazing teachers from whom I learned a lot about the nature of reality (or, perhaps, non-reality).

From them I learned about struggling with, and moving through, different levels of consciousness. I gained a great deal of respect and compassion for their process of trying to discern what was "real" from what was delusional; I felt this more strongly for those individuals who continued to experience their lives as a tortuous journey at times, even with help from the pharmaceutical world of psychiatry. Having experimented quite a bit with hallucinogens during the '70s, I felt I had some sense of what they might be experiencing. I, however, could "come down" from my state of non-reality, whereas theirs just continued.

I found in my work that I frequently felt more of an affinity with the patients than with those who were treating them. I became so adept at deciphering the seemingly nonsensical and delusional musings of the patients that the psychiatric professionals frequently called me into staff meetings to assist them in gaining a better understanding of the people they were treating.

I was told I had a "magic touch" in being able to understand and connect with individuals who had previously been considered lost causes and who were, effectively, just being maintained. Secretly, I couldn't help but wonder if my prior use of psychedelic drugs, my psychic gifts, and my deep involvement in nontraditional healing better served my close connection with these special individuals than anything I had learned in school.

I became rather passionate in my attempts to understand their realities, and if I placed myself in the right frame of heart and mind, I was able to form an instant connection with many of those who were considered unreachable. Like any of us, these folks responded very positively when they felt cared for and safe. It was during this time that I began to have a deep sense that perhaps all of the patients were not so "crazy" after all. Although they certainly suffered from chemical imbalances that were terribly distressing to them and to their families, perhaps these unique individuals were also part of a larger evolutionary shift. In the future perhaps all human beings would be able to part the veils and see into the archetypal realms; they would become walkers between the worlds, able to travel lucidly to other realms of consciousness, while not losing touch with this reality.

I worked with these "mentally ill" individuals to explain their illness and how it was affecting their grasp on external reality. I used what most of the professionals around me considered a novel approach, one considered to be impractical. This approach grew out of my authentic relationship with them, as opposed to seeing them as "patients." Rather than deny their delusions, hallucinations, and different realities, I spoke to them about the separate realities that exist on many levels of consciousness. I acknowledged the various levels they spoke about, giving them some validity. The caveat, however, was that the day-to-day reality of the physical world was the one they had to learn to live and function within if they were going to be able to have some semblance of normalcy in their lives.

I found that when their subjective awareness was validated, many of these individuals began to settle down, become less delusional, and relate to me from a place of mutual trust and respect. Their faith in our relationship allowed me to hold space for them as they shared their fear and paranoia, as well as their hopes and dreams. I was able to be a supportive guide for what was actually taking place with them, not only in this dimension, but on other levels as well.

This may not seem strange or out of place in our present era, but in the '70s and early '80s I only knew a couple of other people who believed that these individuals should be told their diagnosis. Norma McLaughlin was an incredible supervisor and friend, and Louise Andrusky was another cherished mentor and friend on the mental health board. The three of us often felt like lone wolves as we stuck to our guns and went up against "the system" on numerous occasions to do what we knew was right for our clients. The prevailing belief at the time was that mentally ill patients would not be able to comprehend their dilemma, and that therefore it would simply be a waste of time to explain things to them. I found this to be totally false with most of my clients. Many of the individuals I worked with were relieved to hear the truth from a medical and psychological perspective about what was "wrong" with them. Their subsequent understanding brought more trust and cooperation, and better functioning overall. Their quality of life improved and their hospitalizations were reduced. Families were grateful to be able to keep their loved ones at home and to know that they had allies in the mental health system.

It was around this time that I began to grasp the idea that the best way to assist anyone who was struggling with reality on any level was to be really present with that person—to be real, direct, honest, and authentic; and above all, to open my heart and hold space for whatever the person was feeling. We are all delusional on some level, meaning we all have thoughts and feelings that make sense to the ego, but perhaps not to the rational mind. Who is to say which reality is correct?

The Shamanic Breathwork journey that you will read about here takes the journeyer through many alternate levels of consciousness, the validity of which would be questioned by standard mental health and medical models. However, these alternate realities bring some of the most amazing healing transformations—so much so that there can be no denying their effectiveness. For instance, many of the stories that are shared after a Shamanic Breathwork journey might sound farfetched to the "normal" world, but when understood archetypally and shamanically, make perfect sense. The proof is in the many examples of change we see in people's lives. Some of these examples are contained in the pages of this book.

When I think back to my time with those early clients at the mental health centers, I feel a deep sense of gratitude. They taught me so much about how to really listen and hold space for intense processes, and how to open my heart and mind. They taught me that miracles can and do happen if we trust the process and offer empowerment to the wise one in each of us— no matter who we are!

A few years after I started this work, I moved to Florida with my family and continued to be employed in the mental health field. After working in another day treatment program for those referred to as "chronically mentally ill," my focus began to shift from that program to a new field. I was given the opportunity to work with substance addicts and their families, first through the local mental health center, and later at a treatment center. In the recovery field I once again found that many of the traditional methods of treating addiction were not as helpful as the alternative approaches that had been therapeutic in my own healing.

Substance abuse was an issue in my own life. I had used drugs in my youth, until age twenty-one. I had, however, continued to abuse alcohol until age twenty-nine, when I realized something had to change, and I became a member of Alcoholics Anonymous.

In AA, I began to work the twelve steps, and my chemical addictions were totally arrested. For me these twelve steps were deeply and personally spiritual, and were able to ground my naturally sensitive nature. They gave me the foundation I needed to be truly sane and sober in what I realized was a rather crazy world. I had many powerful, mystical experiences right from the very beginning of my entry into recovery, and these informed my healing process on a daily basis.

One of my most powerful mystical experiences happened early on in my recovery. After just a few days I had such an overwhelming urge to drink that I didn't think I could stay sober any longer. I followed the simple advice of my sponsor* and humbly got on my knees and asked my newly found Higher Power (God as I understand God to be) to remove my obsession to drink. I suddenly felt very tired and lay down. I awoke about four hours later feeling quite altered, and surprised that I had slept so long. I went into the bathroom and realized that I was feeling very different. I noticed while I was brushing my teeth that I felt as if I were filled with light, and suddenly I heard the words in my head, "I no longer want to drink." In that moment I realized that the obsession and compulsion had been lifted from me.

That was more than twenty-six years ago and I've never longed for a drink again. Anyone who has suffered from addiction to alcohol or drugs knows what a miracle it is to have something like this happen so early in sobriety. I have had many such experiences in my recovery and discovery since that time, but this was a major turning point. I realized that something greater than my ego had lifted me up into a higher level of consciousness on that amazing day. I believe I underwent a powerful shamanic shift, an ego death and spiritual rebirth that formed a sturdy foundation for the rest of my life. I knew that as long as I kept my spiri-

---

*Sponsors are individuals who have been sober for a substantial period of time and, as part of their ongoing recovery, assist a newly sober person in working the twelve steps.

tual condition in check, my addictions would cease to be a problem.

That is why getting sober is called *recovery* as opposed to *recovered*—ongoing healing is happening at higher levels of consciousness and is a necessary part of sustained recovery. I am happy to say that, one day at a time for more than twenty-six years, this has been the case for me. It is truly a never-ending journey.

Once again, I found I had a "magical touch" with the addicts and their family members, and many individuals with whom I worked enjoyed solid recovery from a life-threatening illness. I went back to college during this time and obtained the degrees that were now required to do the job I was already doing. My colleagues respected me, but I often felt as if I were going to be "found out"—it seemed to me that I was always out on a limb, flying by the seat of my pants, and breaking the rules about how I was supposed to relate to my clients. I hugged them, shared some of my own story, used intuition rather than textbook approaches, and showed them that I truly cared. I remember one facility director telling me that I needed to be careful with what I was doing or he might have to fire me; in the same breath, he told me that I had an amazing talent to help others heal. I was not quite sure what the double message was meant to convey, or what to do with it.

In my late twenties I met Jacquelyn Small, a well-known psychospiritual teacher, author, and founder of the Eupsychia Institute,* who inspired me greatly. Never had I met anyone like Jacquie. Her first words to me at a Kentucky addictions conference were, "Hello, kindred spirit." She won my heart and trust immediately, and I recognized a soul connection that I'd missed since my beloved grandmother's death when I was twelve years old. Jacquie and I formed an instant bond, and I consumed everything she wrote and eagerly awaited her monthly newsletter,

---

*Eupsychia (Greek for "psyche's well-being") is an educational institute and service organization founded in 1975 by Jacquelyn Small. Its mandate is to be a training and healing program for professionals and others seeking knowledge and experience of personal transformation and soul-based psychology. The concept of eupsychia was coined in 1962 by Abraham Maslow, the father of self-actualization theory and one of the founders of transpersonal psychology.

Small Talk. A few years after we met, she became my main breathwork teacher. She introduced me to Holotropic Breathwork, another important step that enabled me to eventually make sense of my life.

But first, my life came apart.

When I began the breathwork with Jacquie I had already been sober for a few years, and I was ready for the next level of my spiritual journey. I was feeling restless and as if I had reached an end point. I could not imagine what was yet to come and I was confused about what the next right step was or how to find it. My first breathwork session with Jacquie reactivated my inner healer, and another major shift in my conscious awareness began. This inner knowing began to be more present in my daily life and made me increasingly aware of what was not working in my marriage, on my spiritual path, and in my career.

Through several sessions of breathwork, and entering training with Eupsychia Institute, I became aware that I needed to make many changes in both my inner and outer life. Over the next few years I was guided into a new life, but this required that I deconstruct my old life, a life that from the outside appeared to be working just fine, thank you very much! However, even though it had been a good life on many levels, it had come to an end and I had to face the fact that my marriage was ending and my way of working in the world was changing.

I realized that I needed to quit my job and that I had to let go and trust spirit and my inner voice to guide me through these enormous changes. It seems so long ago now, but at the time I felt as if my entire life had been turned upside down and I had to completely trust that I was doing the right thing. I was totally motivated by continuing to do frequent breathwork sessions that enabled me to hear my inner voice more clearly and to release emotional blocks to my freedom and sanity. In a relatively short time I established a new ground of being and re-created some stability in my life, with the understanding that life travels on a spiral path; to be reborn again and again means one must also be willing to let go of the old life when the wheel turns, in order to be fully alive and soulfully embodied.

During these times, Small was working closely with Stanislav Grof (the founder of Holotropic Breathwork) and his wife Christina, teaching and training students to become Holotropic Breathwork facilitators. Holotropic Breathwork is a transpersonal psychological approach that accesses different states of consciousness in order for healing to occur. It integrates insights from modern consciousness research, anthropology, various depth psychologies, Eastern spiritual practices, and mystical traditions of the world. The word holotropic means "moving toward wholeness" (from the Greek *holos* = whole, and *trepein* = moving in the direction of something). In essence the process creates a controlled setting wherein a person's psychic processing is amplified through a specific focus on the breath, thus facilitating the psyche's innate capacity for healing.

I was completely hooked from my first Holotropic Breathwork session at the Red Roof Inn ballroom in Nashville, along with approximately one hundred fifty other individuals. I wasn't completely sure what had just happened, but I knew that my life had just made a radical turn for the better.

Until my first breathwork experience I did not really have a context in which to explain or understand the many mystical and psychic experiences I had been having since birth. During my very first session I was able to completely surrender to the breath and the altered state it created, and travel through multiple levels of consciousness. In this altered state I became acutely aware of the energetic patterns of these multiple levels, the creative matrix that they originated from, and ways they manifested through symbols and images in my psyche. Even though at that time I did not have the sophistication or language to fully describe what I had experienced during my session, some part of me "got it," and that understanding has never left me. You might say I experienced a paradigm shift and an enlightenment of some kind. This new level of awareness motivated me to step out of linear thinking and enabled me to recreate my life in previously unimaginable ways.

This was the beginning of my stepping away from my past

preoccuption with formal education and fully onto the path of shamanic consciousness, because now I was deeply convinced of its merits. I felt validated instead of weird and out of place in the world around me. I learned that these states of consciousness were desirable and could lead to a more fully embodied, passionate life in the outer world as I shifted from ego agenda to my soul purpose. I also found the energy that had been stuck in my body and energy field and had finally been freed, and I could now utilize it to make major changes in my everyday life. I found clarity in my visions, courage in my character, and a release of life-force energy (kundalini) that surged through my body and moved my spirituality into deeper and more meaningful areas of experience.

I frequently tell my students that during this time, "I realized I wasn't living in Kansas anymore, Toto." From this first experience I felt as if—as paradoxical as it might sound—I had found "home"—the place I had been looking for all of my life.

I also knew from the first session that I would somehow take this work back to my clients, friends, and the world. In my excitement I found the courage and motivation to take time off from my regular work at every opportunity, and travel to wherever a Holotropic Breathwork training was happening. It was not easy to explain any of this to my family and friends, but I was certain that it was where true healing was taking place. My own healing journey was a living example of the process.

Small eventually parted company with the Grofs and created the Integrative Breathwork process. I decided that this was the path of learning I wanted to follow. While I had great respect for the Grofs' work, my deeper connection and training was with Small's breathwork style and psychospiritual programs. To my mind they had a deeper psychological approach and included more in-depth processing with psychodrama and addictions work. A significant contributor to some of the psychospiritual, psychodrama, and addictions work at Eupsychia Institute was Small's friend Sue Jane White, a true wise woman who became an incredible mentor to me as well.

I was truly fortunate to be in the close company of, and work alongside, incredible teachers and healers over the next several years at Eupsychia Institute. Some of the guest teachers at our gatherings were Marion Woodman, Barbara Marx Hubbard, Ram Dass, Larry Dossey, June Singer, Peter Russell, Fred Alan Wolf, Gabrielle Roth, Matthew Fox, Jeremiah Abrams, Malidoma Somé, Shakti Gawain, Andrew Weil, Robert Moore, and Swami Beyondananda (Steve Bhaerman), to name just a few.

During this time my love affair with the healing power of the breath was continually deepening through various forms of breathwork. I became acquainted with many types of breathing processes, and I grew in my understanding that they all, at their core, involved opening the flow of life-force energy inherent within us. This energy is called *kundalini, prana,* or *chi,* depending on the culture or tradition encountered.

I had several very intense kundalini awakenings and experiences during breathwork sessions, and each time this occurred it was as if centuries of dysfunction and old belief systems were incredibly dismantled. My life began to transform itself in amazing ways; my understanding of the nature of so-called reality was shifting dramatically, and I felt my spirit taking quantum leaps in consciousness. I encountered energetic beings from many different realms, some of whom became my spirit allies and helpers as I developed my skills of being in multiple worlds at once.

During the time that I was a trainer with Eupsychia Institute, I continued to have many of what I now know were shamanic experiences. I had stumbled upon these experiences, rather than seeking them out, but they always made me more aware of different levels of reality and allowed me to walk between the worlds. I found that my breathwork experiences began to bleed over into my everyday reality and open up unexpected portals of chance and synchronicity that irrevocably changed how I viewed my life, its soul purpose, and the world. I began to feel a new sense of empowerment and became a consummate choicemaker. My private practice in alternative healing was booming—quite stunning given the fact that I lived in a small, ultraconservative town in western Kentucky. The truth was that the work was alive within me, and people's souls are drawn to the true light of healing once they are exposed to it. This overcame many potential (and actual) objections to what I was doing.

My burgeoning interest in the shamanic world eventually led me to deep exploration of Native American traditions and other earth wisdom teachings. Seneca Wolf Clan Grandmother Twylah Nitsch first appeared to me while I was in a deeply altered state of consciousness.

Grandmother Twylah Nitsch was born in 1913 on the Cattaraugus Indian Reservation in upstate New York. She was raised by her grandparents, medicine man Moses Shongo and his wife Alice, and trained to become the lineage holder of Seneca wisdom and leader of the Wolf Clan Teaching Lodge. This role was prophesied before her birth and was passed on to her after her grandfather's passing, when she was just nine years old.

Daughter of a Seneca mother and an Oneida-Scotts father, Grandmother Twylah was a direct descendant of Chief Red Jacket, a renowned Seneca orator whose discourses are still studied by scholars today. The Seneca are among the original members of the Five Nation Peace League known as the Iroquois Confederacy and are the acknowledged philosophers of the league.

Seneca society is composed of various clans. Grandmother Twylah's clan, the Wolf Clan, teaches the wisdom, philosophy, and prophecy of earth history, namely that all creatures—all creation—are members of the one family born of Mother Earth, and that our destiny is to reclaim that oneness. Gram, as she was fondly called by many, brought students into her home to learn the ancient ways firsthand. She formed the Seneca Indian Historical Society, a school without walls, and began holding councils and numerous workshops, and disseminating her teachings through a home-study correspondence course.

Her Seneca name of Yeh-Weh-Node—"She whose voice rides on the four winds"—was prophetic. She spread her sacred ancestral teachings across the world to such faraway places as Australia, Africa, Holland,

Germany, Poland, Canada, Israel, Russia, Japan, the British Isles, Italy, and across the United States. In April of 1999 she received the prestigious Living Treasures of North America Heritage Award in recognition of her life's work.

I met Grandmother Twylah in dreamtime meditation, a powerful spiritual practice I was learning from a Cherokee teacher and friend at that time, Teresa Mt. Pleasant. During my inner journey, Grandmother's spiritual presence made itself known, and when she stroked my head and called me Gentle Star Wolf it had a life-changing effect on me. It took me several years to actually track down Grandmother Twylah in the outer world. When I finally arrived at her home on the Cattaraugus Indian Reservation outside of Buffalo, New York, she asked me (rather firmly) what had taken me so long (she had appeared to me several years prior to my actual visit). I was quite shaken and answered that perhaps I would have found her sooner if she had told me her name and given me directions to where she lived!

I spent the next few years learning the ways of the Wolf Clan energy. This included the cycles of truth emanating from my vibral core and walking in trust, stability, dignity, love, and gratitude. And although I became a dedicated student and granddaughter of Gram Twylah, my true path is a path of synthesis, which means I learn by my own direct experience and often blend many teachings from different lineages that speak to my heart. Gram always encouraged me to be true to my vibral core—my inner divinity—and to listen to my heart and spirit. Perhaps this was her greatest teaching to me. She used the words, "Go to your within, within, within. This is the place of your vibral core, the essence of your true being."

I once said to her, "Gram, I honor and love you and all that you have taught me, but my path is to take what has meaning in my life and integrate it with the other paths and lineages that speak to me; I will not teach it exactly as you do." Her response was "Great, Star Wolf, there is only one Grandmother Twylah and I don't want to be cloned!" She told me she knew my heart and trusted who I was, and knew that my work would reach many people on the planet. She said that was why she had called me to her, so that the teachings may live. She knew that I would not lose the heart of what she was sharing with me and so many others in the world.

She explained to me that the path of the wolf is to be a type of scout, a pathfinder, a way-shower. She said the wolf spirit person was a thinker as well as a healer, and could navigate her way on the shamanic path through various multiple levels of consciousness. She said the wolf person would have a vision and follow it with her whole heart, and then take that lesson and knowledge back to the rest of the clan. The wolf energy is also about being able to see the bigger picture and envision a better world; the wolf can be both visionary and prophet. The wolf is a natural teacher and shares what it has learned with others, thereby passing on the wisdom to future generations.

I visited Gram Twylah at home on the reservation where she taught me directly. She once visited me at my home in California and attended a workshop I was offering, where she shared her teachings with my students. She also sent her son and daughter-in-law to teach our Venus Rising groups in California, and sent me lessons in the mail. We spoke fairly frequently by phone, although she really didn't like to talk much on the phone. One of the ways she taught me from the beginning, even before I had met her, was through the dreamtime. She confirmed that meeting when we first met on the physical plane.

Gram gave me lessons on finding, naming, and talking to the stone people (rocks). She spoke to me about the wisdom of the animals (creature teachers) and the standing people (trees). She also spoke to me about the Great Star Nations—the many different Native American people who believed they originated from the stars. She told me with a twinkle in her eye that we were all from the stars and that we came here to learn how to be "real human beings." She said that if we could just see the invisible ones who were waiting in line to get an "earth suit," we would thank our lucky stars for our bodies and our journey around the sacred wheel of life. The Pathways of Peace and the Cycles of Truth were two of her foundational teachings that focused on entering the silence of our "within," finding our true power by living from the truth of our vibral core, and radiating the soul qualities of wisdom, integrity, stability, and dignity—which, in turn, would create inner peace and happiness in our lives.

Gram passed on to many of us "wolfies" what her beloved grandfather had taught her, that following the twelve Cycles of Truth and the Pathways of Peace would help us to preserve our wholeness, walk in balance, and fulfill our life's mission. She shared the importance of truth; that we must learn, honor, know, see, hear, speak, love, serve, live, work, share, and be thankful for the truth. The Pathway of Peace is living in harmony with this ancient philosophy.

She believed in peace and frequently spoke of becoming a peacemaker, a philosophy inspired by a great sixteenth-century Native American named Dekanawida. Dekanawida succeeded in uniting the Iroquois tribes in a confederation that still continues. This confederation was used as a model by Benjamin Franklin and several other founding fathers when they were formulating a government for the newly emerging United States. The tenets of the peacemaker's philosophy were peace, unity, and the power of a good mind.

Grandmother Twylah often spoke of Dekanawida and encouraged all those she taught to become peacemakers—first in our own hearts, then in our families, and then in the world around us. She believed it was the responsibility of all of us to carry the seeds of peace and the message of peace into every aspect of our lives and the world. One of her favorite sayings was, "All for one and one for all."

She was truly one of a kind and holds a special place in my heart.

The path of the wolf encouraged me to step more fully into my role as a visionary pathfinder and way-shower for others. Grandmother Twylah asked me to pass on what I was learning from her, in addition to my own inner experiences. She had many students and followers (although she wouldn't call them that) and we all referred to her as Grandmother. When my own paternal grandmother passed away,

Grandmother Twylah told me that she was adopting me as her spiritual granddaughter, and I joyfully accepted her invitation to be connected to her in this deeper way.

My journey was intertwined with more breathwork experiences and other shamanic teachers, including other Native American and Mayan teachers. It was during this time that the vision of developing a method of breathing in ceremonial space, and incorporating valuable earth-wisdom teachings and rituals, emerged as a burning desire on my soul path.

Contributing to this desire was my connection to Jeremiah Abrams, an amazing teacher and author of several books relating to Carl Jung's work on the shadow, archetypes, and the concepts of individuation and "sacred marriage." Many individuals who have done extensive shadow work through the Shamanic Breathwork process now say that meeting the shadow has become the cornerstone of their shamanic healing path.

Jung said that "meeting the shadow" is the apprentice piece of soul work, and sacred marriage is its masterpiece. The sacred marriage occurs when we open to what is known as the beloved, and the beloved can come in many forms. It can be our higher power or an idealized image of the Divine as a God or Goddess. The point is to find deep self-love and have a deeply spiritual relationship with our own spirit, soul, and human self. The key to loving others is to love ourselves.

Although my relationship with Jeremiah shape-shifted over a period of seven years, it was through both our personal and professional processes that we began the process of integrating breathwork with Jungian work. We taught many workshops together across the country. Some of our most important work was done at the Skyros Center in Greece, at Esalen Institute in Big Sur, and at other sites in California and around the United States.

I had been fairly familiar with Carl Jung's teachings prior to meeting Abrams. However, it was during my close association and collaboration with him that Jung's work became part of a powerful map for the journey of my soul. Each time I have made a leap in consciousness on my life's journey, I have always felt compelled to share my new level of healing and awareness with others around me. Since my early twenties I have had the great good fortune of working with scores of individuals and groups by assisting them in transforming the pain and suffering in their lives and consciousness. I have personally assisted thousands of rebirths, energy release work processes, and soul returns (which will be explained in a later chapter). I lost count long ago of how many workshops and training groups I have facilitated over the years. I have been on a constant search for greater methods of healing for more than three decades, and I have dedicated most of my life and work toward this end.

It was a combination of these factors that led to the birth of Shamanic Breathwork and to the creation of the Venus Rising Institute for the Shamanic Healing Arts during the spring equinox of 1996. Venus Rising provides a place for individuals to come together for profound transformation through shamanic healing circles and the Shamanic Breathwork process. Individuals who wish to propagate the healing work can also train as facilitators of the Shamanic Breathwork healing arts.

Our institute is currently in the process of shape-shifting into the Venus Rising University in western North Carolina at Isis Cove.

3
TRUE LIFE EXPERIENCES WITH SHAMANIC BREATHWORK—PART ONE

Change

*This is where I yank the old roots
from my chest, like tomatoes
we let grow until December,
stalks thick as saplings.
This is the moment when the ancient fears
race like thoroughbreds, asking for more
and more rein. And I, the driver,
for some reason they know nothing of
strain to hold them back.
Terror grips me like a virus
and I sweat, fevered,
trying to burn it out.
This feat is so invisible. All you can see
is a woman going about her ordinary day,
drinking tea, taking herself to the movies,
reading in bed. If victorious
I will look exactly the same.*

34

Yet I am hoisting a car from mud ruts
half a century deep. I am hacking
a clearing through the fallen slash
of my heart. Without laser precision,
with only the primitive knife of need, I cut
and splice the circuitry of my brain.
I change.

ELLEN BASS

The following are accounts of persons who have undergone Shamanic Breathwork. There are additional accounts in a later chapter of the book. These amazing individuals have inspired me and my work more than words can express.

DIVINE JUSTICE

In the middle part of the 1990s, my life was coming undone. I was a successful lawyer with a second career as a reserve army officer with U.S. Special Forces. However, I was also an alcoholic and my disease was progressing rapidly. At the same time, old ghosts and memories from my days in the 101st Airborne Division in Vietnam were coming back to me, and on a daily basis I was dealing with a delayed onset of post-traumatic stress disorder. The two conditions fed off each other. The more I drank, the worse the PTSD became. The worse the PTSD, the more I drank. I was in total and complete denial about both conditions.

After my life came completely undone and I'd lost my job, my family, and my reputation, and gone to jail for a while, I finally got treatment for both alcoholism and PTSD. I got into recovery.

I worked with many therapists and counselors and they helped; however, my life still lacked direction or a grounding from which I could successfully move forward. I was missing something and I felt stuck. One of my therapists finally told me, "There is more to unraveling the mystery of you than just psychology." He had some experience with Shamanic Breathwork, and he invited me to a weekend workshop facilitated by Brad Collins. I had no idea what to expect.

My first breathwork experience shattered me to the core. It was as if a laser beam pierced through all of my barriers, protectors, facades, and ego-based shields and went straight to my soul. I was laid open. I was physically and emotionally spent but spiritually charged in a way that I could not quite comprehend. I did not know exactly what to make of it, but I knew something huge had happened to me. It frightened me, but I knew I had to continue.

I went back to Shamanic Breathwork and attended another workshop, this one facilitated by Linda Star Wolf. I had a similar, if less dramatic, experience. In the process I discovered parts of myself—parts that were severely wounded and parts that could heal. I still did not understand the process, but I knew that I had been given the gift of a great healing tool.

I stayed with it and attended a couple of eight-day workshops. Then, I attended SHIP* and the transformation accelerated. The teachings were helpful and illuminating. I was touched particularly by the shadow work we did. I discovered the part of myself that sabotaged so much of my work and subconsciously kept me from meeting my full personal, professional, and spiritual potential. In SHIP, I confronted my shadow and turned him into an ally. In the process I experienced two profound mystical experiences during separate breathworks; these opened me completely and allowed me to consciously connect with divine power and divine love. This was no small step for a no-nonsense military officer and hardened trial lawyer.

Immediately following SHIP, I tried the biggest case of my career against a major HMO that had misdiagnosed a brain tumor as "panic attacks" for seven and one-half years. The HMO defended the case ruthlessly and aggressively at every level. They denied everything and

---

*SHIP is an acronym for Shamanic Healing Initiatory Process, a concentrated program of accelerated breathwork healing. It will be described in greater detail in chapter 9.

offered only nuisance value as a settlement. After two weeks of trial and three days of deliberation, the jury found the HMO guilty of negligence and solely responsible for the death of my client. They awarded a multimillion-dollar verdict. The money could not bring my client back, but it held the HMO accountable and helped the widow build a new life.

I could not have obtained that justice without the power and love that I discovered within myself at SHIP. I could not have done it had I not turned my shadow from an enemy to a friend who was there to help me through challenging times. I carried that with me throughout the trial and shared that power with everyone in the courtroom. It gave me the ability to reveal the truth and help the jury to get to justice.

I do not know exactly where my life will go from here. There is still work for me as a lawyer. I left the military behind several years ago, but wherever my path leads I will stay connected to the work of Venus Rising and Shamanic Breathwork. The process continues for me.

PAUL HENDERSON,
WASHINGTON

THE KUNDALINI CATERER

My first Shamanic Breathwork experience came to me about fourteen years ago when I was stuck in a bad marriage. I had been miserable for years, married to someone I now believe was an alcoholic. The abuse was mostly verbal anger; he never struck me, but would punch holes in walls or doors. I always found a way to cope, hoping the problems would go away on their own. I really felt on some level that my goodness, understanding, and loving support would somehow overcome the problems.

Years passed—eleven to be exact—although the misery of this abusive, codependent relationship was apparent from the beginning. The real wake-up, shake-up call came after a miscarriage, at which point I realized that if I had had the child, I never would have left the marriage.

My codependent feelings intensified when I realized what I knew my soul needed to do. I went into extreme overwhelm about what other people would think, and how much pain my husband would feel if I decided to leave.

I began searching, reaching out for support. My spiritual path was the first thing that came forth to comfort me. I started exploring alternative healing modalities for the body, mind, and spirit. I started a practice of daily meditation and prayer, along with yoga, to support my process. Somewhere along the way I was directed to Linda Star Wolf as a counselor. Our first session was focused on my family-of-origin wounding, and I was cracked wide open. She held loving space for me as I told my story and began to connect this wounding with my current codependent relationships.

I began to attend Shamanic Breathwork groups as part of Linda Star Wolf's healing practice, and my world began to open up. I had never felt so much connection as I did when watching and holding space for others as they shared their process. I was attracted to the strong sense of spiritual connection, and realized that it was vital for my own growth. I loved the open-mindedness and total acceptance of each person's individual path of healing. Everything about Shamanic Breathwork inspired me to really look at myself.

Through the Shamanic Breathwork process I began to get in touch with my body. The emotional release that came from touching and working with the chakras led me to take classes on energy healing and massage. I began a massage business in which I incorporated many things I'd learned from working with the body during Shamanic Breathwork. I added guided meditations and smudging, along with drumming, to allow my clients to receive messages from their own inner knowing.

Years passed and I went through the Shamanic Breathwork training program and began leading my own Shamanic Breathwork groups, and developed my own style of purification lodges. The lodge became a place where we would journey through the Five Cycles of

Shamanic Consciousness from Star Wolf's teachings. In this process I use the body, sounding, soul returns, and energy releases, all of which came through my Shamanic Breathwork training. I later became the Shamanic Breathwork bodywork teacher for Venus Rising Shamanic Healing Arts.

So many things in my life have changed since meeting Star Wolf and doing Shamanic Breathwork. I have relocated to Isis Cove in western North Carolina and created the Kundalini Catering business, inspired by a vision that Star Wolf had after she tasted a pot of soup I had made for a workshop in Kentucky. She knew, somehow, that I had what it took to hold loving space for others and provide nourishing food for the people who came through our program. She knew that I would be more than just a caterer; I would be a creator of sacred space through the food I prepared.

The things that have changed in my life since my encounter with Shamanic Breathwork and Linda Star Wolf are too numerous to even count. Never in a million years would I have dreamed that I would be sitting up on a mountain with all the members of my soul family doing what I love to do for a living. Probably more than anything else, the gift of believing in myself and staying conscious has been the most rewarding of all.

SARAH JANE FRIDY (MANY HEARTS),
NORTH CAROLINA

STEPPING INTO SOUL PURPOSE

As a housewife and mother whose children were getting ready to leave the nest, and a part-time hypnotherapist and spiritual director ready to move into full-time work, I was on the lookout for the next new technique to assist in my own growth, as well as that of my clients and business. An acquaintance raved about the results she was getting from breathwork, and I decided to try a few sessions. Immediately, I was convinced of its transformative value. However, I knew I would need to travel to get adequate training, so I began to research breathwork training programs on the Internet.

I returned several times to Venus Rising's website. Shamanic Breathwork was a different type of breathwork from what I had experienced, but my soul could feel the call. My ego, however, had all sorts of practical reasons why I should not spend the time and money necessary to commit to a program I knew very little about. A few months after my initial pull toward Shamanic Breathwork, I met Anyaa McAndrew and found out that she was actually a part of the Isis Cove community. She highly recommended that I try SHIP—at that time, a one-year commitment of five, five-day sessions. The synchronicity of meeting a powerful woman who was a Shamanic Breathwork facilitator—a training program to which I was already drawn—confirmed my decision to do SHIP; it was an obvious next, right step.

Shamanic Breathwork facilitator training turned out to be so much more than just another tool in the tool belt. The first year of training helped me move through family-of-origin issues I thought I had dealt with long ago. Many relationships I thought were incapable of change have been transformed. A few have been released. There are so many wonderful new people in my life as we continue to grow a community of conscious, heart-centered individuals here in the Twin Cities and in cities across the nation and beyond. This soul family is weaving the web of a new paradigm. Each soul brings his or her unique gifts to the whole. I have been able to release old patterns and truly step into my soul purpose as a shamanic minister, teacher, and guide.

I have now shifted my focus from individual hypnosis sessions to facilitating groups and assisting others with making deep, remarkable changes in their lives through Shamanic Breathwork and other circle work. Deep individual healing and the community we are creating are the keys to the global transformation we are now experiencing. I am blessed and honored to be a part of it.

DEB IRESTONE (STARWALKER),
MINNESOTA

HEALING OURSELVES—
HEALING OUR LOVED ONES

Almost fifteen years ago, I met Star Wolf at Esalen Institute in California. I had signed up for a workshop on the shadow that she was co-facilitating. The workshop included breathwork, and although I didn't yet know it, it would be a turning point in my life. Breathwork has helped me through almost every major issue in my life, pushing me past the limiting beliefs I had created, forcing me to move through stuck emotions, and giving me the strength to make decisions that have saved my life.

In the spring of 2002 I went through a six-month process of breathing once a month. We had a small group of women from different walks of life, yet we all had issues that were holding us back or keeping us stuck. In my case, I was in a six-year relationship with an alcoholic who was falling deeper into his disease and taking me along with him. I lacked the ability to walk away, and I could not see how life threatening this situation had become for me. About halfway through the process I had an especially powerful session that left me in a state of deep introspection. I had asked that we cut the cords that bound my lover and me, and my mandala reflected the despair that I felt. I drew a woman quietly drowning in several inches of water, yet unable and unwilling to see that the air was only inches above her nose and mouth.

That night I had a nearly violent altercation with my lover that left me feeling unsafe in my own home. The next morning that image of the woman came to me, and she gasped for air and lifted her head. I was finally ready to be done with this, and I immediately called the police and filed a restraining order. Without the power of the breathwork, I am certain that things would have escalated and one or both of us would be dead today. For one of the first times in my life, I started to defend myself—to set boundaries.

I have seen the power of calling forth the inner shaman, of allowing spirit and breath to move through my body and bring forth exactly what I need to grow and heal on my path. As I look back over the past fifteen years, the biggest leaps I have taken have been near, or shortly after, time spent with Star Wolf that always included breathwork. It has helped me to heal childhood wounds and reclaim lost parts of myself, given me strength when I needed it, and allowed me to see and understand obstacles to my growth. I have done years of therapy, and although they have been helpful, none have given me the inner change that is the gift of breathwork.

As I write this I am in the process of another major life change. It started with deep depression that sent me back to Star Wolf and breathwork. There is still much left to do, but already there have been significant changes in my life. As a result of the changes he sees in me, my twenty-year-old son is now healing his wounds and addictions through breathwork. Within six months after I started, my lover is now doing his healing work through breathwork and working on his issues. It is so true when they say that we do this work for ourselves as well as for our friends and family. The healing does branch out and touch the lives of others.

MEGAN BEACHLER (SACRED FLAME),
CALIFORNIA

DIGGING FOR GOLD

I came to Venus Rising in December of 2005 with a background in dance, ritual performance art, and international spiritual activism. I was born in the United States and did much of my sacred work on the continent of Africa with my (then) husband; at that point we had been married twenty-seven years. Our most recent project was a two-year pilgrimage to South Africa, Swaziland, and Mozambique in spiritual response to the pandemic of HIV/AIDS (2003–2005). It was truly one of the most painful experiences of my life. The constant work with PLWA (people living with AIDS) and their families, the shocking deaths of those close to us, and living on the road without a home of our own for over a decade—a lifestyle that was not in alignment with my essence—took a tremendous toll on my life-force energy and my marriage. By the end of the pilgrimage, I was physically, emotionally, mentally, spiritually, and financially bankrupt, and my marriage was shattered. I was in my fifty-fifth year.

When I returned to the States after the pilgrimage, a good friend brought me to visit Venus Rising, and I was later introduced to Shamanic Breathwork as a psychospiritual tool for personal healing. I entered the SHIP training program the following year and began to journey deeply into my wounded soul. As a woman in transition and a spiritual being, the ritual and ceremony of Shamanic Breathwork was the soulful catalyst I needed to inspire change. It brought me tremendous healing and transformation.

Now, three years later, I can say that I am a different woman. The glimpses of my past, present, and future revealed during my breathwork journeys gave me hope, understanding, and clarity about who I am; powerful messages from my inner divine and my spirit guides and allies also helped to facilitate forward movement in my life. One such instance saw me visited by Anubis, the ancient Egyptian shaman and heart surgeon. He removed, repaired, and replaced my heart and performed several additional procedures on me over time until my heart no longer ached from the traumas it had endured.

Dropping below my ego mind directly into my heart and soul during my many breathwork sessions has allowed me to release feelings of abandonment from my childhood; helped me to understand how those childhood and adolescent feelings prompted disastrous decisions in my adult life (especially in my marriage relationship); and given me hope that I could correct my codependent behaviors and the manner in which I had been living my life. An added surprise from this work was the feeling of wholeness that has returned to my being as I continue to reclaim lost pieces of my soul.

I have been encouraged by the practice of Shamanic Breathwork to change my life into the life I want to live, thus freeing myself from earlier, inauthentic living. Empowered by the images, interpretations, and integration of my journeys, I have unraveled the remnants of my troubled life and am in the process of recovery—redirecting, redefining, and reinventing my life. The process has helped me to decipher the puzzle of my right livelihood, illuminated the path I am to follow, and fortified me with tools and strategies that I will incorporate into my medicine as I assist others in finding their own divine pathways to healing. I now hold certification as a Shamanic Breathwork Master Practitioner, and it is my truth that opening myself fully and completely to Shamanic Breathwork has birthed my new life.

In closing, I openly acknowledge that I hold Linda Star Wolf and the Shamanic Breathwork process in the highest regard, and I offer my support in the form of this testimonial.

IN LOVE AND GRATITUDE,
MYRNA CLARICE MUNCHUS (AMAI BUTTERFLY DANCING
HEART/CHANGING WOMAN/SOARING EAGLE),
PENNSYLVANIA, SOUTH AFRICA, AND NORTH CAROLINA

SOUL AWAKENING

When Star Wolf introduced me to Shamanic Breathwork some dozen years ago, I was fast approaching the age of forty and feeling I had precious little to show for my time on the planet. However, since then the self-discoveries I have made and the deep emotional healing I have received through the process have allowed me to step into my authentic vocation as a professional animal communicator. I suspect I would still be crammed in a cubicle doing the clerical tasks I did for twenty-eight years, if not for the psychospiritual insights revealed by Shamanic Breathwork.

Animals have greater comprehension of life energy than most humans, and being able to work with this energy is one of the keys to telepathic communication with them. Self-doubt effectively shuts down the energetic connections, and I certainly had an abundance of skepticism and doubt. I had had a great deal of training in animal communication and other intuitive practices, yet it was Shamanic Breathwork that opened the door for me to truly explore and come to trust the reality of the spiritual and energetic worlds.

I recall one breathwork session in particular that expanded my awareness and strengthened my spiritual bond with animals. The entire process was filled with lessons from animals I personally know, as well as the oversouls of entire species. For example, the spirit of beaver advised me to, "Abandon the Puritan work ethic and adopt the beaver work ethic: Work is play and play is work." In my mind I heard so many animals encouraging me, teaching me, that I could not even identify everyone. My heart and my energy field were wide open.

It was in the midst of this beautiful sense of community that I felt Star Wolf kneeling by me. My conscious mind realized she was performing a soul return for me. As she blew the energy into my body, I felt a wave of joy. Later she told me how she had experienced my soul retrieval, and I was amazed. She described seeing a snowbound, frozen lake surrounded by woods. Incongruous in the white landscape, a large green frog told her he was the guardian of a piece of my soul, and it was time for me to have it back. Frog hopped over to a hole in the ice and explained that it was hidden deep under the water.

Calling her allies, wolf and beaver, Star Wolf dove beneath the ice and saw me as a teenager, tangled in seaweed and frozen in place. Beaver gnawed through the strands, and wolf pulled us all up out of the water. On shore the animals came to my aid. Buffalo gave me his robe. Beaver brought wood, and snake rubbed a stick around and around to light a fire. As she watched my face regain color and begin to thaw, Star Wolf looked around and saw, through the trees, animals gathering from every direction. For a moment she was at a loss for words as she told me the story. Then she exclaimed, "It was like the whole zoo!"

The animals told her they had been keeping this piece of my soul safe for a very long time until I was ready to have it back to use it. This piece represents my instinctual love of life, and they told Star Wolf they had protected it for me because I'm a spokesperson for the animals, and their survival depends on me and people like me (and yes, at the age in which I appeared in Star Wolf's visions, I'd been emotionally withdrawn and mildly suicidal). Star Wolf's shamanic story and own breathwork experiences were powerful motivations for me. Instead of feeling lost and alone, I now have a sense of support and community. I no longer have my old abject terror of change, and I look forward to moving into new roles of service as a practitioner of the shamanic healing arts.

KAREN CRAFT,
IOWA

RELEASING PAIN AND ANGER
FROM THE DISTANT PAST

I met Star Wolf and Brad in 2000 in Clackamas, Oregon at a weekend breathwork workshop. I instantly knew I wanted them for my teachers, because they taught with such love and compassion. I had never heard of breathwork, but was excited and a little nervous. I had been working in the corporate world for many years and had just left a thirty-year marriage. When I heard about this workshop, my soul called me to attend.

I loved the loud music and after doing the breathwork by breathing deeply for a few minutes, my body began moving to the music; soon after, I started feeling all this anger coming up. I began making noises, yelling, kicking, and screaming. I was given some pillows and started beating them with my fists and screaming profanity. My rage was shocking to me and I couldn't stop, and I also knew it needed to be released. I had no clue I was holding so much anger in my body. A couple of breathwork facilitators were helping me and I was kicking and hitting the pillows, calling them names. All this anger was directed at my dad . . . at my abusive childhood. When I left home at the age of sixteen I thought I had left it all behind, and that I was just fine.

I finally became so exhausted that I just had to lie there, and then all this grief came up and I sobbed and sobbed. After the breathwork was over I was amazed, but also embarrassed for being so loud and angry. After being processed by Star Wolf, I knew how important this work was and knew I wanted and needed more.

All of us in the group got together to figure out how we could receive more teaching and breathwork from these incredible teachers, and SHIP was born. I felt so happy and blessed to be accepted into this process. I remember crying when Star Wolf called to tell me I had been accepted into the SHIP program. SHIP changed my life. I continued to have many more breathworks like the first, going deeper into my grief, anger, and pain. With the deep processing and family-of-origin work that I undertook through the breathwork, I realized how deeply I had buried all my wounds and turned the anger and shame into myself. I had ended up in a marriage copying all my family-of-origin issues. I didn't realize the mental and emotional abuse I suffered there was just as bad, or worse than the physical abuse I had endured when I was a child.

I am so grateful for this work and all the amazing ways it has changed my life . . . or should I say, saved my life. I am also grateful for the incredible gift that Star Wolf gives, a gift of holding me with such love and compassion. It enabled me to go deep and do the work I needed to do, so that I could step into my power and my authentic self.

In 2002 I attended an eight-day Venus Rising workshop in California. When we broke for lunch the first day, spirit led me to go up to Star Wolf and guided me to say, "I would love to do Reiki on you." Star Wolf said, "Great, let's do it outside this afternoon." I walked away, astonished that I had made that offer! It was definitely spirit-driven as I could barely utter my name in a healing circle, let alone offer to do Reiki on Star Wolf. I was a nervous wreck, but borrowed a sheepskin to put on the ground for Star Wolf to lie upon.

As I was saying a prayer and calling in my spirit guides and Star Wolf's spirit guides, I could feel the whole large area fill up. While I was doing Reiki on her, turkey vultures and butterflies were flying overhead. We were surrounded by trees, and five deer walked out of the trees and all five stopped when they saw us. They backed up a few feet and stood and watched the whole session. It was magical and the most amazing, incredible session I had ever done.

Later in the week Star Wolf met with me and told me she had received a transmission of Shamanic Reiki symbols, and asked me to be Venus Rising's Shamanic Breathwork Reiki teacher. I was stunned, and doubted I could ever be a teacher. However, Star Wolf had belief in me, and because I trust and honor her judgment and wisdom, I accepted.

She has changed my life by helping me to believe in myself. I have now taught many Reiki classes and am a Shamanic Master Breathwork Practitioner and do my own breathworks. My life has changed beyond belief, thanks to this work and to Star Wolf and Brad. I am grateful.

BARB WESTOVER (THREE HAWKS DANCING),
OREGON

FROM PSYCHOTHERAPIST TO SHAMANIC PRIESTESS

I met Star Wolf at a shadow workshop in 1995. As a transpersonal psychotherapist with a thriving practice in Atlanta, I was looking for new tools for my trauma clients. In my mid-forties, supporting my depressed husband in chiropractic school, I was unconsciously looking for a way out of my unhealthy situation. I discovered my suffering during two breathwork sessions that week; it was something I had clearly been in denial about before. I had both experienced and facilitated breathwork in past years, but this was different. I loved the theory and the overview that went with this work. The way each person's breathwork journey was processed and integrated went deeper than anything I had experienced before. I felt seen and had new insights. I was motivated to experience and learn more, so I was the first to sign up for a new training program Star Wolf was starting the next year.

Our little Good Luck Soul Group met eight times around the country for two years, learning, growing, and changing our lives. A year after I started the program I got divorced, and blossomed as a Shamanic

Breathwork practitioner. This was the single, most powerful tool for deep and thorough transformation I had ever found! My clients, both those with trauma and those who simply needed to get "unstuck," all benefited. I started a few monthly breathwork groups and quickly incorporated Shamanic Breathwork into my practice in many different ways.

I created shorter versions so that I could even facilitate a breathwork in a one-hour therapy session. I sponsored Venus Rising in my Atlanta community so that my friends and clients and I could experience weeklong Shamanic Breathwork events. In 1997 I was initiated as a priestess, and a few years after that I started facilitating priestess circles at the prompting of some of my female clients. I began to create a version of the Priestess Process that I later called the Shamanic Priestess Process. The Venus Rising Aquarian shamanic principles of good shadow work, conscious death and rebirth, the cycles of change, and, of course, Shamanic Breathwork itself were so much a part of me by now that they naturally extended into my work as a priestess. Later, Shamanic Breathwork was integrated into other versions of my priestess work that evolved over time.

Now fourteen years later, I cannot imagine doing therapeutic work without using Shamanic Breathwork as a central modality. I cannot imagine not having it available to me when I feel called to do some personal work. Recently, I lost both my mother and my dog, a beloved companion of fifteen years, within a two-month time period. Shamanic Breathwork is helping me move through my grief in a way that is right and sacred. I am eternally grateful.

ANYAA MCANDREW (WHITE FOX),
NORTH CAROLINA

BASKING IN THE SUNLIGHT OF SPIRIT

My name is Alyson and I am an alcoholic. I was introduced to Shamanic Breathwork about ten months ago when my alcoholism had my life dangling by a thread. I had just survived a suicide attempt and had spent time in a state hospital to detoxify from alcohol poisoning when I was referred to the transformation process at Venus Rising. I was, you might say, willing to go to any lengths to recover from my alcoholism and suicidal tendencies.

The first time I experienced the Shamanic Breathwork process, I was blown away. In the process I was able to recover the part of my soul I had lost when I was raped as a young girl. I'm not sure exactly how to explain it. The breathwork was a spiritual experience that surpassed anything I'd ever known to be possible. I, a grown woman who had been traumatized as a child, was able to release the fear and anger I had held for more than two decades. But it was more than just a release. I was able to see my child self and take that little girl into a place of safety. I began to heal major wounds. I was on my journey of becoming whole.

I have breathed eleven times at Venus Rising this year. I've done Transformation House and SHIP, and have attended a couple of one-day workshops. Each time, I uncover an old wound and begin to truly recover. There have been times in my life that I have been abused, and I can confront my abuser in my breathwork. For most of my life I have mistreated myself. I am able to face myself as my worst predator in Shamanic Breathwork. There are feelings I had never been able to understand or communicate in a healthy way that I have been able to feel, express, and release safely in Shamanic Breathwork. In breathwork, I blast away spiritual blockages and restore the parts of my soul that my alcoholism, depression, and hard living had laid to waste. Each breathwork opens my heart and mind and strengthens my connection to the God of my understanding . . .

I am ten-months sober, and I work a program that is an inspiration to many who have been in AA for years. I attribute a great deal of my recovery to the work I do in the Shamanic Breathwork process. My life is rich, and I finally bask in the sunlight of the spirit.

ALYSON BAUMRUCKER (WOLF DRAGON),
NORTH CAROLINA

STEPPING OUT OF MY COMFORT ZONE

My journeys with recovery and Shamanic Breathwork began within a month of each other in 1994. I believe that the combination of these two has saved my life. My first Shamanic Breathwork experience was with Star Wolf in Iowa; in the process integration group after the breathwork, Star Wolf, whom I had never met before, suggested to me that I needed to decide whether I wanted to live or die. Needless to say, I was quite taken back by this because I was in a deep depression and suicidal. However, I was intrigued with the breathwork and continued to breathe off and on over the next few years. I used to say that I had a love/hate relationship with breathwork. I hated some of the places that it took me, and I loved it because I could really begin to see how it was working in my life. This process was opening me up in a way unlike any of the other modalities I had ever experienced. Over the years I had been hospitalized countless times for my depression and suicidal tendencies, and had been in an inpatient drug and alcohol treatment center for thirty days.

My healing really began when I stepped out of my comfort zone of the Midwest and attended breathworks in other parts of the country; my world as I had known it began to fall away. Indeed, Star Wolf has said that if you do not want to change, then do not do breathwork. I can be a bit of a slow learner, and yet, we all *get* things when we are ready. Star Wolf planted the seed with her invitation to me to decide whether I wanted to live or die in 1994, and the seed began to take root several years later when my soul was ready. This is when I finally understood that what she was asking me when we first met was if I was ready and willing to die to my old self and be born into a new way of thinking.

I was hitting yet another wall in my life in 2004 and reached out to Star Wolf and Venus Rising for help. I was considering coming to their new center in North Carolina and doing a personal intensive with them. They suggested that I come and do the SHIP program. I was basically a noncommittal person and had no idea how I was going to be able to do the SHIP process, yet I knew that I had to. During the third initiation of the SHIP process, the shadow, I was in such a deep, dark place that I did not want to come to the session. However, upon getting here I realized that it was my ego that had not wanted to come, yet my soul knew that I must.

The mandala that I created after my breathwork at that time was interpreted as a tombstone coming up out of the ground. A divine intervention team was formed consisting of Venus Rising staff and my SHIP-mates, and I was encouraged not to go home or return to my job at that time. I came for five days and stayed for eight weeks. I never returned to my job.

I now know that I have been through many life/death experiences. This is a gift of sorts—a gift of experience. I believe that breathwork has played the biggest role in my personal healing. It has opened and healed me more than my many previous years of treatment in mental health facilities and with professionals. Upon writing this, it became clear to me just how much of a healing tool Shamanic Breathwork has been. My recognition came when I realized that I had been hospitalized for mental health issues only one time, for ten days, since beginning my journey with breathwork. Prior to my first breathwork in 1994, I had been in and out of the system for about twelve years.

KATHY MORRISON,
NORTH CAROLINA

WALKING THE PATH OF SELF-REALIZATION

Breathwork changed my life. That's a pretty generic claim, isn't it? How many times have you heard something like that—this changed my life, or that, or something else? However, in my case it is absolutely true— the Shamanic Breathwork process changed my life.

In early 2000 I had hit absolute rock bottom in my life, but I did not know it. I was living in a loveless, totally codependent and unsatisfactory personal relationship. My partner and I were completely and totally enmeshed with each other. He was an addict with severe psychological problems that remained untreated despite his regular visits to a psychiatrist. Our house and lives were a wreck. My partner ran the household through his illness and addiction. I held the household together financially and emotionally, taking care of all that needed to be done. I had taken on all of the responsibility in our relationship without any of the power.

I am a lifelong alcoholic and addict, although by early 2000 I had quit drinking and using. What I had not recovered from was codependency. It was killing me. I longed to change my life, get out of the dead relationship I was stuck in, and strike out on my own, but I was terrified to do so. I was paralyzed.

On Valentine's Day, 2000, I found myself sitting with a small group of people in Star Wolf's living room hearing about the Shamanic Breathwork process. With some fear and yet willingness, I lay down on my pallet and began the deep, repetitive breathing. The music was loud and all encompassing; it very shortly blocked everything out, and off I went on my first journey. I cannot tell you today what happened during that first breathwork session. What I can tell you is that my life began to change—not immediately, but irrevocably. The following July I went to my first weeklong workshop. It was there that I finally understood the extent of my codependency—a realization that brought me to my knees. I came home from that workshop, told my partner we were separating, and went to my first Al-Anon meeting the very next day.

Now, some nine years later, my life looks completely different. I moved from my beloved California to Isis Cove, I work on the staff of Venus Rising, and I make my living by facilitating workshops and helping to support the beautiful people who come here for healing and transformation. I haven't talked to my ex-partner in almost six years. One of the saddest aspects of my transformation was that I had to leave him behind. He was not willing to change, and ultimately, I was not willing to stay the same.

Throughout this time I have "breathed" regularly. The immediate effects continue to be subtle, but the transformation in my life and personality is spectacular. I've done many things in my life—I came of age in the '60s, and I've spent a lifetime in self-examination and analysis—and nothing, absolutely nothing, has fostered the change that Shamanic Breathwork has brought in my life. It is since I began regularly experiencing this fantastic process that real transformation has occurred, and I have finally begun to walk the path of true self-realization. I am, and will be, forever grateful. (Plate 25 of the color insert is a picture of me with the artwork I created to express the new person I have become as a result of my involvement in Shamanic Breathwork.)

RUBY FALCONER (BLACK PANTHER WOMAN),
NORTH CAROLINA

4

The Shamanic
Breathwork Experience

· ·

In transforming ourselves,
we transform the world.

STAR WOLF

Each Shamanic Breathwork session is always a unique experience and journey. The process itself seems to know how to magically take you exactly where in consciousness you need to go for greater healing and transformation. The following is a description of the way Shamanic Breathwork sessions are typically offered in a group or workshop setting. It is important to note that this process can be modified for individual sessions or different group sizes. Shamanic Breathwork can even be done alone, if there is adequate preparation for the sacredness of the journey. (Journeying alone is discussed in chapter 11 of this book.)

Shamanic Breathwork in groups occurs in pairs that consist of the journeyer and the co-journeyer. Prior to beginning, the assembled participants choose a partner with whom they feel a connection. The two decide who will journey first and who will journey second. Each journeyer will find a comfortable spot in the room, lie on a mat, and establish preferences (breathing agreements) with their co-journeyer. Some individuals prefer not to be touched at all during the experience, while others are open to whatever occurs.

During the process the co-journeyer serves a vital, supportive purpose as a nurturer, grounding cord, and guide to hold the sacred space while the other partner journeys. The co-journeyer serves as a soulful companion and bears sacred witness to the psychic and physiological process of healing that occurs while the journeyer is in an altered state of consciousness.

In addition, there is always at least one facilitator who oversees the entire group. The main responsibility of a Shamanic Breathwork facilitator during a group session is to stay fully present for the Shamanic Breathwork journeyers from the beginning of the session to the end, including the sharing process afterward. A facilitator "holds space" with his or her presence and can perform a number of other functions based upon agreements made with the journeyers. The facilitator's intention is to empower and assist in the awakening of the participants' inner shaman and wisdom keeper. The breathwork facilitator may also engage in some energetic bodywork if a journeyer requests it.

The facilitator will sometimes offer soul return and energy release work (see chapter 7 for more information on these processes), as well as focused bodywork to help release "stuck energy" and to create cathartic releases for a journeyer. The Shamanic Breathwork facilitator is present to assist the journeyers, but always remains aware that the shaman is within each of us; thus, the facilitator does not try to superimpose an agenda on the person breathing, even when processing with the journeyer afterward, during the sharing session.

A journeyer can signal the facilitator not to interfere with the journeying process by touching or attempting some sort of bodywork process, and/or to stop the session at any time. There is a definite advantage to having a trained facilitator present, not only in the Shamanic Breathwork journey, but in doing any kind of altered states inner work.

Various books offer shamanic journeys for healing, training, and transformation, and they are wonderful ways to get help in developing a spiritual path or deepening a pre-existing path.

At Venus Rising we begin the Shamanic Breathwork session by smudging each person in the group with smoke from burning herbs (sage, cedar, and/or sweet grass). A smudging tool, such as a fan made of feathers, is used to impart emotional, physical, and spiritual purification. This particular ritual is a common practice among Native American and many other spiritual traditions that may use incense, the ringing of chimes and bells, or holy water instead. When done in an intentional, respectful, ritual space, the smoke attaches itself to negative energy and, as it clears, takes the negative energy with it; the negative energy is released into another space where it will be regenerated into positive energy. The essence of smudging is to clear and expand the auric field and life-force energy.

Prior to the actual breathing process, the lights are dimmed, candles may be lit, and the group is led through a specific meditation; this helps each person to connect with whatever is most sacred, which will guide the sacred process. Ego agendas are released and intentions are set in a process of bringing the true desire of the journeyer's heart into conscious awareness, and using prayer, mantra, or affirmation to support the manifestation of that desire. As with goal setting, it's important to be aware of what it is they hope to accomplish so that they can direct their life-force energy toward that end. However, whenever I enter into a Shamanic Breathwork journey, I affirm my intentions to my spirit guides and helpers and then follow up with these words from teacher/author Shakti Gawain, "This or something better, Creator." For many, this is a time to connect with divine forces, a higher power, Mother Earth and Father Sky, archetypal forces, power animals, or aspects of the inner, wise soul.

The primary facilitator then begins a slow, rhythmic drumming that resonates with the heartbeat of Mother Earth and with the participants' hearts. This increases conscious connection with the body and with higher consciousness. When the facilitator senses that the group is centered and attuned to receive their experience, the selected music for the journey is slowly turned up as the drumming subsides. At this point the breathing portion of the journey begins.

A WORD ON MUSIC

Before taking the reader through the specific elements of the Shamanic Breathwork journey, it is important to explain the role of music in the process. In Shamanic Breathwork sessions we work with chakra-attuned music to open the chakras and allow the energies that are "stuck"—creating blockages to the life-force energy—to become as vibrant and clear as the music. Breathwork removes or dissolves obstacles to the flow of energy.

There are many types of breathwork. Some use music and some do not, but among those that do, I acknowledge my early breathwork teacher, Jacquelyn Small, as one of the true masters of teaching how to create a magical recipe for the musical breathwork journey, rather than just playing random pieces of cathartic music. Jacquelyn taught that aligning the musical journey with the chakras creates a gradual opening into our energetic field, as the music shifts from tribal to more heartfelt, higher chakra music. This opening stimulates any trapped or repressed energies, including experiences and memories associated with the chakras. Many such blockages are linked to life experiences and traumas, including past-life experiences.

Once the energy has moved through a particular chakra and released any stuck emotions, thought forms, or energetic force lodged there, the chakra begins to relax into an open channel through which the life force can pass into circulation throughout the entire chakra system. This allows the physical body and the energy body to regulate the kundalini (life-force energy) once the blockages have been removed.

Each chakra is addressed during the breathwork journey, and specific music correlates directly with this progression, ascending from lower to higher chakra energies. Selected tracks usually do not contain recognizable lyrics, as these could possibly alter the experience from one of the journeyer's soul to one suggested by the music itself. Often, however, lyrics in other languages, sounds of human vocalization, indigenous chants and prayers, or lyrics otherwise unrecognizable to the journeyer are present in the music.

We have seen that the power of chakra-attuned music activates emotions and energies within the body, mind, and soul, but why does music play such a large role in expanding the breathwork experience? How does sound facilitate experiences directly aligned with our intentions? An important relationship between music, sound, and the element of water may help us begin to understand. The research of Dr. Masaru Emoto has shown the way that intention and sound can have dramatic physical effects on water at the molecular level. Through experimentation, Emoto has deduced that the purity of one's intentions has a dramatic effect on water's molecular structure; and that a large composite of intention—as in a group process—will amplify this effect. Perhaps most significant to the Shamanic Breathwork process, Emoto found that water crystals become aligned and beautifully structured when music is projected onto them.

The implications for the human body are significant, given that human beings are typically composed of 65 to 75 percent water. By setting our intentions for wholeness and healing in both the beginning meditation and the selected music, journeyers are opened to larger, whole-body transformative processes experienced not only on the psychospiritual level, but also down to the cellular level.

The vibrational forces of the music assist in unlocking trauma and other memories that have been encoded at a cellular level. If the memories stay repressed they continue to create discord among the body, mind, and spirit; this is sometimes referred to as "soul loss." When the memories are activated and animated, they are expressed, and a catharsis occurs that often brings completion to both psyche and body. With this expanded consciousness the memory can be experienced and healed in ways that are difficult to access through traditional psychotherapy.

A WORD ON THE BREATH

As the music begins, the Shamanic Breathwork journeyer begins to breathe deeply in a rapid, rhythmic fashion; this is a continuous breath, without pauses between inhalations and exhalations. As the journeyer continues to breathe deeply, energetic flow is enhanced by the increase of oxygen. Most people typically use only a small percentage of their upper lungs.

Those who engage in deep breathing experience a sort of super-oxygenation that differs from hyperventilation. The brain, in its super-oxygenated state, is able to unlock energetic, spiritual, and physiological channels not typically accessed with normal breathing. Over the years many researchers have offered a variety of explanations for why this method of deep, rapid breathing creates chemical responses and altered states in human beings; however, what I personally experience and witness in others cannot be explained by traditional science. It is, as Stanislav Grof has stated in his research, "beyond the brain."

By using the power of our own breath, we tap into a secret reservoir of healing. When we begin to breathe deeply and rapidly for an extended period (usually around ten to fifteen minutes), the ego begins to move aside, allowing the higher self to emerge and begin to pilot our consciousness to where we most need to go for healing and heightened awareness. Each journey is a different experience, and the breath is the portal through which journeyers access altered consciousness and cathartic release.

PROGRESSION THROUGH THE CHAKRAS

The journeyer lies down with eyes closed or covered with an eye mask, and begins the aforementioned deep-breathing exercise. The music is attuned to the seven chakras, which hold the memories waiting to be released from these vortexes of energy. (Please see plate 1 of the color insert for more information about the chakras.) Typically, the first two or three chakras (the lower chakras, starting with the base root chakra and the sacral chakra) respond best to an earthy energy, such as drumming, pulsing, and sensual rhythms. Depending on the length of the breathwork journey, music attuned to these chakras is played for about twenty to forty minutes.

The next phase of music is attuned more to the middle chakras, such as the solar plexus chakra, the heart, and the throat, but may also dip back down to the base and sacral chakras; it also begins to have more of a story line. We frequently use theme music from a film or some other form of dramatic music for this middle section. This kind of music often has the effect of opening the journeyer to his or her individual melodrama. This phase lasts from twenty to thirty minutes before leading into a different type of music that addresses and opens the heart, upper throat, fifth, sixth, and seventh chakras.

This final section of the journey is guided by music that has an ethereal, or celestial (some might say New Age) feel to it. These are the sounds of harps, violins, or music that otherwise opens the heart and lifts the spirits. The heart music and the higher chakra music usually last around twenty to forty minutes, again depending on the length of the entire session.

During each of these segments or phases of the Shamanic Breathwork journey, the participants are focused on breathing until they do not have to think about it any more. Breathers are instructed to, "Breathe until you are surprised." As the breathing continues, the journeyers will eventually begin to return to autonomic breathing as they enter altered consciousness. There are periods of intense breathing (especially at first), and then more relaxed breathing as the session continues; however, this often varies, as each person reacts differently to various musical stimuli. Bodywork, energy work, and the experiences of other journeyers in a group setting also may trigger a response in the breather.

Many times during a session a journeyer will have an experience, then slow the breathing, then suddenly wish to start accelerating the breathing again to reach another level of consciousness. In some instances people breathe intensely for only twenty minutes or so at the beginning, and it takes them through the whole journey. If there is an attempt to *program* the breathwork, it will not work effectively.

The final stage of the Shamanic Breathwork session moves from ethereal seventh chakra energy into grounding, heart-centered music with lyrics. Familiar music and the sound of the human voice gently bring the journeyer back to a waking state of conscious awareness. During this music the facilitator begins to softly and rhythmically play the heartbeat of the drum and call the person back by asking the journeyer to, "Take a deep breath, exhale slowly and fully, and begin to gently return to this space and time, bringing back only that which serves you." Upon "returning" from a Shamanic Breathwork journey, individuals are encouraged to proceed with care and intention, as they are still in an altered state of consciousness and possess a widely expanded auric field. Immediately upon completion, the person who has just completed a journey is asked to symbolically express that journey by creating an expressive art form through the Shamanic Shakti Art Process. These artistic creations take many forms, including large drawings, mandalas, mask-making, poetry, sculpture, or journaling, and will be more fully discussed in the following chapter.

THE FIVE WORLDS AND ELEMENTS OF SHAMANIC CONSCIOUSNESS

The truly transcendent power of Shamanic Breathwork lies in entering into one or more of the five worlds (altered states) of shamanic consciousness. Here the journeyer may enter into a number of different layers of reality, or worlds—the sensory world (energetic, physiological responses); the rebirthing world (related to the person's actual or symbolic birth process); the interpersonal/historical world (the person's relationship to self and others in the world, including personal story line); the archetypal world (mythical story lines relating to the transpersonal realm of consciousness); and the void world (no-thing, no-mind state of consciousness). Each of the five worlds of shamanic consciousness relates energetically to one of the five shamanic elements of water, earth, fire, air, or spirit.

The Sensory World—the Element of Earth

The first world of consciousness often encountered during the Shamanic Breathwork journey is the world of the senses, or the earthly sensory realm of consciousness, where all of the senses may be heightened and exaggerated. Participants often report amazing visions of light and other images, colors, sounds, smells, tastes, and tingling sensations throughout their bodies. Sometimes an experience may be particularly energizing to a specific sense, such as being visually flooded with a myriad of colorful geometric shapes or images, or a strong fragrance of flowers, or perhaps of cookies baking. I remember one such breathwork session where I could detect the smells I associated with my grandmother, who had passed away when I was a child. This compelling smell in the sensory level later led me into a whole hour of spending time with my beloved grandmother. During this time I was able to tell her good-bye— something I hadn't had the opportunity to do in this reality.

My grandmother Mammy Jones was an important figure to me in so many ways during my childhood, and although she passed away right after I turned twelve, she has continued to be a powerful influence and force in my life. I think of her as a spirit guide to this very day. Mammy was a renegade Baptist who believed in fairies, extraterrestrials, and all manner of spirits, both visible and invisible to human beings. She taught me at an early age to talk to animals, trees, rocks, and God. In fact, she taught me that God's spirit lives in everything around us.

Mammy believed that all of creation was loved and cared for by the Supreme Creator. She was generous and fun-loving, with a terrific sense of humor. My grandmother could find the magic in any situation and taught me how to read the "signs and omens" that were always speaking to us in our daily lives. As the only child of two hardworking young parents, I spent many happy days with Mammy and my grandfather, Pappy, at their home on Grapevine Road. We spent a tremendous amount of time outside in the garden, the nearby woods, and with the farm animals in the "chicken yard."

They had no phone and there was reception for only a couple of TV channels, so we entertained ourselves in the evenings by singing and telling stories on the porch swing, while Pappy smoked his cigar to keep away the mosquitoes. During this wonderful time, I learned how to hear the fairies speak, look for UFOs that frequently crossed the night sky, and begin to understand what frogs and other night creatures were communicating to us.

I was never lonely or afraid. I felt the unconditional love of my grandparents, but it was my Mammy that touched my soul so deeply and imprinted in my heart and mind the magic of being alive and loving "all creatures great and small." She reached out to others less fortunate, and I think it was her influence that made me initially want to become a counselor. I have tons of Mammy stories, but I'll save them for another book!

It was Mammy who taught me to interpret my dreams when I was just a little girl. We talked about our dreams every morning when we awoke, unless they were bad dreams; it was important not to discuss those before breakfast. She told me that the dreamtime was as real as this world, and that telling dreams before you ate and were fully grounded left open a portal through which those images and scenes could manifest more fully and come true. So if my dreams had been bad ones, I was very careful not to tell my dreams until I'd had something to eat.

Shortly before Mammy left this earth, I awoke one morning very upset from a dream I'd had about her death. She comforted me and asked about my dream, and even though I told her I wanted to wait until after breakfast, she insisted that I tell her so that I could calm down. I did tell her the dream and she reassured me that she would never leave me. When she passed away a few months later, I felt that her death was somehow my fault. It took many years before I was able to revisit this traumatic event and heal the guilt, grief, and fear I had felt around Mammy's death.

When she passed from this level I felt pretty lost, since most of my days and nights had been spent at her house. My grandfather sold their place and moved in with my parents and me for a short while. So the person, place, and animals that I loved most of all vanished, virtually overnight; in some way, so did I.

My Shamanic Breathwork journey allowed me, as mentioned above, to tell my Grammy good-bye. This was incredibly healing for me, since it had haunted me for more than thirty years. The importance of this world of consciousness should not be underrated. It is in this realm that we can finally begin to let the ego take a vacation, and get in touch with our bodies and the life-force energy running through the body. We can stop the tedious mind chatter and laundry list of things to do, and allow our kundalini life-force energy to flow. In this world, free association, instincts, and intuition begin to guide us. In turn, we are led to other levels of consciousness, if that is where we are supposed to go at that time.

This sensory state of consciousness is often experienced early in the Shamanic Breathwork experience and precedes deeper cathartic releases (although it may be experienced at any time during the session). It is often an enjoyable shamanic level of consciousness.

The Rebirthing Level—the Element of Water

The world of rebirthing—utilizing the shamanic element of water—is a powerful place of healing and reprogramming for many individuals. This has certainly been true for me; I have experienced major shifts of transformation while visiting this realm during a Shamanic Breathwork session. If you enter this realm of consciousness, there are a variety of meaningful experiences—or birth patterns—that you may reexperience. The birth pattern is imprinted at the time of one's actual birth, the time of our birth process in coming into the world. For example, the birth itself may have been natural, induced, cesarean, or one in which drugs or forceps were used to enable the process. There are as many birth patterns as there are people. The actual way we enter the planet sets an imprint that is often replayed in the way we make changes in our day-to-day lives.

For instance, I was born two weeks early and I find I am anxious to get things done, and am usually ahead of my time with ideas. My mother had an induced labor and was given ether during her labor. As a result, I often feel that I make sudden changes and move very quickly and easily, but in pushing through to the end, I become exhausted and almost anesthetized. My husband, who was born two weeks late, is much more relaxed than I am about getting things done, and will procrastinate until the last minute and then get it all done quickly.

Birth is a natural and beautiful process, but it has become a mechanical, medical procedure for many in the contemporary world. While medical interventions may sometimes be necessary, this is the exception rather than the norm. Medical interference during the birthing process has precipitated a whole host of far-ranging complications.

The rebirthing that may be experienced in the Shamanic Breathwork process is often an intensely physical undertaking. This is particularly true when it becomes evident that the journeyer is moving into a birthing/fetal position. This is something a trained facilitator recognizes, and responds to by engaging the person in focused bodywork. The facilitator may offer physical resistance and create a type of birth canal with arms wrapped around the journeyer, allowing the person to crawl through to freedom.

The process and length of time it takes for a person to rebirth can vary due to an individual's actual birth process (caesarean, breech, drugged, or other traumas). Rebirthing can be one of the most healing of all Shamanic Breathwork experiences. It is also not a one-time experience. Any time there is a significant life change, the archetype of birth may emerge in the consciousness as the energies begin to shift.

In working with thousands of individuals, I have been able to assist them in resurrecting their old birth patterns and reprogramming their original birth into one that is healthier. Entering the shamanic world of rebirthing will eventually lead us to a more instinctual and natural way of birthing change in our lives, which carries over to how we meet and go through times of challenge.

Although rebirthing is a very important process that often arises naturally for shamanic breathers, until recently I had never trained in, or experienced, Rebirthing-Breathwork, as taught by Leonard Orr. Orr developed his process after finding that experimenting with the breath brought him back into his own birth and allowed him to heal the accompanying trauma of that event. Further experimentation between 1962 and 1974 revealed improved functioning in his clarity of thought and sense of well-being. An estimated ten million people worldwide have practiced Rebirthing, and many have become Rebirthing practitioners.

In the spring of 2008 I received an unexpected call from Orr. He was going to be teaching in North Carolina, and a mutual friend had told him about our retreat center. I had long been a fan of his work and jumped at the chance to meet him at last.

In the course of our meeting, while listening to Orr speak about his intimate connection to a rather famous, proclaimed immortal—an Indian avatar named Babaji—I suddenly felt a rush of energy and inner knowing that Babaji was the true spiritual grandfather of Shamanic Breathwork. Babaji had taught Orr many things that had been incorporated into his Rebirthing process. One of the things Babaji emphasized was the importance of incorporating the four elements—water, earth, fire, and air—into daily life, and invigorating them with spiritual energies.

Those who know Orr know that he is very connected to the elemental world. Every morning he spends time under water in the bathtub with his snorkel; he sleeps by a fire or with candles lit around him at night, and preferably on a mat upon the earth or floor; and he faithfully practices breathing exercises several times daily. He immerses himself in the healing vibration of the elements as frequently as possible. He shared with me that this is what the guru Babaji taught him he must do in order to attain immortality. It was then that I realized that the teachings of the Spiral Path of Alchemical Transformation (which relate to the Five Cycles of Shamanic Consciousness and the elemental world that had birthed through me to create the Shamanic Breathwork process) had its origins in Leonard's work with Babaji during the 1960s. It was as if I had finally found my long-lost ancestral roots that linked directly back to the master, Babaji.

The Interpersonal/Historical World—the Element of Fire

The interpersonal and historical world, with its often-fiery chaotic energies, is an amazing place to revisit and release old patterns of dysfunction inherited from our families of origin and our culture. In particular, experiences of our formative years tend to emerge in interpersonal journeys.

Trained therapists realize that where and how we grow up, the nature of the caretaking we receive, and from whom we receive it are some of the most influential factors affecting personality. Often there is underlying dysfunction (oftentimes stretching back several generations) that has not been recognized on the conscious level. These invisible influences affect us profoundly. Shamanic Breathwork journeyers often tell us that in their breathwork sessions they have been able to access core issues that had escaped them in traditional counseling or treatment. "I got more out of my Shamanic Breathwork session than a year of talk therapy" is a common testament to the deep interpersonal experiences of many breathwork participants. Many individuals enjoy relief and happiness as they shift from ego adaptations formed in childhood to a newfound sense of freedom and original soul purpose.

The interpersonal/historical world does not come without its challenges, however. This level of consciousness can induce a wide range of emotions and seems to bring up some of the greatest personal trauma and energetic charges. People often express anger, grief, sadness, loss, frustration, anxiety, and fear. Once fully released during a session, the results are astounding; a return or new realization of clarity, direction, hope, peace, deep relaxation, courage, and renewal of spirit are the rewards of confronting one's past.

This demonstration of healing at such a profound level was what first sold me on breathwork. My first several breathwork sessions were spent in the fires of transformation, revisiting and reexperiencing many old traumas of my life. During these sessions I was able to express repressed, pent-up feelings of anger, grief, and guilt around several events, and bring them to completion. In addition to releasing all those negative feelings that were having a negative effect on my health—both physical and mental—I felt a real in-my-body shift around some key dysfunctional patterns. The breathwork gave me the ability not only to express and release old patterns, but also to awaken another level of consciousness within my psyche that could witness my journey at a much deeper level of awareness. This witnessing has increased over the years and has resulted in tremendous change in every area of my life, empowering my path in ways I never could have imagined at the time. I now refer to this "awakened one" within me as my "shaman within." My initial experiences with breathwork formed the cornerstone of the Shamanic Breathwork programs that I teach today.

The Archetypal/Mythical/Transpersonal World— the Element of Spirit

In this world of spirit consciousness you might experience anything! The possibilities are truly unlimited. Psychic blueprints that come to us from the collective unconscious and beyond often make themselves known in the Shamanic Breathwork journey. While these transpersonal experiences sometimes can appear unrelated to our everyday, normal way of living, they are always connected to the personal at levels not readily apparent.

Perhaps embodying a wolf running through the woods, or soaring above the earth and seeing with the vision of an eagle is something your inner spirit needs to experience in order to heal. It is not unusual to connect with deities or sacred figures that carry powerful symbolic meaning to one's soul path, without having prior knowledge of these figures. It is in this shamanic world that many people have the deepest spiritual experiences of a lifetime, whether with nature or with celestial figures, spirits, or angels.

The Void World—the Element of Air

At this level of consciousness, all content disappears and one is left with emptiness, or what Buddhists often refer to as the state of "no mind." The nothingness and spaciousness might be confused with sleep, but there is much going on beneath the surface. This level often creates a deep sense of well-being and letting go of the ego's attempt to control reality. In this space people report that they feel new information or inspiration being downloaded into their subconscious mind, and perhaps even into their DNA.

After experiencing this world of the void during breathwork, journeyers will often have sudden awareness, or resolution, of an issue that the conscious mind has been unable to reconcile. They may have a new insight, inspiration, or creative idea that seems as if it came out of thin air. The spontaneous answer to a troubling situation that triggers the release of old, binding patterns is a surprising and exciting element of the healing process, and often occurs in the void realm of shamanic consciousness.

5

PROCESSING THE JOURNEY

. . . .

After breathing, the journeyer (still somewhat altered and assisted by the co-journeyer) engages in "sacred scribing," as well as one or more expressive art forms that we broadly refer to as the Shamanic Shakti Art Processes.

In sacred scribing the journeyer describes specific experience(s) from a session in detail. The co-journeyer scribes the journeyer's account into a journal, and relates back and scribes his or her own experiences during the journeyer's Shamanic Breathwork. This process allows for integration and grounding, as well as for the journeyer and co-journeyer to briefly process together their experiences in the session. (See chapter 7 for some personal accounts relayed via scribing.)

The Shamanic Shakti Art Processes use various forms of artistic expression to convey one's experience. It may include what we refer to as "bigger picture" drawings, mandalas, clay creations, paintings, poetry, journaling, or some other sort of expressive art. The artistic expressions of images and visions encountered during the breathwork journey through the "bigger picture," are extraordinarily powerful tools in the Shamanic Breathwork process.

While initially Venus Rising put much emphasis on the drawing of mandalas as the primary artistic expression for integrating breathwork experience, over the last few years we have expanded the focus of our integrative work to embrace all of the Shamanic Shakti Art Processes mentioned above. The artistic expression embodied in these processes is meant to give full access to the unconscious and conscious patterns that are animated by the breathwork.

The various Shamanic Shakti Art Process expressive art forms are merely suggestions—starting points from which the journeyer's experience comes to artistic life. Almost invariably the experience pours from the journeyer's psyche onto the paper or is molded into clay or another material. This expressive arts process allows the journeyer to quietly reflect upon a powerful experience, using the materials as a form of soulful expression to encapsulate that which words alone cannot convey. The expressive art piece that is presented to the group in the sharing process is both a reflection of where the individual is now and a "preview of coming attractions."

Embedded within each individual shamanic creative art piece is often essential information for the journeyer about the meaning of images, symbols, and motifs experienced during the Shamanic Breathwork journey. These images, symbols, and motifs are interpreted both literally and for their underlying metaphorical meaning and archetypal themes. Archetypes are present in every culture and have been recorded by dreamers across time and from all walks of life with remarkable commonalities.

Psychologist Carl Jung and many others have postulated the existence of a number of core archetypal forces, including the archetypes of the shadow, anima/animus, divine couple, child, trickster, and the self. For men the core archetypes also include king, magician, warrior, lover, and *puer*, or eternal boy. For women the core archetypes also include maiden, mother, crone, and high priestess.

Engaging in a spirited dialogue with the archetypal forces expressed in our art allows us to integrate material that may otherwise exist outside of our waking consciousness. In this process of recognition and integration we have the opportunity to fully engage with core archetypes and purposefully invite them into our consciousness, so that we may live and learn their lessons, rather than resist them unconsciously.

Following is a brief description of the Shamanic Shakti Art Process from its creator, Judy Red Hawk Merritt, Ph.D. Judy is a graduate of the Shamanic Breathwork process, a Soul Recovery Practitioner (practicing soul return and energy release work), and a key member of our staff at Venus Rising.

THE SHAMANIC SHAKTI ART PROCESS

The Shamanic Shakti Art Process is about opening the self to inner knowing, inner voice, and insight (the soul). We dare to encounter the language of the soul by opening the whole self to the materials of soul expression (various art media including paint, clay, fabric, nature and found objects, drawing materials, plaster of paris, mask materials, and so on). We find and investigate the art in the heart; the heart in the art. To do that, we must "hear" with the inner "ear." The words art, ear, and hear are all contained in the word "heart."

This act of heart-centered creation—of bringing into life reflections of self, spirit, and soul—is an innate God/Goddess-given gift to every living being. We all have witnessed the act of creation in the natural world around us in spider webs, the spirals of seashells, and the bird's colorful plumage and flight, song, and dance. The Shamanic Shakti Art Process is about reconnecting to that natural, perhaps more childlike self who made mud pies and sandcastles, flower crowns, and willow branch bows and arrows. This natural self invented songs and dances, played dress up, and leapt and twirled. This is a part of every person's essence that creates and imagines as easily as breathing, and as unselfconsciously. It is the sacred, natural, united self.

This is the self who lives in what M. C. Richards calls "the crossing point,"* the adult union of mind, heart, body, spirit, and soul as a source of creation. We may first have to confront negative voices from the past—like the inner critic, who might say, "That hill can't be purple,

---

*M. C. Richards, *The Crossing Point: Selected Talks and Writings*

that turkey can't be green, that line isn't straight, that person is silly looking"—and give ourselves over to creative, flowing energy. Then, through the act of creating that is not based in judgment or criticism, we can heal the shame under which much of our creativity has been buried.

Imagine the creative flow like the sap of a tree. The flow begins in the roots in the earth, then flows up through the trunk and out the branches to the leaves. In so doing it nourishes all parts of the tree. For many of us our creative sap retreated, much as tree sap does in winter. This retreat muffled our self-expression so that we were unable to express our soul's true manifestation, particularly in school and later in our work, but often in our family of origin as well. We can retrieve that part of the soul that was lost, and which we stopped listening to and recognizing. Relearning how to recognize and listen to the soul can lead us into the state of original integrity, authenticity, and wholeness that is our birthright.

The Shamanic Shakti Art Process invites the return of the inner artist, and like the thawing tree in spring, encourages reconnection with the creative life flow and deep inner wisdom. We are all the artists of our lives, creating our own realities, making it up as we go. Deep inside we remember this truth and long to be open, once again, to the artistic self.

As a process and practice, the Shamanic Shakti Art Process takes the individual deeper into the self. The process is grounded in shamanic practice; everything is done in ritual and ceremony, and with the belief that the healer lives within each individual. Through the act of smudging and setting the intention for the Shamanic Shakti Art Process, the shaman within is called to awaken, enliven, and charge the process with healing and revealing energy.

The shakti energy is intentionally activitated either in the Shamanic Breathwork session or as a separate process at the start of a Shamanic Shakti Art Process session. The shakti energy steps up its circulation throughout the body and provides the shaman within with the stamina needed to build the relationship among, for instance, the painter, the paint, and what shows up on the painting surface. Stamina is needed to be able to stay with the painting, the process, and the breath; and to stay present in the moment. The individual drops into self (the shaman within) and the universe of knowing and connection (the shakti) that is part of every human being's cellular and psychic structure. If painting is the medium of expression for a particular session, the painter is encouraged to, "Paint until you are surprised;" to persist to the edges of the senses and through to where the deep knowing lives and will show itself.

This stamina sustains the act of commitment to become present for ourselves. Others can mirror parts of ourselves to us, but this is a passive experience. To stay with ourselves in any process is a very active process of will, one that often requires a physical, mental, and spiritual commitment to pushing forward with what feels uncomfortable. Traveling through ourselves to where the deep knowing lives requires an act of surrender. We surrender the ego's agenda to the soul's agenda; to know the language of the soul so that we can live in right relationship to our divine self.

Through painting, for example, the Shamanic Shakti Art Process forms onto the paper—or whatever the surface on which we are creating—a visual representation of feelings, which are preverbal body experiences. All feelings are initially sensations in the body before being given a description in verbal language. Verbal language allows us to censor feelings and is many steps removed from the actual, initial, felt experience of the feeling sensations themselves. If the individual can allow the feelings to borrow the hands, the brushes, the paint, and the eyes until the creative expression is complete, until every last fragment of awareness has been expressed, explored, and put into the creation (the painting, the collage, the sculpture, the mask), he or she will be able to see the language of the soul in what is created.

At the end of the session the individuals gather to share their experiences. This step is necessary in order to more fully understand and integrate the soul language. The Shamanic Shakti Art Process takes the individual into the right hemisphere of the brain, there to experience expansion and connection with the Divine. Jill Bolte Taylor has eloquently lectured and written about the hemispheres of the brain in her book, *My Stroke of Insight*.

Through the Shamanic Shakti Art Process we can find the freedom to commit and surrender to exploring the cellular memory of past trauma that lives in our body. Exploring a memory through this process can lead to healing that memory on the cellular level, thereby opening the very cells of our bodies and allowing them to expand and receive the connection to the Divine through the language of the soul.

Upon completion of everyone's scribing and expressive art processes, the circle is reconvened for a sharing and integration (processing) session. This particular session serves a number of functions. It is an opportunity for all participants to become energetically grounded, and for the Shamanic Breathwork facilitators to ascertain if those who have journeyed require additional processing. If so, the facilitators often will engage the journeyer in an energetic process or psychodrama to allow the journeyer to more fully complete the breathwork experience.

The group's main function at this point is to facilitate integration and understanding of the journey. This includes deep interpretation of the expressive art process. Each of the Shamanic Breathwork facilitators is highly skilled at holding sacred processing space and interpreting participants' shamanic art pieces, due to extensive experience from their own inner journeys, as well as their knowledge of archetypes and symbology.

The facilitators engage the journeyers in a dialogue about the breathwork experience and what meanings they make of the symbology emerging from their shamanic art pieces. In this dialogue, the facilitators talk about understanding the power of the archetypal images and may discuss specific experiences with which they assisted, including soul returns and energy release work.

During this group process, the individual journeyer also has the opportunity to receive feedback and support vital to the integrative process. The co-journeyer served as the individual's sacred witness during the journey, and now each member of this group holds the sacred space for the journeyer's unique and cathartic experience. By bearing witness to this journey, each member of the group supports the individual and allows that person to take in feedback and more fully integrate fragmented aspects of the self.

For those who have struggled, or continue to struggle, with addictive patterns in their lives, the Shamanic Breathwork process is an incredibly powerful tool for recovery. Most addictive behavior is rooted in the shame, pain, or abuse people experienced in childhood, or at other times in their lives. The process allows individuals to deeply access these repressed feelings and states of trauma in a way that supports a cathartic and healing experience. This healing happens not only in the breathwork session but also is integrated and realized through group processing.

When we are able to have corrective physical, emotional, and spiritual experiences around our trauma, we are less likely to seek addictive behavior as a familiar way to stay numb or dissociated. The experience of powerful healing in a group setting also creates an opporunity for learning to trust that groups can have a healing energy, and that one doesn't have to struggle with addiction and recovery issues alone. The group setting creates a unique alchemical vessel. We will further explore addiction and recovery issues later in this book.

6

THE SPIRAL PATH AND THE FIVE CYCLES OF SHAMANIC CONSCIOUSNESS

· ·

Working as an agent of change and shamanic minister for individuals seeking answers to life's difficult questions, I frequently hear statements such as, "I feel confused and stuck and don't know what to do," or "I wish I had a map to show me which way to move through this situation." I, too, have felt lost and longed for direction and guidance at various crossroads in my life. My own longing for a deeper understanding of how to move through change in my life without so much drama and pain motivated me to search for that "map." This search eventually led me to the discovery of the Spiral Path of Alchemical Transformation and the Five Cycles of Shamanic Consciousness.

The Spiral Path of Alchemcial Transformation and the Five Cycles of Shamanic Consciousness comprise the first initiation in our more concentrated breathwork process, which is known as SHIP. Because this first initiation is so important and pivotal to the entire process, we devote this entire chapter to fully articulating what it is and its profound significance to the Shamanic Breathwork process. This map of the Five Cycles of Shamanic Consciousness is the very core essence and foundation for teaching people how to shape-shift an old paradigm and create lasting change in their lives.

There are five very distinct archetypal cycles of healing and change that we all experience in our everyday lives. The amount of ease or dis-ease and stress we experience is largely determined by how well we are able to manage each cycle of shamanic consciousness along the way. Each cycle has a distinct mood, feeling, and set of identifiable characteristics that distinguish it from the others. These five cycles act as keys that open our psyches to a deeper understanding of our inner terrain as we move through change. The five cycles provide a map of alchemical transformation that clearly illuminates both the positive and shadow aspects of our psyches.

By gaining a better understanding of the element connected to the cycle you are currently negotiating, you will be better able to embrace the characteristics of that element and utilize it as a guide during your process. Shamans have always interacted with the natural and super-natural elements of this world. By closely examining your sacred scrib-ing, art drawings, mandalas, masks, poetry, sculptures, and other sacred artistic expressions through the lens of the Shamanic Shakti Art Process, an interpretation can be made that will help you recognize your present cycle of change. This will provide an inner knowing, a tool that offers guidance in navigating changes—welcome or unwelcome—and the abil-ity to proceed with awareness.

While certain cycles of shamanic consciousness may feel much easier or more desirable than others, every cycle is equally important and cannot be skipped or ignored without paying a high price. There are no shortcuts through the cycles, yet by bringing focused atten-tion to where one is on the journey, the process can be accelerated. The key here is timing—the most important element of every sustain-able change. Even though each cycle must reach its natural conclusion before the next can begin, the process is not linear, but multidimen-sional, and may be accelerated and supported in a number of ways. If we can recognize, accept, and fully embrace our current cycle, we can proceed into the next phase with far less fear and struggle than we usually experience.

The basic map that I discovered while working with people in the Shamanic Breathwork process is the Spiral Path of Alchemical Transformation and the Five Cycles of Shamanic Consciousness. It is based upon the spiral approach to life, rather than the more familiar linear/patriarchal approach that has dominated the world for more than two thousand years. The spiral path is the sacred marriage of the masculine (yang), linear path to the feminine (yin), nonlinear path. When the circular feminine and straight-line masculine energies merge, the result is the spiral path. We still move in circular orbits, but each time we revolve around the circle we expand further beyond the limits through the spiral. If it were stretched out, this spiral would look like a circle traveling through space, or an expanded Slinky toy.

It is important to note that each cycle, like all things in life, has both a light and dark side. A person going through a particular cycle will often embrace the light aspects and welcome the cycle and its inherent gifts. Conversely, many people will reject the shadow aspects of a particular cycle and resist its lessons. Even though we may not want to experience an unpleasant aspect of a cycle of shamanic consciousness, it is extraordinarily necessary for us to experience the *whole* journey in order to fully understand and integrate it into our lives.

When we align ourselves with these cycles and the symbol of the spiral, we understand it as an ongoing journey. We can postpone cycles, but we inevitably move through them in this life on a continuous basis. By becoming conscious of this process and being able to identify the images, feelings, characteristics, and elements, we are able to embody the sense of empowerment and self-mastery that accompanies a life created through intention.

I have been writing and teaching about the spiral path and the Five Cycles of Shamanic Consciousness for the past thirteen years. I have been assisting others with change and transformation around their issues for more than thirty years. Throughout this time I have encountered and practiced a wide variety of models for healing, guiding, and counseling from medical/psychological models to highly alternative energy and experiential models.

One of the most frustrating experiences in working with others in the process of change is seeing them get "stuck," or regress in their process. We all feel stuck sometimes when facing a challenging issue or when temporarily reverting to old behavior, but it is very disconcerting to see someone lose consciousness and revert to extremely unhealthy and perhaps dangerous situations and experiences from which they never emerge, or only emerge after severe consequences.

One of the most common places for this to take place in is the area of addiction. Many addictions can bring about disease and early death, or contribute to severe mental illness. At the very least, addictions rob us of our vital life-force energy, joy, creativity, and the ability to live a rewarding life.

The simple truth is that our culture doesn't offer a healthy model for change. Change is not a linear process; it does not follow a straight line, nor does it happen in a circular fashion. To keep going round and round in the same old circle indicates that no real movement is happening. It is kind of like quitting taking drugs because you were arrested and afraid of going to jail, and taking up alcohol instead, because it is legal. All this does is trade one negative addiction or behavior for another.

The spiral path is really an alchemical transformation map of shamanic consciousness. The spiral movement takes us through sequential experiences of symbolic death and rebirth on the pathway of changing something in our lives. Change travels in a circular motion on the spiral path, but it is more like orbits than circles, and each orbit moves us beyond the present situation to a more expanded level of awareness or consciousness.

The spiral path may not travel in a straight line, or what is often referred to as a masculine or yang-like manner, but neither does it move in a circular, feminine, or yin manner. The spiral is a powerful symbol that allows us to become both receptive and dynamic in becoming aware of the change needed and the ability to move forward on the path of transformation.

The emerging spiral paradigm is a path for the times we are in, and grasping the concept of the spiral and the ability of the Five Cycles of Shamanic Consciousness to change our lives is the single most important shift we can make in order to awaken and truly shape-shift ourselves and the world around us.

For a shamanic teacher, therapist, or perhaps even friend or supporter, it is easier to assist others in their journey if armed with a working knowledge of these cycles. It is difficult, if not impossible, to help someone stay the course through various cycles of change if we are unaware of what the person is going through and do not trust the process.

From the perspective of shamanic consciousness, we understand that the great wheel of life consistently turns and moves us through many sequences of death and rebirth. With this awareness we understand that there is nothing to fear if we can stay awake and utilize the resources that will help us to progress through each cycle *consciously.*

Often, traditional psychotherapists, teachers, physicians, and healers actually interfere with, and corrupt, the process of death, rebirth, and change because of their own fear and lack of understanding. Their actions are not meant to be malicious; they simply misunderstand the way in which people really change and grow. However, using the Five Cycles of Shamanic Consciousness as a template and map for change allows procession through these cycles with a certain amount of faith, trust, grace, and ease.

THE FIVE CYCLES OF SHAMANIC CONSCIOUSNESS AS AN ALCHEMICAL MAP FOR CONSCIOUS CHANGE

Each of the five cycles is typically associated with a color, an element, positive aspects, negative aspects, and one or more archetypal experiences. Each cycle of growth and change includes both positive and negative aspects that will mirror the journeyer's birth pattern. Unless a healing modality is engaged to shift the archetypal birth pattern, it will most likely remain the same throughout a person's entire lifetime.

Below we explore the five cycles and the unique aspects and expressions of each. Please also refer to the images in the color art insert of this book that were drawn by individuals when experiencing either the positive or negative part of each cycle.

Cycle One of Shamanic Consciousness: The Water Cycle

Element: Water

Archetypal experience: Revisiting the conditions of our entry into this lifetime through our original womb experiences and birth process. Being in the void. Connecting to oneness and Source prior to conception.

Colors: Deep blue/indigo, or pastels of blue, green, and lavender. If the waters are polluted they may appear murky and ominous, with swampy green-browns and blacks.

Positive aspects: Peaceful, relaxed, meditative, gestating, blissful, floating, "being" as opposed to "doing," satiated (all needs met), inspired, receiving messages or downloads of information, and feeling a sense of oneness. (See plate 2 of the color insert for an example of the light aspect of this cycle.)

Negative aspects: Lethargy, apathy, narcissism, laziness, sloth, perfectionism, obsessive/compulsive planning, regression, and helplessness. (See plate 3 of the color insert for an example of the shadow aspect of this cycle.)

The first cycle on the map of shamanic consciousness is the water cycle, related to womb-like experiences. It is often associated with a sense of floating. In the water cycle there is a sense that nothing is really happening or needs to happen. This may be an authentic stage where one is simply moved to rest and be free from struggle. In our contemporary, fast-paced, goal-oriented culture, this cycle is often neglected and dishonored—we do not allow ourselves the time to just be. On the other hand, addictions are often related to trying to return to a womb-like state. This regression to the first cycle is where we may feel comforted, safe, and nurtured.

From time to time, we all get stuck in the various cycles; however, to be fully healthy, we must move forward into subsequent cycles at the appropriate time. Many individuals stuck in a water cycle will have a variety of amazing inspirations and ideas, but cannot ever seem to get motivated into action. They procrastinate. There is never a good time to take concrete action or create a serious game plan. They are always in the getting ready or dreaming stage of "one day." They may be obsessive/compulsive in their need to be perfect, making it very difficult to birth things into the real world. These individuals are clearly stuck in the watery womb of the first cycle. They are dreaming their dreams without manifesting them.

In contrast, someone who has been a workaholic and real go-getter may need to enter into the water cycle to temper a fiery nature and avoid burnout. This might include going to a meditation retreat, taking time by the ocean, or sitting by a fire reading a good book.

People who have had a negative womb experience tend to feel that it is not safe to be born—to make changes and move forward—and experience an ongoing syndrome of being "out there" and disembodied in their lives. It can feel like helplessness.

Cycle Two: The Earth Cycle
on the Map of Shamanic Consciousness

Element: Earth

Archetypal experience: Beginning to travel down the birth canal. Family of origin and inner child issues arise.

Colors: Earthy tones, black, dark greens, and shades of brown. If one is feeling really stuck, the colors may be dense, dark, and ominous.

Positive aspects: Grounding, realistic recognition of limitations, creating a plan, reasoning balanced with creativity, humility, identifying old patterns and sorting things out, breaking out of denial, getting honest, taking stock, and coming to grips with what is not working. (See plate 4 of the color insert for an example of the light aspect of this cycle.)

Negative aspects: Constriction, feeling stuck, uneasiness, fear, feeling unsafe, feeling victimized, resistance and inability to change, overwhelming feelings, repetition of old patterns, and depression. (See plate 5 of the color insert for an example of the shadow aspect of this cycle.)

For the majority of people facing change, the second cycle of shamanic consciousness is one of the most difficult. Because of feelings of helplessness, and sometimes hopelessness, a person may experience an overt or covert sense of depression during this earth cycle. People may seek medical and therapeutic assistance to help them to feel better. At this point in the process, there is a growing restlessness that eventually turns into extreme discomfort if a person is resistant to change or in some kind of denial about an outer world situation.

Even for a willing soul, this stage will still cause some discomfort; for a period of time there is some confusion as to what to do, and decisions appear unclear. There is a distinct feeling that there is no escape from the present situation. We hear people say, "I can't stay in this situation, but I don't see any way out of it either. I feel like I am suffocating." Comments like this are confirmation that someone is speaking from the earth cycle. This cycle deals with having outgrown your present circumstances and feeling the squeeze to move on. It brings up limits and boundaries issues for most of us.

On the lighter, positive side of the earth cycle is someone who willingly embraces the need for grounding energy and begins to explore options and break through illusions. Being in the earth cycle allows us to slow down and make grounded decisions, which can bring some relief and prepare us for necessary changes. The earth cycle is where the realistic ego's needs must be met, and is one of the places in which linear thinking and the ego can be engaged in a helpful way. Before we can take the ego to the fire, it must be strong and grounded.

Cycle Three: The Fire Cycle of Shamanic Consciousness

Element: Fire

Archetypal experience: Opening of the cervix—light at the end of the tunnel, transformation. Shadow issues emerge. Images of death and rebirth, such as the phoenix rising from the ashes.

Colors: Brilliant reds, oranges, and yellows. If one is feeling out of control the colors can appear to be bold and chaotic, and blacks and other darker colors may be mixed into the reds.

Positive aspects: Creativity, movement forward, taking action, alchemy, passion, intense sexual and kundalini energy, and empowerment. Hopeful, courageous, energy of transformation. (See plate 6 of the color insert for an example of the light aspect of this cycle.)

Negative aspects: Anxiety, constant chaos, rebelliousness, emotional volatility, impulsiveness, hyperactivity, struggle, acting as a perpetrator and becoming abusive, addictions running rampant and "acting out," and projection of blame, anger, and rage. (See plate 7 of the color insert for an example of the shadow aspect of this cycle.)

The third cycle of shamanic consciousness is related to the element of fire and brings with it an even greater urgency to create change. This cycle is a place of powerful transformative energies. There is often a feeling of "now or never," "getting off the fence," and, as the Nike ad says, "Just do it!"

When people are experiencing anxiety, anger, or impatience, they are often somewhere in the third cycle of the transformational journey. Rather than trying to alleviate these symptoms, it is important to find a way to express emotions in a safe space, which often frees up the stored energy so that it can be used in a more productive and creative manner. This release into creative action is what facilitates our birth into the world and into new energies. Many people are afraid of the power of this cycle and the anger or energy within themselves. When this power is disowned there is a tendency to revert into the earth cycle and become temporarily stuck in the process, or to strike out and project anger or rage onto another. In fact, any time we regress to a previous cycle, this reversal of progression through the cyclical process may make it more difficult to regain forward momentum for a period of time.

In the third cycle a person's life may be in complete chaos, turmoil, and confusion. This is the negative aspect of a fire cycle. In order to have what we really desire, we have to release certain aspects of what we have. While we may not tear down the entire house, we may have to make a complete mess while remodeling. If we can remember this and remain conscious during the shift, we can have the patience to know things will eventually come back together at a higher octave in an elevated way. On the other hand, if all we do is tear down walls without reconstruction, we often find our lives completely out of control with no sense of purpose or direction.

During the third cycle we often must confront our past, as well as our present and impending future, and make decisions we have been procrastinating about, or afraid to make. It is up to us to do our part, to take the leap of faith and step out without knowing what the outcome will be. The aspect of our consciousness referred to as "the shadow" often rises up and makes itself known during the changes we are making. Others around us may be disturbed, hurt, or confused with our changes in behavior, even if they are in our own best interest and are positive in nature.

Cycle Four: The Spirit Cycle

Element: Spirit—the supernatural or transpersonal element, as opposed to the world of natural elements.

Archetypal experience: Transformation is in process without any more struggle; surrender, letting go, and opening to imminent birth. The miracle of birth is being accomplished. Divine intervention, supernatural beings, and spiritual allies appear to support the journey.

Colors: Green, white, beautiful pastels. These are soft colors, almost invisible as they arise during a more disassociative, out-of-body state of being.

Positive aspects: Trust, humility, calm, inner peace and knowing, relaxation, feeling comforted and held energetically, release of attachment to outcomes of any situation, nothing matters, everything matters, everything is seen as sacred (even the profane), the impossible seems possible, and miracles do, too. (See plates 8 and 9 of the color insert for an example of the light aspect of this cycle.)

Negative aspects: Humiliation; giving up as opposed to surrendering; ego feels deflated or defeated as it is forced to let go of its defenses, self-serving plans, and agenda. Because of trauma and other issues, one can become somewhat disassociative and escape into the transpersonal realms of consciousness, into a state of "spiritual bypass." (See plate 10 of the color insert for an example of the shadow aspect of this cycle.)

The fourth cycle of shamanic consciousness is the elemental spirit; it has a supernatural, transpersonal quality to it. This cycle occurs when we can surrender ourselves completely, without attachment, to outcomes in any given situation. We experience faith in ourselves and in the process. In this cycle we turn everything over to our higher power, or to something greater than the ego's control. It is when we know we have done our part to cocreate change and that it is no longer up to one person alone.

The Twelve-Step program of AA refers to this as, "Turning our will and our life over to the conscious care of a higher power to do for us what we cannot do for ourselves." This is an act of surrender to something greater than the human ego and requires letting go without conditions or limitations.

In the fire cycle there is the need to use our will to push. In the spirit cycle there is the need to stop pushing, to move through resistance and connect with our higher power or higher self. Here we allow ourselves to surrender until we are somehow mysteriously moved to the other side of the situation. This is not to be confused with passivity or with the watery aspects of the first cycle. Often, there is confusion that in the not doing, nothing happens. The fourth cycle calls for the active use of will; it is difficult work to let go and trust that everything will work out in the end.

The fourth cycle of spirit actually brings water, earth, and fire; emotions, physical body, and mind into the highest transformational energy field of being and heart. This is the place of the supernatural—that which transcends time and space. This is a cocreated place between human and the spirit, where the soul finds embodiment. In this place and time we open ourselves and fully surrender to the archetypes and to God/Goddess. We surrender ourselves to the Divine, where magic, synchronicity, miracles, and transformations occur. It is the place of high alchemy and change.

One of the negative aspects of the spirit cycle would be becoming complacent and taking no personal action of responsibility. While we do have to "let go and let God/Goddess," it is important to remember that spiritual growth requires footwork and action; surrender is a verb. It is in this cycle that we may experience grace. One minute we are standing on the edge of the chasm, and the fire is pushing us forward toward the abyss; and in the next moment we are freefalling into a whole new way of being. What once seemed impossible now begins to form into our new reality. This necessarily leads us into the next and final cycle before we start all over again with something else.

Cycle Five: The Air Cycle of Shamanic Consciousness

Element: Air

Colors: Sky blue, gold, silver, brilliant celebratory colors

Archetypal experiences: Rebirth, awakening, and embodying shamanic consciousness. Becoming enlightened, becoming the teacher, freedom from limitation, and visionary experiences.

Positive aspects: Rebirth, visionary perspective, embodiment of spirit. Integration of body, soul, and spirit. Becoming the teacher, longing to serve, being in touch with the "big picture," regeneration, celebration, peace, freedom, enthusiasm, generosity, gratitude, spaciousness, clarity of vision, and purpose. (See plate 11 of the color insert for an example of the light aspect of this cycle.)

Negative aspects: Religious fanaticism, arrogance, burnout, overidentification with the archetypes, aloofness and disconnection from the heart of humanity. In one's head intellectually; or conversely, airheaded and not grounded. (See plate 12 of the color insert for an example of the shadow aspect of this cycle.)

When you reach the fifth cycle of shamanic consciousness, you are in the completion stage of an orbit—a rebirth. It is a time for celebration! This is the air cycle and represents greater understanding. We expand our consciousness to see the bigger picture. This cycle is connected to the elements of air and spaciousness.

Air allows us to take a deep breath and incorporate the elements of our whole experience. It is a place of becoming the teacher and being willing to share our experience as a teacher, writer, counselor, leader of some kind, and mentor. From this place of embodiment we have a much bigger picture, and the journey, along with all the lessons learned along the way, begins to become much clearer. We can see like the winged ones. All the chakras are opened, allowing breath into the lower part of the body.

At last, there is room to breathe! It all makes sense and the struggle is over. We are beginning to live the changes we have been trying to make all along. Gratitude, vision, and clarity are three principle characteristics of this stage. There is often a feeling of wanting to share what has been learned, or gained, from one's experience with others. It feels as if there is an opening, where once there was a wall of doubt, confusion, or pain.

Even though there may be much excitement, joy, or even relief during this cycle, there is also a period of adjusting to this new reality. One of the images that comes to mind is the butterfly that has emerged from the closed chrysalis state in all of its beauty and glory, yet needs some time to dry its beautiful wings in order to fly. Another image is that of the powerful phoenix rising from the flames and ashes into the sky.

While is it a joyful embodiment, it is also a felt sense. One of the biggest pitfalls is feeling that we have arrived—we are not able to hold the understanding of beginner's mind simultaneously with the wisdom that has been gained. An example of this is a teacher who is unwilling to do any more personal work, believing that an apex has been reached and there is nothing left to learn.

Upon entering this cycle, the sense of change in the body is visceral, as is the change in surrounding environments. It is important to recognize, and take note of, all that it took to get to this incredible place of renewal and change. You will need this memory to assist you as you embark upon the next *spiral of change* that is surely just around the bend.

7

Soul Recovery—Soul Return and Energy Release Work

. . . .

More than two decades ago I was working with Teresa Mt. Pleasant, a Native American friend and teacher who taught me many things, including a method of healing that she referred to as "getting rid of negative energies and returning lost spirit parts." I have modified and renamed these shamanic healing methods, calling them "energy release work" and "soul returns." The essential process remains the same, and the results are as powerful as ever.

During healing sessions with my Cherokee friend I realized that I had already been doing similar processes in the inner child/addictions work that I had been teaching, albeit in a more mainstream way. Because we were not restricted by the formal rules and regulations of mental health and treatment centers in our work together, we were able to go much deeper into the origins of what she referred to as "lost spirit parts." Not only was I able to experience greater insights on my spiritual journey, but also I was able to truly internalize them in my body, mind, and spirit. It was through these kinds of journeys that a flame was rekindled within my being, revealing a path that was to deepen over time. Eventually I opened and embraced the special gifts of my childhood, gifts that I had repressed in my attempts to live a "normal" life.

At this time I was simultaneously learning more about breathwork and realizing just how powerful these healing methods were. Between the breathwork and the shamanic work, my psyche opened and I was catapulted into a whole new dimension, which eventually led me to the heart of Grandmother Twylah Nitsch and her powerful Wolf Clan teachings. The combination of breathwork with energy release/soul return work was a natural synthesis for my own healing journey, and I became eager to share its beneficial gifts with others. I soon found that in order to do this to the best of my abilities I would have to leave the institutions I worked for and step out on my own.

The institutions simply were not open-minded enough or geared to the true heart of healing, and couldn't, or wouldn't, take the risk of employing these healing methods—even though they worked. A director at one of these centers once told me, in private, that I was one of the best counselors he had at the center, and that the clients and clients' families loved me. These clients had all shown tremendous improvement in their mental health issues over the course of my interactions with them. In that same talk he also told me to either stop employing some of the weird methods I was using, or at least be discreet while using them. Shortly after this encounter I realized that I would not be able to continue to work in a system that prevented the full expression of what I had to offer to others for healing their lives.

I remember thinking *I must be crazy to leave secure employment, with good benefits, to strike out on my own and offer a method of healing transformation that no one will understand.* I am sure many others around me thought the same when I shared my plans with them. The truth was that I felt an irresistible urgency to answer my own soul's calling, and I knew deep down that I could no longer avoid what my spirit was guiding me to do.

Almost twenty years ago I opened my first independent alternative healing practice, called Recovery and Discovery Counseling Services, right on Main Street of a small town in western Kentucky, population 15,000. My work was an immediate success, although given the fact that I was in a small, Bible Belt community, it was not without its challenges. Some of my clients would sneak in the back door of my office building to avoid being seen coming in for treatment with the weird woman who used strange, unorthodox counseling methods for emotional clearing and healing. But while my clients may have been somewhat intimidated by the unfamiliar treatment they were receiving, one thing was clear to them—my form of therapy worked!

Word soon got around, as it often does in small towns, and I had a very mixed experience with the people who lived there. The effectiveness of what was happening overrode many of their fears, and some of my harshest critics eventually showed up to do "that breathing thing."

One woman, a children's agency director who later became a good friend, told me she was actually warned by some of the religious far right, who also worked in social services, to stay away from that weird woman using strange methods of healing. She said she used to drive around downtown looking for me, even though she had no idea what I looked like, thinking that maybe she would spot me with horns growing out of my head or something.

I had several confrontations with some more conservative and narrow-minded individuals and groups during this time, but I held my ground and kept doing the work. This made me stronger in my convictions, allowing me to trust more deeply in the healing transformational process I was involved with, and to become even more determined. It wasn't always easy and at times I felt like trying to go back to my old life, but something inside kept me on course, and I knew that I was learning how to walk in my spiritual truth and from my deepest truth.

Over time the mutual trust, respect, and love my clients and I felt for each other deepened and grew. A majority of them were women, and many of them are dear friends to this very day. My first breathwork group there consisted of a group of amazing women who named themselves the Wild Wolf Women's Circle. I facilitated their group for a year, doing breathwork on a monthly basis. I had the privilege of witnessing the rapid transformation of these wonderful, high-spirited women as their lost soul parts returned and their spirits found freedom from the darkness of repression, so prevalent in towns like the one in which we lived. The work I did with these trusting souls laid the foundation for all the trainings and healing work I do today. I bow with an open heart of deep affection to these lovely ladies, and some brave fellas, who took the risk and trusted me with their hearts and souls as we explored these accelerated healing processes together.

THE WORK ITSELF

During a regular breathwork journey, trained facilitators may become aware of a journeyer's need for a soul return, or to release blocked energy before the soul piece can be successfully returned. This awareness often occurs during an intense bodywork session, but it can also occur while a facilitator simply scans a breather's body and auric field. The facilitator's hands are placed where they feel intuitively guided; eyes are closed and the breathing is slightly elevated as the person enters deeply into the journeyer's energy field.

Although I truly believe that the shaman lives within each of us, sometimes it is necessary to receive assistance from another in order to access this inner healer. Just as an intact, healthy immune system can usually ward off illness and disease, there are times when intervention and medical treatment are also required. The first step is to empower and encourage the journeyer to awaken to the inner shaman and do whatever healing work is possible on his own. The facilitator may then utilize other methods such as bodywork, energy release work, and soul return, if appropriate. The intuitions of the journeyer and the Shamanic Breathwork co-journeyer, or group facilitator, are heightened during this process, which creates a great opportunity for radical transformation for the journeyer. I have both facilitated and witnessed the healings that take place during these amazing journeys thousands of times over the years.

A variety of experiences may occur during this time. Often the facilitator will experience a vision, or short journey, during which that person will retrieve some "lost" part of a journeyer's past experiences (even past-life experiences) and return it to the present for healing and release (soul return). However, as stated above, many times before a soul return can happen, it is necessary to dissolve one or more obstructions to the journeyer's energy field by using blocked-energy release methods. Facilitators detect these oppressive obstructions in many forms. They may emerge as dark, ominous, or otherwise threatening images (for example, creatures, dark amorphous masses, ball-and-chain symbolism). The facilitator may attempt to release the oppressive presence in a variety of ways: by engaging the energy in a dialogue, questioning what aspect of the soul it is protecting or for what it is compensating; by negotiating the release of the lost soul piece (recall the earlier discussion of spirit lawyering); or by transmuting, rather than dissolving the negative presence.

The facilitator may use a personal spirit guide/totem in conjunction with one of the journeyer's, to assist with the release and return. The facilitator usually symbolically releases the soul parts and energies through a variety of methods such as cupping hands and blowing the energy of the soul parts into the person's energy field, into the earth, or skyward—allowing the natural elements of nature to transmute them. Sometimes rubbing the hands together quickly and placing them over, or on, the energetic field and body of the breather completes this process. Crystals and other stones are sometimes used, in addition to other sacred healing tools. These are only a few of the methods that advanced facilitators may use while working with a person, either in a private session or within a group Shamanic Breathwork session.

The purpose of touch in Shamanic Breathwork is purely in the service of healing. It is important to note that many who have experienced physical and sexual trauma need to be reassured that their physical boundaries will be respected and maintained. It is explained in detail to each of the participants that, during the process, the facilitators may ask a journeyer to receive structured, focused bodywork. The facilitator will scan the journeyer's auric field and then place hands on the chest, shoulders, feet, head, or other appropriate body part to facilitate the release of repressed emotion and memory in the body. The journeyer may request at any time not to be touched, and this should be respected immediately.

The Shamanic Breathwork facilitator identifies specific areas of the body where emotions appear to be blocked as a result of conscious and unconscious repressive mechanisms. By placing hands strategically on the journeyer's "stuck" places, it becomes possible to physically and energetically assist the journeyer in identifying, releasing, and often resolving repressed emotion or trauma. This is an essential aspect of the process, since the facilitator can utilize somatic techniques, which traditional psychotherapists are neither permitted, nor trained, to utilize.

GUIDELINES FOR THE SHAMANIC BREATHWORK FACILITATOR DURING SOUL RECOVERY WORK

When a facilitator is conducting a soul return or blocked energy release for another person, the following guidelines are very helpful to the process.

1. Always come from an open, grounded heart. Nothing will truly work unless your heart is open and grounded in the truth.
2. Truthfulness creates integrity.
3. Integrity centers you in your higher self, which creates trust, an essential condition for successful healing. It is very important to have trust in the process as well as self-trust, so that as a facilitator you will be able to fully trust the process and the intuitive "hits" or flashes of understanding you receive while working with Shamanic Breathwork journeyers.
4. Trust inspires confidence and feelings of self-worth.
5. Self-worth births stability, which creates the grounded energy needed in order to be a solid and safe space holder for others.

6. Use truth as your protection and boundaries as your strength.

7. Find your symbols and give them meaning before unwanted symptoms come looking for you. Everything in life is symbolic: the clothes we wear, the food we eat, the music we listen to, and the icons we choose to honor. By learning more about which symbols we are intuitively drawn to, and what effect they have on our lives, we can really begin to see the deeper meaning behind them. As our consciousness changes, so will our symbols begin to shape-shift. We may find that something that we have long been attracted to—like a particular animal such as the wolf, or hawk, or horse—has a much deeper meaning in our lives than it did when we were younger in our conscious awareness.

There are layers upon layers of hidden meanings present in the outer symbols we unconsciously choose, and inner searching eventually reveals their healing energy for us, and why they are our medicine. Symbols are the outer expression of the language of the soul, and their metaphoric meanings are filled with clues that will help to heal others, as well as ourselves. If we fail to pay attention to the symbols that our souls guide us toward, they may turn into a lower form of energy, called a symptom, in order to seize our attention. Symptoms inform us that something is not working and that we need to pay attention in order to restore balance to some aspect of our lives.

Once you begin to have a sense of what is meaningful to you and what symbols are yours to use—a crystal, a cross, a feather, or perhaps your favorite dog who has passed to the other side—they will begin to appear, or call to you in synchronistic ways and download their messages of healing to you. When you are self-aware and have a strong connection to what has meaning for you, you will feel the connection with your spirit allies and can assist others in finding theirs as well. Then you will experience self-confidence and a sense of empowerment when working with others.

8. Your experience and the symbols that are speaking to you

become your medicine. Sometimes these symbols may have been in your awareness for a long time, and at other times you will engage entirely new symbols filled with energetic meaning for you and for those with whom you are working.

9. Create a purification ceremony wherein you smudge, burn or apply oil, sprinkle herbs, ring bells, chant, immerse yourself in water, or utter sounds or tones. While sometimes toning and sounding are used during a session, typically the purification process happens at the outset of the process in order to set the atmosphere and clear the air, and to help create sacred space.

10. Find your symbols for protection and use them. The symbols for protection are your spiritual symbols that empower you to travel between the worlds and to part the veils of consciousness. An example might be surrounding yourself with a golden light, or placing a glowing web of protection around your auric field so that you neither take on anything that is not yours, nor leave anything of yours with the journeyer. Set safe energetic boundaries around yourself and the Shamanic Breathwork journeyer.

11. Call upon and invoke your sacred allies, animal spirits, angels, and any helpers you choose to assist you with your healing work.

12. Turn over the outcome and results to the Greater Power of your understanding (God, Goddess, higher self).

13. Create a private, safe, and sacred space in which others can do their healing work.

14. Explain the soul recovery process to them briefly.

15. Take them on a guided meditation to help create relaxation and an open state of being.

16. It's important to use many methods to help create the altered state, such as music, breath, drumming, dancing, singing, chanting, bodywork, art processing, and so forth.

17. The altered state is essential to help others to gain a larger perspective into their world.

18. When you journey you may have to bargain or make a deal as a spirit lawyer with different aspects of the psyche, in order to create a pathway home for the soul piece that has gotten off track.

19. When you return, release the soul piece into the other's energy field. You may do this by cupping your hands and blowing the energy into different areas of the journeyer's body or energy field. Anything else you feel you need to release you may do by blowing it into one of the four elements: the earth, air, fire, or water. All of the *neters,* or nature spirits, have the power to neutralize the negative energies and return them to the great field of plenty to be recycled for renewable energy.

20. Assist your person in coming back with drumming or soft music.

21. When you journey for another, trust what comes to you; and when you come back from the journey, share the soul return and energetic release work that you did with the journeyer in a loving, nonthreatening way. Allow the person to guide you—with body language and other subtle clues—as to how much she is ready to hear. It is unnecessary to tell the person every detail, as the work has already been done and her spirit and body have registered it completely.

22. Help the journeyer to ground by doing expressive art forms such as the Shamanic Shakti Art Process, which may include a wide variety of art forms. Also a snack and a drink of fresh water will help ground the energy.

23. Help the person to realize that unless he cares for the returned part, it may fade from his life again, much as a dream will, and its message will be forgotten unless attention is paid to what it has to teach. It is very important to honor the process in an ongoing way.

24. Cultivate your sense of humor and your intuition, and use them both in the work that you do.

25. Offer ongoing support to the person who has journeyed or refer her to someone who can continue to support her journey, such as a counselor, shamanic minister, drumming circle, talking stick circle, meditation group, or sponsor.

26. Express gratitude for the journeyer's willingness to heal and transform his life, and for allowing you to be a part of his journey. Encourage each person to celebrate life, transformation, and the gifts he has to offer as a result of doing soul recovery journeying and healing—not only for himself, but also for the world.

TRUE LIFE SOUL RECOVERY JOURNEYS

The following twelve accounts are of the work done, in pairs, utilizing blocked energy release work and soul return. The first person's account in each pair represents the story from the journeyer's point of view; the second account is that of the co-journeyer who facilitated the process and held the sacred space.

i. Tena Turek (Windraven)—Soul Recovery

Tena Turek/Windraven (journeyer): During the breathwork I was with a white tiger who took me to a pond surrounded by every species of large cat. I was told to take a good long look into the pond, where I could see into the depths of my soul. I was told I was now the leader of the entire feline kingdom and needed to rebirth into my new role. After I did that I prepared for a celebration by grooming myself. During the celebration I summoned two cats at a time and sent them out into the world. They later returned to me with gifts that needed to be blown into my chakras. I was given the gifts of grounding, life-force energy, power, unconditional love, the courage to speak up and tell my truth, intuition, and a connection to spirit. I was then told to open up to the abundance of the universe, so I raised my arms above my head in gratitude and opening. During my integration journey I met my fourth grader who was called stupid by her teacher, and I also saw myself in a past life as a dancer in a men's tent where the men were seated at tables around the perimeter and the girls danced in the center. As I was coming out of a spin I was stabbed in the belly by one of the men because he did not like my dancing; he said I wasn't good enough. The feeling that I am not good enough has been a core issue for me all my life. (Plate 13 of the color insert is a picture of me with some of the artwork I created after my breathwork session.)

Terry Walker (co-journeyer): My co-journey with Windraven was very dramatic. With touch and mental telepathy I sent Windraven all the love and support I possibly could. I wished her a happy, successful journey and off we went. She became a tiger prowling and growling and hissing through the forest. She was angry and troubled. Windraven asked me to put up resistance; she had this strong need to push. So on my knees I did that, and she nearly knocked me over. Howling very loudly she rebirthed anew. I held her abdomen and encouraged her as she went through this. Proud and majestic, she called in others to come. She was confident, gifted, and felt good. I sent her love and stroked her back and head. She proudly licked herself the way a cat would. She then proceeded to lie down and rest, holding her hands to the heavens to give thanks and connect. Then she brought them down and crossed them over her chest. I placed my hands over hers, over her heart. I also gave thanks to the Creator, to Windraven for her new empowerment, and for being fortunate enough to be part of this wonderful soul recovery.

◎ ii. Terry Walker—Soul Recovery

Terry Walker (journeyer): My journey took me through the chakras. It started with a young girl of around fourteen running away from fire and chaos to a wooded area surrounded by animal friends. Then a goose took her away on an incredible adventure to an island, a river with ducks, and a leap over a waterfall; and finally up into the sky to a place of empowerment and peace. The last vision was of a beautiful, pink quartz crystal shining magnificently: the symbol of unconditional love. My journey is expressed in my shakti art piece. (See plate 14 of the color insert.) This soul journey process and creating the shakti art was incredibly transforming for me. It would have taken me years and years of therapy to accomplish what was achieved in this soul journey recovery session.

Tena Turek/Windraven (co-journeyer): When I was a co-journeyer for Terry I felt heat in her belly and there was a fire burning off everything that was holding her back. The fire needed to be contained so it wouldn't get out of control. When the fire was out, a confident, self-assured young woman in a business suit and stiletto heels was there and anxious to come back, but she said she didn't need the suit and heels and put on something more comfortable. Next I had my hand on Terry's heart and there was a group of children of all ages in her heart who were lost, sad, and struggling. They came up my right arm, passed through my heart and down my left arm, back into her heart. The third thing was that I was clearing a bunch of worms out of her head and putting a seesaw in to create balance.

◎ iii. Judy Merritt (Red Hawk)—Soul Return

Judy Merritt/Red Hawk (journeyer): I am aware of going into the journey space with a huge headache and feeling as if I will vomit. My intestines have been bothering me for weeks now . . . we call that "being in process." I am aware of being very still throughout the journey. At one point, I am burning hot all over and have the sensation of being covered with feathers, as though I am either growing feathers and turning into my Red Hawk self, or a huge bird is lying on me. It felt suffocating to have the huge bird lying on me, and I didn't want Pat's/spirit's hands on me. As I type this, the image of being "incubated/hatched" comes to mind for the first time, and the next part makes a different sense: the urge to curl up on my side, as small as I can be, as still as I can be, barely breathing, in despair.

My mandala paintings represent a red speck suspended between a gray heaven and earth, and a close examination of that speck reveals fire and turmoil, with perhaps a way out—a toxic womb, or perhaps, what conception is like; and not unlike the roil and toil of the earth and the heavens being conceived and birthed through fire and explosions. And I so long to be reconceived, gestated, and born anew. As I lie on my side, I despair of being born/hatched again . . . the struggle of hatching myself is highly overrated. I am angry, yet I have not the strength and desire to crack that egg, to beat wings against that cocoon. I just want someone to find the egg, take it home, tend to it lovingly, maybe even knock back from the outside to let me know someone is out there, so that I have hope to come into love and tenderness and kindness in this world. Perhaps I can just quietly die inside the egg . . . I am aware that Pat is at my back and I am powerless to respond . . . perhaps she is knocking on my egg. (Plate 15 of the color insert is my artistic expression of this experience.)

Pat Cummins/Shamasees (Sheewho) (co-journeyer): I called in my guides and personal totems and asked that my personal ego step aside so that I could become a heart-centered, transparent soul return practitioner for my partner in this journeying between the worlds. I'm grateful for this opportunity and appreciative of whatever level of trust my partner can open to me.

The drumming began and I was called to go in. Judy Stillwoman lay motionless upon a blanket. I shape-shifted into a form known unto me as Shamasees. There were cave-mothers chanting and circling outside a cave. It was a circle of women . . . chanting and calling for Judy cave-child to return. "Return, return, return to the mother . . . return, return, return to the mother." Undaunted by the hours, they circled and chanted for the longest time.

A rather large gatekeeper blocked the cave entrance—a Motherbuddha, who wouldn't let the cave-mothers enter. A cave-child within could hear the women calling, and she was terrified. Looking back outside from whence she had come, one could almost hear her saying . . . "One mother was bad enough—why would I be dumb and stupid enough to respond to a whole tribe of them?"

Yet there was a yearning . . . a yearning that eventually became irresistible.

Cave-child tapped Motherbuddha on the back and climbed up to her shoulders, where she peeked over. Perched there she could watch unseen as the women circled. Silently she watched the women circling and calling her to return. "Return, return, return to the mother."

Listening and watching the chanting women, a desire to join the dancing emerged. This desire grew bigger and bigger with each circling round. Eventually, her yearning to join in became larger than her fear. Slipping through the gatekeeper, cave-child cautiously revealed herself . . . a girl nearly thirteen emerged. She appeared to be shy and anxious, unsure and yet determined, simultaneously scared and hopeful.

The circling cave-mothers made space for her to join the enchanting dance. Last I saw her, she was dancing, chanting, and circling round . . ."Return, return, return to the mother."

Shamasees's heart fills with joy. Blessed be the witness of such attending.

Next, as shamanic soul return practioner, I simply sat beside Stillwoman's motionless form; her hands were overlaid upon her belly. At some point there was a calling to place my hand on top of hers. For a while my hand gently rested with the up and down motion of Stillwoman's breath.

Slowly Stillwoman removed my hand, and soon after turned onto her right side.

Her feet crossed, one atop the other. Time passed. Stillwoman's body curled into itself. Shamasees stood to gain a larger view. Witnessing from that angle, she sensed a chrysalis had been formed about Stillwoman. Each time there was an urge to touch or interact, I held back. Something sacred was happening and I didn't want to damage this process in any way. I simply sat and held loving space for this butterfly's emergence.

I don't recall the exact sequence, but somewhere in the journey

Shamasees had seen needlelike points sticking everywhere in a motionless child. The needlelike points were long-spined stickers, or prickly pears. Shamasees began to pluck them out. They were needles. Shamasees gathered handfuls of them, and laid them into a pile upon the earth blanket. The needles were laid aside and saved . . . lest the child-butterfly-Judywoman might need them later for basket making.

Shamasees recalled from her own life journey that, "Whatever takes you in can also take you out," and "Whatever takes you out can also bring you back."

The possibility for healing comes and goes both ways.

The drumming shifted and Star Wolf's familiar voice invited us to begin returning.

Shamasees/Sheewho knew there was a backdoor to the heart, and so lightly placed her hand upon Judy Stillwoman's backdoor heart. The touch seemed to be accepted. Slowly and gradually this touch expanded to other areas of Stillwoman's back. It seemed as though some sense of embodied touch was now being returned to Judy: woman-child-of-then. As soul journeyer, it was my hope that a new sense of caring could be imparted. I felt blessed to have shared this partnered soul return journey.

Returning from the journey and into the room, Judy and I made eye contact and shared brief whispering. I felt some trepidation about an earlier commitment to leave the session early. I hoped that this newly returned Judy could hold and receive additional support.

So it is . . . blessings of the journey.

⊙ iv. Pat Cummins (Sheewho)—Soul Return

Pat Cummins/Sheewho (journeyer): Judy was the shamanic Soul Recovery Practitioner who co-journeyed on my behalf. I was journeying to let go of fear and become pure of heart, so that I could pass symbolically through the needle's eye, which was a wooden staff that I'd brought with me. I'd found the staff several years ago while walking in the woods.

I also had a desire to retrieve my twenty-three-year-old self, an aspect of myself that had gone underground as a result of a job loss. There was an attendant sense of anger, shame, and failure that I'd locked away for nearly forty years. I'd not been aware of this need for retrieval until my arrival at the Cove. The first night I had a dream. The next day, Star Wolf offered a teaching that triggered my dream memory. I knew that I must seek out my twenty-three-year-old self and return her respect and enthusiasm, in order for me to step out more fully as a shamanic practitioner.

I was surprised that when I found her, I also found my two-and-a-half-year-old self, who had been adopted.

I began journeying on a path that seemed to be in a jungle environment (perhaps Peruvian). I was shaking a tin can rattle. Animals alongside the path began to journey with me.

Almost out of nowhere a pyramid structure appeared. It was the Temple of Shame and was constructed of beer cans. At twenty-three, after losing my job, I had turned full-heartedly to alcohol to drown my feelings.

A large woman figure blocked the temple entryway. She was formed of sticky tar, pinecones, leaves, dirt, and feathers. The journey group touched and rocked the mounded statue. She began to loosen and feel their touch. My journey-self asked, "Will you let us see and be with her who is hidden away in shame?"

The mounded statue woman immediately covered her eyes and said, "If I let you meet with her, she might be mad at me." The statue cried. She told the story and cried.

Then there was another shamanic journey into the jungle. This group was being led by the twenty-three-year-old, who was carrying a tin can rattle. She was surprised to discover that the Temple of Shame was now only a miniature that sat on a mound of dirt where two streams merged into one. She recognized the intact etchings, even though they were now tiny. Time had surely changed things.

Where the Temple of Shame once stood, someone had built a large and shiny new temple by melting and recycling the aluminum cans, and inlaying the structure with gold and multicolored gemstones. A beautiful, yellow-golden sun woman sat in the portalway. I recognized her as the Liquid Light of Living Grace, whom I've met in other journeys. One must pass through her to gain entryway into this temple of everlasting grace. I moved toward the light.

Next, I stood and leaned fully into the staff, and knew a felt-sense of my heart's piercing. With the help of a butterfly's weavings, my vision heart-self was passed back and forth several times through the needle's eye.

Blessed be. No longer limited by the hindrance of old belief, there is a sense of true returning.

⁘

Judy was there to help in every way, and as my spirit asked, she helped to make it be. At one point she blew a shamanic aura about me with her breath, which seemed to give me form. As the drum called us back, we lay beside each other, and even as I knew she was Judy, she also doubled as my returned selves (ages two and twenty-three).

This was a life-changing journey and I had difficulty condensing it for speaking. Bless Judy, she touched and spoke to me . . . asking that I take a moment to go within and retrieve that which was essential. (Plate 16 of the color insert is a picture of me with some expressive artwork I created following this breathwork session.)

Judy Merritt/Red Hawk (co-journeyer): Before her shamanic breathwork, Pat shared that her intention was to be rid of the shame of her twenty-three-year-old self. I did not know the story of that shame, and felt that I didn't need to know. This is an intuitive process, a soul-directed process, not one of facts. My role as a co-journeyer is to be handmaiden to my journeyer. I assist my journeyer's process, taking cues from her/his direction, sometimes hearing, seeing, or feeling something intuitively related to the journeyer's inner experience.

Pat knew exactly what she needed and I followed her need and her direction . . . that also included keeping her safe: The "eye of the needle" wood staff she was using in her journey was sharp at both ends; she was altered and would not be aware of injury. While I had no knowledge of exactly what was occurring in Pat's inner journey space, I knew I needed to keep her safe. I also knew I needed help from Star Wolf, who was nearby, since I had only two hands, the staff was long, and Pat was up and very active and interactive with the staff.

Toward the end of the journey, something quite sweet and magical occurred when I felt inside the role of the handmaiden, the priestess ministering to this radiant being who had been made more whole. I was called to energetically wipe away the residual of shame from around her, as though wiping clean a new baby after birth. Then, I needed to honor this new being with the touch of breath around her; she was too delicate and new to touch, as though her butterfly wings needed to dry in the air. So I simply blew around her to dry her off as she completed forming herself . . . it was an honoring, a supplication, a ritual, and a ceremony . . . an incredibly intimate experience.

◎ V. Holly Frey (Dancing Bear)—Soul Return

Holly Frey/Dancing Bear (journeyer): In my first breathwork session the dog I had lost to cancer six months prior came to me with the message that he'd help me from the other side. I also received the gift of power from a beautiful angel, and then experienced a rebirth. In the second breathwork I became a bear walking my path of introspection, nudging folks along the way so we could all be strong and dance together. At first I had felt that this was a path I would walk alone.

I was then taken to Isis Cove and Spirit made it clear to me that I was to keep moving and that I am on the right path. I am not, and would not, be alone. Black Panther Woman returned a nine-year-old child to me who told her that, "They gave my dog away." My family had given my dog away when I was nine years old. It felt really good to have that child come back to me, and to know that my recently lost dog is also with me.

A fifteen-year-old Native American boy also returned. This boy had been ridiculed by his tribe for being a coward because during a battle, he had run back to the women's tent to protect them. Black Panther Woman watched him leap off a high cliff into deep water to prove to himself that he was not a coward. He then danced gleefully in celebration of his power and courage. My path in life is to help other women regain their power, as I have worked to regain mine. I am grateful to have these soul pieces returned to me.

Ruby Falconer/Black Panther Woman (co-journeyer): Holly did not move throughout her journey. She went into it immediately and it was as if she went far, far away very quickly. I journeyed for her twice. I first came upon a small girl about seven or eight years old. She was in a cave, sitting by a fire. She was very surprised to see me, and somewhat angry. I asked her what she was doing there in the cave all alone. She told me, "They gave my dog away." I asked her if she wanted to come back to Holly. She was somewhat hesitant and preferred to sit next to Holly so she could watch her.

In the second journey I came to a place in a forest at the base of a cliff with a huge waterfall. At the top of the cliff I saw a young Native American boy—perhaps fifteen years old or so. I watched as he leaped off the cliff into the river below. He swam to shore and then went into a celebratory dance. He danced and whooped with complete abandon. I approached him and asked why he had leapt off the cliff. The boy told me he had done it to prove he was not a coward. During a recent battle with another tribe he had run to the women's tent to protect them, but the men in the tribe had considered his actions cowardly—they had assumed he was running to the women to hide. He felt humiliated and shamed by the accusations of the men. He knew he wasn't a coward and wanted to prove it to himself. He did want to return to Holly, and after he returned, the young girl also wanted to return.

CHAKRA NAMES CHART

Chakra Names by Number	First Chakra	Second Chakra	Third Chakra	Fourth Chakra	Fifth Chakra	Sixth Chakra	Seventh Chakra
Chakra Names	Root Chakras	Sacral Chakra	Solar Chakra	Heart Chakra	Throat Chakra	Third Eye Chakra	Chakra Chakra
Sanskrit Chara Names	Muldhara Chakra	Svadhishthana Chakra	Manipura Chakra	Anahata Chakra	Vishuddha Chakra	Ajna Chakra	Sahasrara Chakra
Chakra Color Names	Red Chakra	Orange Chakra	Yellow Chakra	Green Chakra	Blue Chakra	Indigo Chakra	Violet Chakra

Plate 1 (above). A chart of the seven major charkas.

Plate 2 (right). The light side of the Water Cycle—healing at a cellular level.

Plate 3 (below). The shadow side of the Water Cycle—a chaotic womb experience.

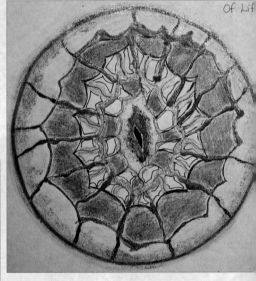

Of Life

Plate 4 (upper left). The light side of the Earth Cycle—emerging from the chrysalis.

Plate 5 (above). The shadow side of the Earth Cycle—feeling stuck and the urge to open.

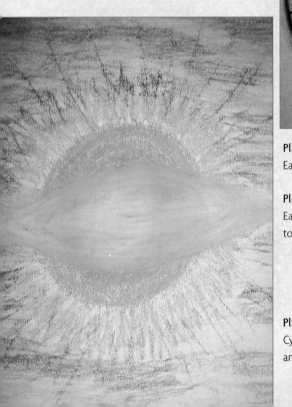

Plate 6 (left). The light side of the Fire Cycle—feeling brilliant, fiery, powerful, and creatively charged.

Plate 7 (left). The shadow side of the Fire Cycle—Venus with horns, representing repressed sexual energy coming forth.

Plate 8 (above right). Another image of the light side of the Spirit Cycle—a lion spirit guide leading the practitioner to the inner beloved.

Plate 9 (left). The light side of the Spirit Cycle—spirit in matter; opening and healing and falling in love.

Plate 10 (right). The shadow side of the Spirit Cycle—a wolf spirit guide coming forth to assist the practitioner in a time of turmoil.

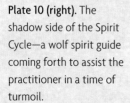

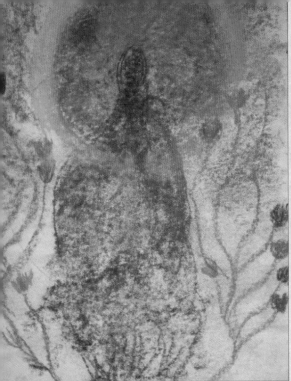

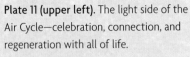

Plate 11 (upper left). The light side of the Air Cycle—celebration, connection, and regeneration with all of life.

Plate 12 (upper right). The shadow side of the Air Cycle—out of the wounded heart a rose in born in a process of wondrous transmutation.

Plate 13 (lower left). Windraven feels empowered and at home at last in the mountains.

Plate 14 (lower right). Terry Walker's art expresses the liberation of her spirit.

Plate 15 (left). Red Hawk's soul recovery involved healing the toxic womb and preparing for rebirth, as expressed in the artwork created following her breathwork session.

Plate 16 (right). Sheewho expresses her process through artwork and her poetry: "She who comes and goes, who gathers as she soews, who gathers, weaves, spins, and sews, the elements of shadow and delight."

Plate 17 (below). The Art Temple at Isis Cove, North Carolina after the creative force has come and gone during a typical Soul Recovery Week at Venus Rising.

Plate 18 (left). Starrfire celebrates the divine union of the masculine and feminine through her artwork

Plate 19 (below). Fireheart shows his artwork, which expresses the resurgence of his life force energy and the sacred union that he experienced during his breathwork session.

Plate 20 (left). Prana during the Soul Recovery Week shows her artwork, which reflects the balancing of her chakras and the aligning of her soul parts.

Plate 21 (left). Sara Claire's artwork expresses Hathor's Horns, created during a Soul Recovery session.

Sara Claire

Hathor's Horns

Star Dust

Plate 22 (above). Star Dust remembers the way to wholeness and her right to existence during Soul Recovery Week at Isis Cove.

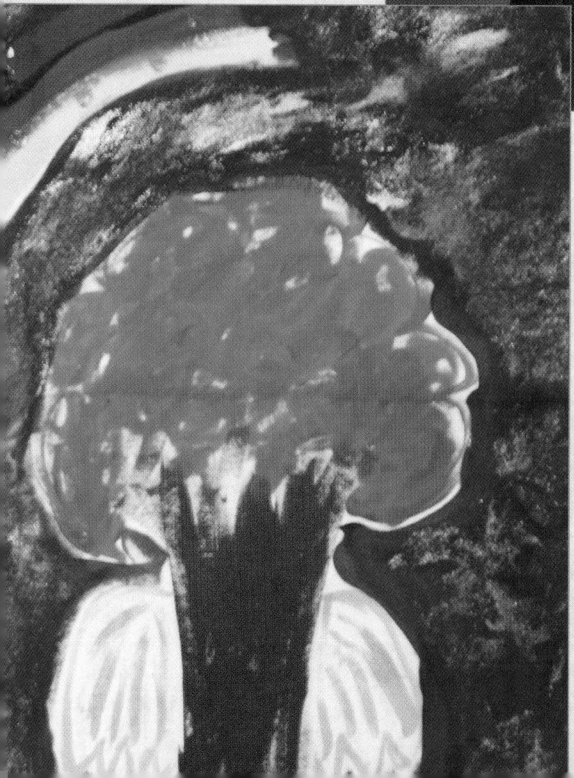

Plate 23 (left). White Tiger Woman creates the Tree of Life in her Shamanic Shakti artwork.

Plate 24 (left). Dancing Bear comes home and heals the child within.

Plate 25 (right). Black Panther Woman returns in her full power and beauty, which is expressed by her artwork

Plate 26 (left). Brad Collins and Linda Star Wolf create sacred space together during the Wise Wolf Council at Isis Cove.

⊚ VI. RUBY FALCONER (BLACK PANTHER WOMAN)— SOUL RETURN

Ruby Falconer/Black Panther Woman (journeyer): My experience with Holly Dancing Bear was magical and synchronous. My breathwork built upon the first one we did in the soul return workshop and involved my going back to a lifetime as Black Panther Woman, where I felt whole and complete unto myself. Black Panther Woman was a medicine woman and a shaman. Holly shared with me that she saw me as a powerful woman, a sphinx, and an elephant. I particularly resonated with the image of the sphinx.

In the mystery school teachings channeled by Linda Star Wolf, the sphinx is the earth altar that receives information from the stars and transmutes it across the surface of the earth. This is very much who I was in the lifetime as Black Panther Woman, and it is an aspect of myself I am reclaiming in my present life as the originator, with Star Wolf, of Shamanic Egyptian Astrology. I am grateful to Holly for her loving care and support, and for her ability to see this aspect of my soul and support it in returning to me.

Holly/Dancing Bear (co-journeyer): Initially Ruby was extremely active, totally becoming one with the black panther—it was quite sensual. Because she was so active my first priority was to keep her safe. I did get glimpses of her as a sphinx. Actually, she was "The" Sphinx—The Powerful One! I saw a sphinx body with her face. Later she was an elephant but returned to the body of the sphinx. She was "The" one everyone came to. At the end, she—the powerful Sphinx—was drinking a beverage of her choosing from the chalice.

⊚ VII. SHARI LOWE (STARRFIRE)—SOUL RETURN

Shari Lowe/Starrfire (journeyer): As I sit here eating some of Sarah Jane's nurturing potato soup, I continue the process of integrating what I think was the most profound soul recovery and integration I have ever experienced. As a facilitator of many shamanic techniques myself, I am in awe of the total immersion into the trance state induced this past week. We began with breathing and co-journeying through breathwork, followed by processing with integration. Then I had the honor of being the "demo" for the "traditional" Shamanic Breathwork journey process.

After this, in pairs, we co-journeyed for each other utilizing traditional methods. Then the final breathwork was augmented with the Shamanic Shakti Art Process and an integration meditation, followed by an additional Shamanic Shakti Art Process.

When I arrived at Venus Rising (an area where my ancestors had lived four to five generations back), I was already in process. During the previous six months I had been dealing with a lot of death. The woman who created the process that I facilitate had died; a client of mine had died over a four-month period; and Michelle—a beloved friend, teacher, and medicine woman under whom I had studied—had been moved to a hospice following a seven-year illness and had died there. She left behind a seventeen-year-old daughter; the three of us had a lot of shared karma. I had been taking care of Michelle's daughter for about two and a half weeks after Michelle had moved into hospice care.

Simultaneously, I had recently had a *huge* soul return piece come up with the realization that I had lost a significant portion of my soul and my divine masculinity when my cousin, who had been born two days before I was, committed suicide just after our twentieth birthdays. I was in college in Athens, Georgia, and he was married with two children and working in Wichita, Kansas. I remembered a part of my soul making the decision that if Billy was dead then I could not be a success, because I should have been the one to die and he should have been the one to go to college. In sharing this memory with someone else I used the phrase, "Billy was my other half," and that is when I realized that a big part of me died when he died.

I cannot imagine a more perfect co-journeyer for the last and final breathwork of the soul recovery workshop than James. James is from Tulsa, Oklahoma, where some of my family lived, and twenty miles from where my mother and uncle were born. He had also lived in Wichita,

Kansas, where my cousin was born; and James and my uncle worked for the same company. Currently he lives in Missouri, some sixty miles from where I was born. What an interesting coincidence?

And now, here we were at Venus Rising, about twenty miles from where my Starr ancestors lived four or five generations prior, in Bryson City. What a container in which to hold the recovery of my soul, which was integrating the part of me that had split off with the death of my cousin/soul mate/other half.

I was the first to breathe. It began with a transformational snake piece. James, my co-journeyer, remarked that he felt as if he were witnessing me shed my snakeskin. The next scene for me was running with a jaguar body. I could see my front paws running through the grass all over this country, gathering pieces of "meat" and taking them back to a crescent moon cave. I became aware that the cave was a temple of sorts and that the sun (the masculine) was shining over me to do this deep, dark, inner work.

That was when I moved out into the cosmos and began bringing back pieces of myself from many, many lifetimes and dimensions. I was in India burning on a funeral pyre as a bride of a Rajput against my will, and pulled my soul from that life. I was in Africa, the Orient, Australia, Germany, France, Ireland, Scotland, and Iceland. There were many Native American lifetimes. Then, with the help of my co-journeyer, I began the process of moving this energy out of my body. James held my stomach from behind and pushed the junk out of my solar plexus. I began dispelling the energy by spitting into tissues all the shame, fear, violence, and abuse I had felt and experienced, both as victim and persecutor.

After this took place, three clear and specific energies were removed from me by James, who was working on my lower back. Once these energies had been removed, I curled up into a ball and became the seed/egg of Goddess, which opened my heart and brought me into the light.

After each of us breathed we did a Shamanic Shakti Art Process. (Plate 17 is a photo of the studio in which we create our shamanic shakti art.) My process was cathartic. There were brushes available and I picked one up, but it didn't feel right, so I just used my hands and the square palette that had held the paint to scrape designs. My piece was seven different layers and included broken mirrors and glitter. The first layer was pure spirit of rainbow love of Goddess. The second layer I painted completely black to represent the veil of separation from Goddess, and then I used the palette to allow some of Spirit to show through the veil. The third layer was my spirit, a bit fiery and chaotic, but freely expressed. Once again I covered that layer with black paint to represent the generational depression, genocide, and suicide in my family DNA, again using the palette to uncover some of the color and texture.

Then the fire of transformation came, and I painted it onto the paper. I placed a few of the broken mirrors on there to represent the recovered portions of my soul, but that wasn't enough. I needed to splat paint onto the paper and I got special permission to go outside and experience the "cathartic" nature of this process.

In the splattering of paint onto the paper I reenacted some of the abuse I had received throughout many lifetimes. I then became the abuser and bounced between both of those poles for a while. I then placed the table with the paper onto the ground and poured all of the mirror pieces onto the paper while the paint was wet. Since I was dealing with a generational aspect, the DNA strand was important to me, so I added that with the glitter, which served as the "stop leak" I had been given in an earlier journey. (Plate 18 of the color insert is a picture of me with another example of some expressive artwork I created following a breathwork session.)

James Gilliland/Fireheart (co-journeyer): Before we started the journey I did some body and energy work with Starrfire; I worked her triple warmer meridian and her heart meridian. Once those energies balanced out, Hummingbird and Hathor wanted to be blown into her chest. When we started the journey, Starrfire became a cobra. As a snake, she was trying to shed her skin; I assisted her in shedding her skin, gently peeling off the old skin. After her old skin had been removed, I observed the way she was adjusting to the new skin; how sensitive it felt and how her senses were heightened.

Next I blended with Starrfire's masculine self, allowing her feminine to feel supported by the masculine from her spine (her core). I observed and supported her in claiming her power. The divine union of her masculine and feminine worked together in releasing what no longer resonated with her. Next I observed as her new paradigm was celebrated. After the celebration of the new divine union, her armored feminine invited the masculine to remove her armor in sacred ceremony. He did and revealed her heart: soft, gentle, and strong in beauty. After the armor was removed, a six-year-old girl—innocent, free, and joyful—came running out of a field and ran into Starrfire's chest. I became Anubis and removed her open heart. Star beings gave (me) Anubis a new heart to replace the heart that had been removed.

After everyone was finished with breathwork and art pieces, Ruby facilitated an integration meditation. I do not have words for this process. Instead I went back into the art temple and created another Shamanic Shakti Art Process piece. It speaks for itself. (Plate 19 of the color insert is a photo of me proudly displaying this expressive artwork.)

VIII. James Gilliland (Fireheart)—Soul Return

James Gilliland/Fireheart (journeyer): In the beginning there was an exchange of kings; the old king gave his kingdom to the new king with respect and honor. The old king offered his wisdom to the new king with the caveat that the new king must not incorporate it in the same manner as the old king had; change was needed. Just as I had become Anubis and removed Starrfire's heart, Anubis now removed my heart and then replaced it. Then I started playing, giving the children who were present within permission to play. It took them awhile to feel safe enough to play.

When the children started playing, they were dancing and joyful.

The dance and playfulness turned into dancing in chaos, with the feminine supporting me (Starrfire was steadying me while I was up and moving erratically, making sure I wasn't going to fall or run into something; she was protecting me). The experience with the sacred masculine and sacred feminine was strong and solid working together. Once I danced through the chaos, the children wanted to feel nurtured from the feminine and the masculine wanted to feel safe in receiving the feminine embodied within: Beautiful!

Soft nurturing breasts, compassionate exchanges of energy, loving nurturing touches. I needed the feminine close and embraced her; and the feminine supported me from the core. I just received and felt love—took it in. Then we went to holding hands in sacred union; walking side by side in equal power and strength. Later we had a sacred ceremony, running kundalini energy from the third eye to the root chakra; just heart energy flowing between the masculine and feminine: Beautiful! Then I just felt myself in the body. Most of the experiences of this breathwork were not doing, but *experiencing/being*.

Shari Lowe/Starrfire (co-journeyer): James's breathwork began with intuitively removing something from his hands and arms. The night previous I had received a message to remove the "gauntlet," and thought this might be what I was doing. In James's experience he was experiencing a "changing of the guard" from the "old king" to the "new (Earth) king." Then I experienced what I felt were dolphins dancing above his head, and that guided me to do some work on his fifth chakra and then his fourth chakra. Then Anubis showed up and sliced open his chest and removed his heart. He then turned to Khnum to rebuild the heart. Immediately following, James reached up and placed my hand onto his heart. Then I began the ethereal task of cleaning the space of the heart area, which used to be full of old debris and gunk.

Nepthys then brought back his heart and once that was in place, James immediately got up to express his "little boy's" playfulness. So I stood grounded as strong as I could to hold him safely as he moved this energy through his body. I did experience some fear, as we were in front of a window and James is about six and a half inches taller than I am, and of strong build. Each time I worried about safety, I just grounded more and called on my heart to guide the process. After about three or four songs of strong, pounding, joyful, and chaotic movements, James collapsed on the floor into a kneeling position.

For me he turned into a knight of Avalon, kneeling for some type of ceremony. I offered the sword, but he wanted the chalice and took that instead. He then proceeded to unscrew the chalice bowl from the stem, and the bowl went up his left arm and the stem moved through his right arm. And both parts reunited in his heart. Once this was complete he lay back down and placed my hand on his heart. Then I imagined a cosmic space station crystal temple where healing work with his heart and chakras took place. When that was complete I held him from behind as the divine masculine, and he received as the divine feminine. We stayed like that until the end, when his "pitcher" was full. For the very last song I placed my hand back on his heart, and my other hand removed some clouded thoughts from his crown chakra. What a beautiful sacred ceremony!

⦾ iX. LAURA WOLF (PRANA)

Laura Wolf/Prana (journeyer): In my soul return breathwork with Sara Claire, I received a very deep healing of my little girl. Cradled in her arms I wept out the grief, shame, loneliness, and despair of a childhood spent without any real guidance or nurturing from a mother too overwhelmed by her own pain to effectively parent me. All of my life I have felt like a motherless child. As Sara Claire tenderly held me, I felt the most enormous download of mother love channeled through her and into me.

I experienced this love as coming from the Divine Mother, the mother of us all. In those sweet moments I felt mothered for the first time in my life. I have often heard stories of people having an ecstatic experience of the Divine that changed everything for them. I now have a visceral experience of Goddess as the Great Mother. I no longer feel like a motherless child. I know in my deep heart, in my vibrational core, that I am loved beyond measure. And for this I am eternally grateful. (Plate 20 of the color insert is a picture of me with the artwork I created following this breathwork session.)

Sara Claire (co-journeyer): As I facilitated Laura in her soul return experience, I, too, received a profound blessing, which I consider the recovery of a lost soul piece. I was guided twice to embrace her in a motherly way, and felt an enveloping nurturing energy flow through me toward her; Divine Mother love for the divine child of God/dess I knew her to be. Having been adopted myself, my sense of maternal loss and abandonment, as well as low self-worth, have been centerpoints of my life's healing. The truly unconditional love that channeled through me allowed me to viscerally know both the giving and the receiving of this energy. I can never be the small, lost child again, and hopefully, compassion is more fully integrated in my life.

◎ X. SARA CLAIRE—SOUL RETURN

Sara Claire (journeyer): As I prepared for my breathwork, I was so totally exhausted from the flux of my external life that I slipped into an altered state before the meditation or music began. I felt safe and at a "still point," which was a welcome relief at that time. When I "woke up," I felt not much had transpired. However, I was aware of an image floating at the fringes of my consciousness. I saw the bold horns of Hathor, ancient Egyptian goddess of unconditional love and alchemy. Instead of the traditional golden or red orb usually depicted between these horns, a vibrating, pulsing spiral appeared. (Plate 21 of the color insert depicts these horns of Hathor that I envisioned in this breathwork session.) I felt that the tremendous mother love I had experienced flowing through me while facilitating Laura's journey was visiting me during my own breathwork, and that the spiral was symbolic of the rapidly changing, spiraling journey I am currently experiencing, both inwardly and outwardly. I felt the love and assurance that the path I am on, though difficult, is guided and blessed. I thank Laura, my co-journeyer, for recognizing my need to sink into this space and for so expertly and lovingly protecting it.

Laura Wolf/Prana (co-journeyer): While holding space for Sara Claire at the beginning of her breathwork, I watched her slip into a very restful altered state. She had been under a lot of stress and I sensed that her body needed this rest in order to be able to receive clarity about her next right action. She remained very still and restful throughout her breathwork, while I did some subtle energy work, extracting some blockages from her first and second chakras, and from her heart and throat. I closed my eyes several times throughout her breathwork to see if I could journey with her. I did not receive any specific visions but simply heard the message to hold the space for Sara Claire to rest; she was getting exactly what she needed. As the chakra-attuned music moved into the upper chakras, I felt guided to gently help to open her third eye, with the message of "opening to a greater vision." Then I was guided to blow "connection to Source" into her crown. Sara Claire seemed to awaken from her journey more rested than I had seen her look in days. After her breathwork she had quite a Shamanic Shakti Art Process experience, even though she couldn't consciously remember anything about her journey. Within the next twenty-four hours or so, I believe she came to great clarity about her next right action. It just goes to show me that there is no wrong or right way to do Shamanic Breathwork, and that the soul always knows just what we need.

🌀 Xi. Star Dust—Soul Return

Star Dust (journeyer): I had been working on a theme of abuse having to do with a ritualistic sexual cult sacrifice that happened to me as a child. The memories are sketchy because of drugs, programming, trauma, and parents who have denied it all. The morning of my soul return journey I received an e-mail from someone who had been there and been a participant. This person verified my sister's and my memories. This was both a miracle and cause for an emotional meltdown.

I started my journey on the back of a huge filthy buffalo riding into a city that shone with only green lights, so I called it the emerald city. Both of these images had come to me in a journey months before, and I tried like hell to change the animal and the journey but it would go nowhere unless I went with the buffalo. Once I accepted the buffalo we started heading to the city of green lights and the journey ended there; it did not return until this breathwork day.

From there the visual image changed to that of purple disks being enveloped by yellow energy and removed from my field, while at the same time I was being filled with the yellow energy. This felt like it was being done for me and I was just witnessing it. Then a tall black woman came in on my left side; she was as black as my field of vision and the only way I could distinguish her was the red line of energy running down the front of her to give her a silhouette. She gave me strength and support. A bunch of little beings that seemed like leprechauns started surrounding me, and I smashed them into bloody little bits. Then I became a black panther and stalked and killed a hyena, shaking it vigorously in my mouth to snap its neck before I ate it. After that I was ready to go as the black panther to my childhood hell to get my soul parts back. I sang to my soul parts to call them back, and found a piece of my sister that I wrapped in healing light to keep safe for her until she finds a way to get it back. These memories have physical pain associated with them that is so intense it reminds me of how much I wanted to die as a child.

The next morning after my breathwork these feelings were back for a while; I was contemplating my life choices and my will to live. I realized why courage has never been a big stumbling block for me, but believing in love has. I decided that morning that it is time to believe in love. I pulled a card from one of the decks in the group room and the image was reminiscent of my mandala. The message of the card was not only of my right to existence, but that the earth and its inhabitants, no matter how small, would sense it and miss me if I were gone. It was the perfect card to go with my thoughts of the morning, and the likeness of the images made it feel even more synchronistically mine. (Plate 22 of the color insert is a picture of me with some expressive artwork I created following a breathwork session in my search for wholeness.)

Stephanie Schwinn/White Tiger Woman (co-journeyer): Before we started our journey, Star Dust shared that some of her issues are connected to living in Idaho. My mother's family is from southern Idaho. Star Dust also shared that I look like some people with whom she has unresolved issues. I called on my woman warrior, Katrina, and my black and white striped tiger to help in this journey. They stood on either side of Star Dust as though they were guarding her. They did battle on her behalf on several occasions throughout the breathwork.

Early in the process it was necessary to do energy release work because her energy was blocked, making it difficult to move further. Later I saw some Russian nesting dolls dancing around a fire. They told me that they were parts of her soul that had left. They told me to tell Star Dust that they can't all return at once because that would be too overwhelming, and that they are safe and happy because of all the work she has done. Eventually two stepped forward and agreed to return. It took some time to discern which parts they were, but they finally told me which aspects they were and agreed to return. They asked to be blown into the same area in which I had earlier performed the energy release work.

From there I just held space for her process. During processing Star Dust shared that her mother's family is Russian, which made me wonder about generational issues in the matrilineal line that may be affecting her today.

◉ XII. Stephanie Schwinn/White Tiger Woman— Soul Return

Stephanie Schwinn/White Tiger Woman (journeyer): This journey was very kinesthetic; the energy moved in the form of tingling. At times that tingling was more intense on one side of the body or the other (male vs. female energies). At one point my legs were jiggling and my head thrust itself to one side. I saw a purple and blue rainbow and angels' wings. Then I saw a large tree, including the root system, and I received this message: "From one tree all humanity came, and to one tree it will return. The time for unity has come. That which does not wish to become united will be pruned off, for it is dead to this time and age." (Plate 23 of the color insert is a picture that I drew of this tree of life following my breathwork session.) The journey ended with a vision of different geometric shapes.

Star Dust (co-journeyer): When Stephanie's journey started she looked very young and alone; she seemed afraid or worried. At first it looked as though she was beside a pond, but it wasn't clear and I wondered if I was seeing a baseball diamond at a park. Then I got an image of Stephanie as a cave woman with long hair, partially combed and partially in dreadlocks. She was wearing a fur wrap and riding a very light-colored horse—white at the back, with grey legs. She was in barren terrain. It was kind of mountainous and there was some snow on the ground; she seemed completely comfortable and at ease with where she was and what she was doing. I placed my hand over her heart center and gave both her and the horse the option of returning to her, and both of them did.

I spent some time with my hands a few inches above her, sending energy to her sacral area and her heart center. Then I saw this bluish, purplish angel standing over her. I have known people who have seen angels, and it seemed like such a gift. I never thought I would see an angel so I didn't engage with it. In fact, I started wondering if I was making things up. Cave women, yes. Angels . . . well . . .

I lay down beside Stephanie and started watching her. I saw the aura around Stephanie's head get very active. There were many colors swirling around in slow-moving waves, and it seemed as though some of this energy was coming in and some of it was moving out. I felt that if I scooped some of the outflowing energy away it would leave more room for the incoming energy, so I did that several times until the colors and patterns slowed down and it seemed there was more going in than out. Then I just placed my hand a few inches over the crown of her head to help amplify and open her crown, so that she could better receive what she was getting.

It was a peaceful experience and I sensed that Stephanie was protected by many diverse spirit beings.

8
THE SHAMAN, THE SHADOW, AND ADDICTION

. . . .

The difference between the addict and the shaman is
sobriety.

LINDA STAR WOLF

Many people who are attracted to Shamanic Breathwork are deep souls—they have lived lives with many light and dark experiences. These include experiences with the shadow, and wrestling with addictive patterns. Therefore, it is important to have a working knowledge about the shadow and to understand why people with strong shamanic aspects often struggle with a number of addictions.

It has been said that both shamans and addicts are people of extremes. Being deeply connected to both of these worlds firsthand, I can readily accept the truth of this statement. It is also commonly known in the world of recovery programs that addicts who become sober are some of the most altruistic, creative, giving, and spiritual people to be found. Many recovering persons discover that they are very sensitive in many areas of their being, and that their various addictions were an attempt to cover up that oversensitivity. This is often the case in premature deaths of famous musicians, actors, and other types of artists.

I shared in earlier chapters that my addictions were problematic in my youth and young adulthood until I dealt with my issues and found a way to step into who I was being called to be in this lifetime. In order to heal, I had to finally accept myself with all my sensitivities and realize I could not participate in some of the casual behaviors that others seemed to be able to "get away" with, without serious repercussions. In that humility, I also began to open back up to the special gifts I had tried to disown. I gradually found the maturity to handle these gifts and offer them back to the world. In so doing, I found that others around me were ready to receive what I had to share.

I discovered that the very things that had made me feel awkward and different from other people over the years—my sensitive nature, my powerful imagination (which had been discredited), and my extrasensory perceptions—were extremely valuable and a large part of my soul's purpose for this incarnation.

Initially my substance abuse was an attempt at feeling normal and comfortable in my own skin. Repressing my intense emotional states through various addictions eventually caused them to fill up my unconscious mind and finally, unavoidably, spilled over into my everyday life. Only when I was able to find a way to move through these intense states of consciousness was I able to harness more of my full power and transform my chaos into healing and creativity. I now believe that the energies that were running through me were connected to the kundalini life force, an energy that had spontaneously emerged simply from the true nature of who I have always been. This energy was fueled by my use of psychedelic drugs when I was a teenager, and by the incredible grief I felt from my grandmother's death when I was twelve years old.

I have been astounded by the hundreds of individuals whose stories are similar to mine. This is not to say that everyone has gone to the extreme places that my path has taken me, but the similarities are there. It seems that whatever we repress into the shadow becomes our sacred wounds. In time, that which we resist will persist until it gets our full attention.

Carl Jung, known for his visionary psychoanalytic theories and concepts, taught that everyone has a shadow. He saw the shadow as disowned parts of us that are deeply repressed into the unconscious mind. He believed that the shadow is that which we have no desire to be, and that because of this, we project it onto others instead of taking responsibility for it. The ego ideal of who we wish to be is what we project through our persona to the outer world. It is through the unconscious self-defense mechanisms of denial, repression, and projection that most individuals are able to keep their shadows safely hidden from themselves and others.

The shadow holds not only the negative parts of us, but in some cases, the brightest parts of the soul as well. Some Jungian scholars say that Carl Jung believed most of what the shadow held was *pure gold*, a psychological metaphor for the ancient alchemical aspiration of turning base metals into gold. In other words, the wounded, unloved parts of ourselves that are hidden away often have many gifts to offer the world. I can honestly say that most of what I have been able to bring forth from my own personal shadow has been transmuted into my *medicine* and has made me a much better teacher and human being.

Nearly everyone experiences addiction at some level—to mind-altering substances, food, sex, TV, gambling (including the stock market), compulsive caretaking (codependency), rage, Internet social networking, or work, to name just a few. Most of us are not aware when our somewhat innocent attempts at self-soothing may be progressing into serious dysfunctional behavior and addictive patterns. Addictions and other dysfunctional behavior are compulsive in nature and become obsessively more so as they progress. Eventually, the very feelings and thoughts that we unconsciously try to control erupt into the outer world, often shocking not only ourselves, but also others around us.

That which we suppress will ultimately, fatefully reemerge in our lives. In other words, we cannot escape ourselves! At some point (if we survive long enough) we will come face-to-face with our inner demons in our outer situations and relationships. In the recovery world this is called "hitting bottom," and there is often a sigh of relief when this happens. When the ego is sufficiently deflated, grace can happen. This is a shamanic death and rebirth that transforms millions of lives each year all over the world. The shaman is known to be one who has faced death and lived to share the healing tale with the community. This is precisely what happens in recovery groups everywhere, and again, can involve any kind of serious addictive process.

The archetypal concept of the shadow as a powerful adversarial ally residing within our unconscious minds, waiting for an invitation into the light of day, is an important one. A sacred quote relating to the dormant power of the shadow is, "If you bring forth what is within you, what you bring forth will save you. If you do not bring forth what is within you, what you do not bring forth will destroy you."* There is a type of hidden wisdom in many traditions that points to bringing the shadow and the light of our beings into each other's presence. Perhaps, as one student recently noted in a Shamanic Breathwork group, the greatest spiritual path any of us can follow is the one that attempts to make the unconscious conscious. I call this "true sobriety." Being sober is not necessarily about not drinking or using drugs. For the person seeking to walk a path of higher consciousness, sobriety requires self-awareness. It requires an ongoing spiritual pursuit of such desirable soul qualities as serenity, balance, integrity, dignity, honesty, reliability, and wisdom.

If someone is serious about spiritual growth, she must be willing to honestly explore the darker, hidden side of her personality. There is an old saying that only the fool believes he knows everything there is to know about himself. Openness and willingness are the keys to the beginning of wisdom.

When the shadow can show itself without fear of judgment, its potency can be tapped for creative endeavors. Jung believed that "in spite of its function as a reservoir for human darkness—or perhaps because of this—the shadow is the seat of creativity."

---

*Gnostic Gospel of St. Thomas

Shamanic Breathwork provides a safe and highly effective way to journey to meet the shadow. If we are ready to commit ourselves to moving forward, healing our lives, and coming into sacred purpose, the shadow will begin to emerge and provide many of the answers about what has been holding us back or blocking the way. When a piece of the shadow is encountered during a breathwork session, the appropriate way to meet that aspect is with curiosity, humility, and an open heart. Remember, the shadow was formed very early in childhood in large measure as a reaction to what significant others and society taught was acceptable.

The formation of shadow is a normal part of the socialization process. In this process the child is simply adapting to what is being continually reinforced in order to feel safe, loved, and cared for, even if what is being repressed is a positive thing. An example is a child of prejudiced parents who learns not to value diversity, or one who shelves artistic potential because it is invalidated as unimportant or frivolous. Many wonderful qualities are lost during childhood, but Shamanic Breathwork sessions are their golden opportunity to finally return. When the shadow becomes an ally and friend, we can begin to take responsibility and deal with addiction or dysfunction with acceptance and love. We find the motivation to practice self-love, self-care, and discipline to do what it takes in the everyday world to transform our lives.

The Dalai Lama speaks often about developing "the warm heart." When we are in a state of mental wellness and practicing self-love and self-care, selfishness falls away and we become better human beings on every level. Our neediness dissolves when we are in love with our divine selves. We have a saying in Shamanic Breathwork, "The light, the dark, no difference." This statement comes from a deep understanding of the need to become whole and to fully know and accept ourselves, as well as others.

I often encounter people who love breathwork, who want to become facilitators and eagerly ask about the process. After I tell them the certification requirements, I often share part of my own journey and ask why they want to do this work. I also explain that to be truly effective as a teacher, healer, and facilitator, a person must be sober and do his own healing work in order to be deeply authentic and grounded. I have had the great privilege in my lifetime of introducing Shamanic Breathwork to many people, helping to heal their lives and transform their spiritual paths; and I have also trained many individuals to become facilitators to do this work. It is some of the most gratifying work I have ever done.

9

The Creation of SHIP (Shamanic Healing Initiatory Process)

··

I n 1994 I met and had an instant soul connection with Brad Collins, who had been trained in Transformational Breathwork by a teacher named Judith Kravitz. Brad and I met at an Embracing the Beloved breathwork workshop that I was co-facilitating for another organization. Little did I know at the time that our immediate friendship would later culminate in something much more meaningful.

When Brad and I magically reconnected in 2000, it soon became very clear that we were meant to pursue our own sacred marriage in relationship with each other—a relationship that we had both been working on within our respective psychic realms. (See plate 26 of the color insert; a photograph of the two of us together.) The creative energies of our union eventually birthed a process now known as the Shamanic Healing Initiatory Process, fondly called SHIP by many individuals who have gone through the process. The SHIP program is often mentioned in the testimonials given in this book. It follows the same process as the breathwork, but is an accelerated program comprised of five initiations and requiring a dedicated commitment over a period of time.

Below is Brad's initial vision and account of a powerful breathwork experience and initiation that, years later, contributed to the formation of three powerful things: the SHIP program, the Isis Cove Shamanic Community in western North Carolina, and his highly transformational men's program, the Shamanic Priest Process.

VISIONARY KING

I came to this breathwork in the middle of major life transitions. I was leaving a twenty-year marriage and a lifelong career. I felt as if my psyche bestowed a lifelong vision upon me.

In this experience I initially was a king who was ready to give up his reign. I felt like I was King Orpheus, who had been unlucky in love and had difficulty entering life fully. Like Orpheus, I was physically torn in pieces and buried; the next thing I knew, I was emerging from the grave as a small child.

A group of very nurturing women welcomed me. I felt like a young prince as I was taken into the circle of women. They raised me and taught me many of the skills I would need to lead a full life. They instructed me on how to live with each of the different elements. First, I was taught how to live on the land and earth. They actually transformed me into a sheep, and I grazed and came to know the land. Next, they taught me how to live in the air, and I shape-shifted into the form of an eagle. I was introduced to the element of water and became a fish. They taught me how to live in the fire, and I shape-shifted into the form of a salamander. Somehow the fire did not burn me.

In addition to being introduced to the elements of nature, I was nurtured by the feminine and loved in all the ways a boy could hope to be loved. The time came in young adolescence where I was escorted up the hill to a group of men. The women placed me under the care of a strong, burly man. He taught me the skills that I would need as a man. He taught me how to hunt, kill, build, and survive.

After several years of mentoring with this strong masculine teacher,

I was brought back into the circle of men. They placed me in the center of the circle and I was circumcised as a rite of initiation. They took me back down to the shore and placed me on a large ship for a voyage. We sailed for many days, far out into the ocean. The ship finally stood still and my attention was brought to the ocean depths. I realized that my bride to be was at the bottom of the ocean. At first I was confused about how to meet her, but then I remembered that I had been taught how to live under water as a child. So I jumped into the ocean and met my bride to be. The best way I can explain this is to say that she was the most beautiful mermaid-like creature I could imagine. We were united in marriage. When our union was consummated, we blasted out of the water like a missile and landed on the shores of an island.

I realized I had to build a raft to return to my native kingdom. I built the craft and began my return journey to the green hills of my home. Although my beloved was with me, I was alone. I could feel her presence, but could not see her. As I neared the shore of my homeland, the beauty of the bright green mountains awed me. I beached my raft and began walking up the hill with my inner queen. I passed beautiful gardens and continued into the center of a small village.

In the center of the village square stood a cathedral with many steps ascending to large open doors. As I reached the top of the steps my parents, who were standing behind me, put a robe around my shoulders. The robe was rich, red velvet, trimmed in ermine. The cathedral was full, and as I walked down the aisle, I realized the gathering was for my coronation. I was crowned king and my queen and I began to rule the kingdom.

Ruling this land as king was very satisfying for me. My days were spent solving problems. My queen and I always found solutions to the conflicts and challenges. The kingdom flourished for many years under our reign. It seemed as if I was king for many, many years. One day I realized that my term as ruler of this land had ended. I knew it was time to leave and go over the mountain to a monastery that was familiar to me.

The monks welcomed me into the monastery and gave me a robe to wear. I was taught many types of meditation and esoteric teachings. I experienced a tremendous feeling of homecoming upon entering this monastery. My tutelage as a monk culminated in a meditation exercise where I went out into the universe and looked back at Earth. Earth from space was more beautiful than I could have imagined.

As I observed the planet from afar, I noticed four crystalline points of light around it. Angels, or souls, were coming and going to and from the planet from all directions in the universe. Words cannot describe this profound vision. As I continued to observe, I noticed a robed, Christ-like figure around the Earth. This figure appeared to have the Earth at the center of its being. As I watched more closely, I merged with this figure and vision. I became the robed Christ-like figure with the Earth in my belly. Contractions began in my body, and I realized I was about to give birth to a new Earth. My breathwork co-journeyer put her hand on my belly and helped me to birth this new Earth.

This breathwork experience has continued to inform and inspire my life and work for the last fifteen years. I established the Shamanic Initiatory Priest Process based on this vision. My sense is that this experience continues to guide my life as I mature.

BRAD COLLINS, NORTH CAROLINA

I well remember this breathwork experience of Brad's so many years ago, because I was his group facilitator at that time. I remember how powerful his recitation of the journey was, and how it made me feel. I have stated elsewhere in this book that sometimes we feel as if we are witnessing "previews of coming attractions." Never has this been more true in my observation and facilitation of another's breathwork experience than the day Brad shared the hero's journey of his breathwork session.

Brad's breathwork experience and his soul essence made a really deep impression on me, and although he lived in Cincinnati and I lived in the San Francisco Bay area, we remained in close contact and became good friends. Six years later, when the time was ripe, we would reunite as soul mates and soul purpose partners, bringing together elements of his vision from 1994 and my vision of the five cycles of change and other work that I had been teaching at my organization, Venus Rising Institute for Shamanic Healing Arts.

Many different catalysts caused us to cocreate the SHIP process. One of those catalysts came from a group of participants, many of whom were already involved in the alternative healing arts in Portland, Oregon, and had attended an introductory, one-day Shamanic Breathwork journey. Many of these individuals loved this one-day session so much that they became excited about being trained in the work we were doing. Venus Rising already had a successful training program that met several times each year in California; it included several eight-day events and a good deal of travel. It was suggested that if enough students were interested in doing another committed training program—this one comprised of five, five-day accelerated training initiations—Brad and I would travel to Portland and teach these condensed sessions.

We soon found ourselves teaching and facilitating the process in a large, lovely home on several acres by the Clackamas River, with sixteen committed, intrepid, shamanic souls. From that circle of beautiful spirits the present-day program that came to be known as SHIP was born. When we meditated upon the five topics and five initiations that would encompass the main body of teachings offered through Venus Rising's existing programs, they emerged organically from both the workshop intensives that were already in place and being taught quarterly, and from Brad's vision of six years prior.

THE FIVE INITIATIONS

Each of the five, five-day sessions introduces the participants to an initiation, beginning with an overview of the spiral path and the Five Cycles of Shamanic Consciousness, and ending with Discovering Sacred Soul Purpose. The five initiations begin with the important shifting away from the old paradigms of linear and circular thinking, to the reemergence of an ancient symbol for alchemical transformation, the spiral. They are as follows:

1. The Five Cycles of Shamanic Consciousness and the Spiral Path of Alchemical Transformation
2. The Family of Origin—the Gift that Keeps on Giving
3. Dancing with the Shadow
4. Embracing the Divine Beloved
5. Discovering Sacred Soul Purpose

Each of these five initiations builds upon the one preceding and leads journeyers to a higher level of shamanic consciousness and wholeness in everyday life. There are teachings, readings, exercises, and a Shamanic Breathwork session embedded within each initiation. They are designed to create fertile ground and sacred space for monumental transformational shifts in people's lives. We have witnessed the miraculous over and over again during these intensive SHIP process groups.

Since its inception, the breathwork process (as well as my own) has continued to morph, as will any true shamanic path. Shamanic work is alive and fluid. Despite having some definitive road markers along the way, it is not dogmatic.

Each initiation is discussed in greater detail below.

The Five Cycles of Shamanic Consciousness and the Spiral Path of Alchemical Transformation

This first initiatory cycle is discussed fully in chapter 6, so we will just briefly recap here. In this first initiation, the journeyer learns about the five major natural transformational cycles that affect us all. Each of these cycles is ruled by a dominant element—water, earth, fire, air, or spirit—and as we work on ourselves, one cycle gives over to the next. The natural world is always changing, as are we, and for this reason, nature is an integral part of Shamanic Breathwork.

The Five Cycles of Shamanic Consciousness are all met and engaged with on the spiral map, or path. Each of the five cycles and its corresponding elements is an important foundational piece of an alchemical map for shamanic transformation and the SHIP program. Because it is a new paradigm map for shape-shifting our consciousness, it is the first initiation and our starting point. Although the spiral teachings may appear simple at first, they may bear repeating several times in order to bring full understanding and proper integration of the teachings. This is due to the fact that we are all so heavily indoctrinated into the linear/patriarchal mind-set that has prevailed throughout the world for thousands of years.

Typically, after our first night of coming together and opening our Shamanic Breathwork circle, we begin the next day with the spiral teachings and activate the energies of change within each participant. The following day is spent doing Shamanic Breathwork breathing and the Shamanic Shakti Art Process. The third day is reserved for sharing the journey with others and employing additional energetic methods that may be needed to support each journeyer.

The Family of Origin—the Gift that Keeps on Giving

The second initiation of the SHIP program involves working with our personal past history, or herstory, of this lifetime. We refer to it as FOO . . . Family of Origin—the Gift that Keeps on Giving. This is an important part of the journey and a powerful initiation, even for individuals who have dealt with family issues in past therapy and counseling sessions.

The SHIP program has a very large lens through which to view, and deal with, FOO issues. It provides a new perspective for the "bigger picture" of why we were born into our particular families, and the lessons we learned in childhood and continue to learn as adults when we revisit the past with shamanic eyes.

Through the breathwork process we learn to see the past not as something to be gotten rid of, but rather as a valuable journey offering gems we now can learn to interpret and integrate into present life. We learn to remember to keep mining the gold whenever our buttons are pushed, instead of sinking down into the depths of despair or feeling stuck at the same old place again. What we learn in the first initiation of the spiral can be applied to whatever comes up; at this higher octave on the spiral journey, we are gifted with deeper lessons and wisdom.

We learn that having been born into our particular family is no mistake, and that we can find gratitude for *all* of our experiences, be they light or dark. That is one of the reasons we say "the gift that keeps on giving." To ignore the tremendous influence of our early childhood experiences and families would be to ignore a very important part of the shamanic training. Many children experienced early life as a kind of war zone, and even in the best of families, people are "just human." Let's face it—the majority of humans on the planet are still struggling with many challenges in order to become, and remain, more conscious.

For many students the second initiation is the most shamanic process, because it is during this journey that the inner child emerges with all his fears, anger, hurt, beauty, magic, and love. As we release the emotions and energies that have been blocked at the emotional and even cellular level, the inner light begins to grow, and the past begins to release its tight grip on our present lives. We call this process "soul recovery," and advanced practitioners often offer soul returns and extractions during these breathwork sessions to help journeyers reclaim lost soul parts from childhood and adolescent years.

A student once laughingly told me she would much rather undergo intense, strange shamanic initiations and ingest plant medicines in a foreign jungle than have to confront her parents in the FOO initiation!

How we came into the world—our conception and actual birth—often comes up during FOO week as well. We examine not only the outer conditions of our family, but also the world around us at the time and circumstance of our birth. It is really only within the past fifty years, particularly the last twenty-five, that the spotlight has focused on birth patterns and processes. Once we uncover the truth of our birth, we can consciously choose how we want to rebirth ourselves into this life, within this same incarnation.

Dancing with Your Shadow

The third initiation teaches us how to stalk, or discover parts of ourselves that may be repressed, or hidden from conscious awareness. Some researchers estimate that we use only about 15 to 25 percent of our brain capacity. Most of what makes us who we are and motivates our actions is largely unconscious, so it makes sense that those who are seeking greater awareness would choose to experience an opening and initiatory experience like the shadow initiation.

Sometimes participants don't know what "shadow" refers to, or they balk at the idea of not having conscious control over something that could come up; but the shadow initiation is one of the most powerful and compassionate initiatory experiences. Even though the shadow can be elusive at times, when it finally does emerge in sacred space it will reveal its secrets, if offered our acceptance and love. As my teacher and dear friend Jacquelyn Small used to say, "The shadow cannot be taught, but it can be caught." It is through the setting of a safe container and the expansion of our awareness—through shamanic-psychospiritual processes like Shamanic Breathwork journeying—that the unconscious mind will slowly begin to release its tight grip and control over what it has allowed to be seen and known.

When we begin to take ownership of the so-called unlovable parts of ourselves, compassion is born, making it much easier to love and accept ourselves. It also becomes much easier to accept and love others for who they are, instead of projecting our disowned lost soul pieces onto them. I seriously doubt that we can really love another until we truly know more about who we are and, in so doing, learn to love ourselves.

So much of what we have repressed is the personal power that we sent underground in order to gain acceptance and approval, and maybe even to secure childhood survival. We will never know what our wholeness is until we can look at the light and dark of who we are in this present moment, change the things we can, and accept the things we can't.

Embracing the Divine Beloved

The fourth initiation is designed to open us to our own divinity, our spirit, and our inner beloved. Many New Age workshops often confuse "the beloved" with their opposite gender of feminine or masculine aspects. This initiation may include working with the feminine or masculine aspects, but is certainly not limited to just those parts of yourself.

It is easy to see why individuals might blindly project their inner beloved onto someone outside of themselves, and therefore perceive the beloved as a specific gender entity. While it is true that individuals show up in life as mirrors of the way we experience our relationship with the inner beloved, it is important to remember that they are a mirror of the "real" thing, so to speak. When we pull back our projections and open to divine inner love, the source of all love emerges, perhaps in the symbolic form of a religious figure, a goddess, or a spirit animal.

It may remain formless and come to a journeyer in a variety of sensations, colors, or lights, or send an inner message of divine love. The inner beloved will often cause an initiate to paint, sculpt, write poetry, sing, or dance. It may create an inner longing to join with its essence and impregnate the initiate's inner being with its sacred purpose for that soul's journey.

This initiation requires the initiate to do the deep inner work of regaining trust in the eternal goodness of the universe, in a God/Goddess/Divine Presence that perhaps cannot ever truly be defined. In the twelve steps of Alcoholics Anonymous the third step is, "Made a decision to turn our will and our lives over to the care of God as we understood God."

This initiation often involves a huge heart opening and perhaps is the first time in a very long time that many of the participants have felt a real connection to what we refer to as their "greater power," or spiritual presence.

Discovering Sacred Soul Purpose

The fifth and final SHIP initiation is Discovering Your Sacred Soul Purpose. Brad and I realized, through the many workshops we have presented, that when one does the work of being both human and divine, the natural flow of energy results in a discovery of one's beingness and an opening to one's sacred soul purpose. The soul purpose is to become open to who we really are at any given moment, and to allow life to live through us from a much higher octave than the ego's idea of who we should be. We often refer to this as moving from the ego's agenda to our soul purpose. We acknowledge and thank our ego for its lessons learned and for its attempts to keep us safe, while asking it to move to its rightful place in our psyches so that the master of our being—our soul—can return and take its rightful sacred place in our lives. Bestselling author and teacher John Lee refers to this state as "emotional sobriety." Emotional sobriety is when the ego is no longer in control; it doesn't move us constantly into regressed states, so as a result, the adult self can come forward in its wholeness.

We explore the idea that the soul has always been right here, waiting for us to remember who we really are so that it can take charge of our sacred life-force energy and begin to redirect our lives in much more amazing and meaningful ways. We see that our sacred soul purpose is more about "being" than "doing," but we also realize the spiritual maxim, "As above, so below; as within, so without." In other words, we are spiritual beings having a human experience and we are here to both be and do on this beautiful planet. It is time to have a new master and the new master is the soul—not the ego. The soul can trust and be much more spontaneous since it doesn't operate from fear and secret agendas. Instead, it is open to love's spiritual essence and flow of energy; and to what is total truth, beauty, and good for the whole being of who we are.

Often during this process someone will be inspired to do acts of kindness or create beauty in the world; this motive comes from a pure and open heart. We see that the universe supports our being true to ourselves. If we give our will over to our higher power, and do what is right for ourselves as directed by that higher power, our actions will be the right ones for us, even though it may not appear this way to our ego or to other people.

We have to remember that many times the ego, rather than the true self, has been in charge, and that we have attracted others who are functioning at that same level. Just because our eyes have opened to another way of being in the world and not of it, and we feel ready to walk at a higher octave, doesn't mean the same is necessarily true for those who are closest to us. They may have difficulty accepting the "new" you, and it is better to walk your talk, rather than talk it too loudly. Practicing compassion and being an example are the best ways to open doorways for others who may then choose to walk through them.

At the end of the fifth initiation we teach that the spiral path has just begun and remind people that this is just one spectacular orbit on the great medicine wheel of transformation, no matter how powerful the experience has been in their lives. We offer supportive suggestions and guidelines both during the workshop and afterward to keep the process going upon the initiate's return to everyday life. (These can be found in chapter 12.) The group experience ("where two or more are gathered") provided by the ongoing committed circle of individuals who return several times to go through these initiations together is invaluable. It is really extraordinary and impossible to describe the way "just right" people show up to support the work in which old patterns are triggered in order to be cleared; a perfect alchemical healing vessel is created for all. In addition to scheduled workshops, the community also communicates via group e-mails and open group call-ins. These extended connections help to create a solid support system for lasting change between and beyond SHIP group meetings.

The SHIP program can be employed by many different types of groups in many different settings. We have offered the entire format in a monthlong setting, for instance. There are many other components to the weeklong SHIP journeys that also may be part of each initiation.

These include community building, mask making, trance dance and movement, and drumming circles; or other types of journeying including soul recovery sessions, working with the archetypes, divining tools, and astrological influences, to name a few.

Spending time in nature is another invaluable way in which we heal, and is an important component of our program. Extended breaks are built into every workshop, and we encourage participants to go out into nature to ground and commune with the nature spirits that live here at Isis Cove—or wherever we happen to be offering our workshop. People love the magic of our little cove and blue mountains, and often spend time sitting by Forgiveness Pond, hiking up to Blue Star Prayer Point, walking the wooded trails to Magdalene Spring, or sitting under the large trees by the creek.

We frequently send individuals out on "medicine walks," meaning we ask them to go out into nature and see what comes to them, or what speaks to them on the inner plane. It could be a tree, an animal, a cloud, or a stone. Whatever appears is a part of the healing energy being gifted to them from the nature spirits and becomes their medicine.

Brad and I trust the SHIP process because we have lived it and live it still; it has become part of our daily spiritual practice. We are both committed to this path and to sharing it with others, because it has helped us to break free from many of our outworn, unconscious patterns of dysfunction. It has given us a much larger view of ourselves, our relationships, and our sacred work together. It is our sincere hope that the combination of our lives, Shamanic Breathwork experiences, and sacred soul's purposes of the five cycles of change and the five shamanic initiations will help to quicken those who enter into this sacred journey with us. We wholeheartedly welcome all individuals who feel ready and are called to join us on this exciting path of embodying shamanic consciousness in everyday living.

10

TRUE LIFE EXPERIENCES WITH SHAMANIC BREATHWORK—PART TWO

FROM IVY LEAGUE TO SHAMANIC BREATHWORK PRACTITIONER

I began SHIP in my fiftieth year and could not possibly have anticipated how life-altering the experience would be. I was an East Coast skeptic, Ivy League-college educated, traditionally trained in psychoanalytic thinking and wary of anything that smacked of *New Age, woo woo* mumbo jumbo. Yet I was inexplicably drawn to Isis Cove and SHIP both for my own personal healing and to explore alternative ways of expanding my healing work with others. In my case, what Star Wolf and Brad Collins hold as one of their core truths of SHIP was certainly well proven by my experiences: "The healing is the training, and the training is the healing!"

Family of Origin (Week 1)*: My mother died a few weeks after this initiation, and I felt called to conduct a shamanic funeral for her. It

---

*Although typically our first initiation is the spiral path and the Five Cycles of Shamanic Consciousness, in this case they were reversed.

was something I was drawn to do from my heart without really understanding why in my head. I went to the funeral home before any of my Irish Catholic family arrived and smudged her body, invoking the six directions and the six elements with my jaguar rattle. I cut the cords for her from this life, as well as between the two of us, and I placed amethyst and rose quartz crystals and a small statue of Kuan Yin in her coffin to guide her on her way. "Unknowingly," this was the first ritual I would perform as a shamanic healer.

The Five Cycles of Shamanic Consciousness (Week 2): I sent my resignation letter to the clients of my full-time psychotherapy practice from an Internet coffee shop on the way to this initiation, and thus quit my profession of twenty-nine years. I held my breath as I pushed the "send" button, not knowing how the path would unfold. Before I had even closed the doors on my office, I had begun introducing my clients to different ways of healing through powerful shamanic practices.

The Shaman and the Shadow (Week 3): After this initiation I went to Mexico for two months to sit at a sacred Zapotec meditation place overlooking the Pacific Ocean and face my fears—the shadows that had held me back. Alone in a foreign country, with little command of the language and free of the distractions of my daily life back home, I sat on the meditation point every day and breathed into the fear, calling the shadow forth. I learned through this experience that "shadow and light, no difference."

Sacred Marriage (Week 4): Returning from Mexico to complete this initiation, I decided not to go back to my career as a psychotherapist, despite having no other source of income. Instead, I chose to explore what it means to be a psychospiritual healer. I had to trust that the universe would support and guide me (not an easy thing for my ego to allow me to do!).

Sacred Purpose (Week 5): I became ordained as a Minister of Psychospiritual Healing and opened a new shamanic healing practice. I have stepped into, and am fully embracing, this new life that thirteen moons ago was not yet in my conscious mind. The SHIP process and the shamanic family I discovered at Isis Cove have truly changed my life path, and for this I am humbly grateful.

Reverend Joe Doherty (Jaguarwolf Joe),
Oregon

My name is Judy Merritt; spirit name, Red Hawk. I have a Ph.D. in psychology, and for twelve years I had a traditional psychology private practice. I have a son who is a professional musician and a daughter finishing her BA; she aspires to study herbal medicine. I was married for twenty-five years. I am a Shamanic Breathwork facilitator, a Shamanic Reiki Level III practitioner, and an ordained shamanic pastoral counselor, teacher, and minister.

Those are the factual parts of my identity, along with being part of a family of origin, a family of friends, and a soul family. I also dreamed the dream of the Art and Energy Body Work Temple (also known as Red Hawk Mandala House), helping to facilitate the fundraising for the construction of the temple at Isis Cove in Sylva, North Carolina in the fall of 2005. The temple, I would say, honors the five-year healing process I have experienced through, and with, Venus Rising. I am now the program manager for Transformation House (a center for healing at Isis Cove); I developed the Shamanic Shakti Art Process described earlier in this book. I teach as part of the Venus Rising team; I teach psychology classes at the local community college; and I live as the "Lady of the Woods" in my cabin on Dove Mountain.

Going back to the beginning of my involvement with Venus Rising in 2003, my self-actualization and individuation process has been to bring forth my soul's agenda for healing and get to a place inside of myself, with like-minded people, where I could heal past trauma and eventually do my soul's work. This connecting took place after my mother's sudden death in February 2003 and my youngest brother's suicide in August of the same year. That was my year in hell, and no verbal, supportive, insight-oriented psychotherapy, which I had been in since my twenties, was going to put this Humpty Dumpty woman back together again. Something deeper needed to happen in the healing process of gathering all the pieces of my shattered psyche.

Martina McBride wrote in a song, "Love's the only house big enough for all the pain in the world." I believe my psyche first shattered like a mercury thermometer on a tile floor when I was six years old. Psychotherapy had helped glue me back together, and the glue held until 2003. For me, the *house of love* is what I needed for my healing to happen on the cellular, heart, spiritual, and intellectual levels. At the deep cellular level of my body, memories of physical traumas reside—being beaten almost to death by my mother, sexual abuse by my father and a cousin, abandonment by my father, and an abortion and a rape in my twenties. (This neuropsychobiology of trauma has been researched extensively by Bessel van der Kolk, M.D.) At the heart level, original betrayals of verbal abuse by my mother and others are stored. At the spirit level, I felt I could rely on only myself, because the connection with God/Goddess and all the beings who love me was severed by emotional and spiritual abuse that I perpetrated through the abortion and continued with more shadow, abusive relationships and addictions. Finally, on the intellectual level, my perceptions were distorted through the abuses, the addictions, and the feelings of the shattering.

To feel those feelings on all levels was to go into Inanna's darkness—to fall into possible madness in that space of deep and profound hurt. My intellect and my highly developed abilities to be disassociative, over-functioning, and codependent were my gifts and my strongest defenses. They protected me from all this traumatic pain by allowing me to go into spiritual bypass until the second shattering, with my mother's and brother's deaths. At that second shattering, to heal meant I would have to go into that darkness with a light and the aid of a guide to ensure my safe return. Healing meant I would need to confront, deal with, and make sense of the psychic blood, guts, and mess of the traumas. To not heal would have meant continuing to live half a life, disconnected to feeling my deep feelings except through my intellect. To not heal would have meant to live in and out of chronic depression, in codependent and addictive relationships with others, and with myself.

Venus Rising, as a community, held that loving space and light as I painstakingly took apart my life as I knew it. They were the guides. In that loving space of those relationships, the trust to use the Shamanic Breathwork process for the deep reexamination and reintegration of my mind, heart, and spirit pieces at the cellular level was created. This process has retrieved and reintegrated the broken off, psychic, emotional, artistic, and spiritual pieces by facilitating and holding space for my rebirth into a second life beginning at age fifty. This is a continual process of becoming more fully alive in the life-death-life cycles of change.

WITH WARM REGARD AND BLESSINGS,
JUDY MERRITT, PH.D. (JUDY RED HAWK),
NORTH CAROLINA
AUN APRENDO [I AM STILL LEARNING]—GOYA

DIRECT EXPERIENCE

The Shamanic Breathwork process has taken me directly to the heart of issues I have carried since my early childhood; issues I had no idea were affecting my daily life as deeply as they were. And it hasn't just made me aware of them. Through the breathwork and the supporting group structure I have been able to work with these issues, making more progress in less time than I would have thought possible. It has allowed me to experience true emotional clarity for the first time in my life. It is not a magic bullet; there is still hard work to do, but the rewards are immediate and profound.

JOHN MALAN,
ILLINOIS

SURRENDERING TO THE BREATH

The breath begins slowly, then gets fuller and expands into the fuzziness that transcends the ordinary consciousness of my everyday palette. I begin breathing fuller breaths, notice where the breath enters me, and allow that place to expand until areas that have felt neglected are communicating their appreciation at being recognized and validated.

Air, sweet heavenly air, of its own almost involuntary volition swoops in and cleanses, embraces, and lifts those areas long left dormant by the lungs' random distribution and patterns—patterns long ago decided upon by beliefs we agreed upon for no-longer-relevant reasons of security; a security long since decrepit in keeping with our newfound challenges and missions on this plane of presence and newfound certainty.

Soon, we feel surrender accompanying us, a companion to be trusted without a second thought, for it arrives from within, and without question as having every right to join our ceremony. For a ceremony it is, a ceremony of gratitude for the breath that has carried us and—as we so frequently forget in our daily doldrums—is the one aspect of our physical intake that could end our existence more quickly than any other.

So we take on that tough verb of surrender and the fuzzy warmth that seeps from deep within our core, and we hold ourselves sacredly open to the companionship of our breath. We join with it to go deeper into our rites of passage, our rights of existence, to claim the gems of our birthright. We swallow ever more fully the magnificent breaths that fuel our being alive and being here now—to feel it, feel it, feel it. "Who feels it knows it, Lord." Yes, I.

And then, in synchronicity with our breathing, our lifeline, we fully allow those things that need clearing to arise from within for their betterment within the breath as well. The breath has no prejudice here; it just opens, clears, and revives.

Allowing, we let go and ride the tide of our existence to the next level of lightness to which our breathing inherently ascends. The breath knows only how to be bigger, fuller, and reverently inclined to ecstasy; it knows no other program. Its sacredness is unquestionable, and the words used to describe its majesty are only worthy if they are spoken so that they embody the breath in their message. That is truly what the breath holds: a message, a promise of higher planes of existence. The simplicity of engaging it merely confirms this.

CHRISTOPHER BROWNE,
OREGON

HEALING MY LIFE WITH SHAMANIC BREATHWORK

I began my SHIP journey in 2002 on my fortieth birthday—the spring equinox. For me it was truly a process of finding my way of being in this world, or finding a successful way of checking out. I had already tried mainstream therapy, prescription drugs, and so on, but those had done nothing but take me lower into my depression and my valley of darkness. I had pitched my tent and was just waiting for the next good reason to end my life here.

My first experience of Shamanic Breathwork had been two months earlier, just seven weeks after attempting to take my life. All my life I had not felt a sense of belonging; not in my surroundings, family, friends, or in this world. My sense of disconnect was ever-present in my divorce, loss of contact with my three children, financially moving backward, and little support structure. I wanted out.

A wise shamanic friend was at a loss as to how to help me, so she suggested a weekend workshop with a Marin County couple that was coming to Portland. In that first breathwork I did much healing from tragedies that were connected to some of my past lives. Both Brad and Star Wolf knew my pain, took me under their wings, and supported my healing process. I proceeded to attend an eight-day Shamanic Breathwork workshop two weeks later. Again, the experience helped so much. I was finally gaining a sense of being grounded that had been lacking in my life. When I returned home, my new friends supported and encouraged me and actually convinced Star Wolf to allow me to join the pilot SHIP in Portland a mere ten days later.

My struggles continued as I processed through each five-day aspect of the overall SHIP process. Continuing to join in drum circles and talking groups, I had one of those "aha" moments. Without thinking or knowing what words were coming out of my mouth, I heard myself saying, "I'm tired of my own story."

I found myself finally looking at life differently. The changes were small at first. I found things I was interested in and pursued them. I started volunteering at a senior center and became a hospice volunteer. In one training session I was asked what had drawn me to do this. I replied, "I'm looking for a reason to live." This was quite a profound moment for all in listening range. I began to allow myself to enjoy this life and to step out of my victim role.

By November of that year I was closing up my house and moving my life to the midwest, after meeting a wonderful soul at a breathwork in Iowa. Today, four years after beginning my new life and training through Venus Rising and the Shamanic Breathwork process, I have a thriving remodeling and repair business, am in contact with two of my three children, and have become a grandparent. I have become involved in the men's priest process and am working to put together a group of men in Des Moines.

If it had not been for this life-changing experience, I firmly believe I would have found a successful way of ending my life. I would have perpetuated the idea that when things get rough, take the easy way out and just quit, instead of finding that shamanic soul within, doing individual healing work, and helping to heal our world.

TIM SCHOFIELD,
IOWA

HEALING THE LOSS OF A CHILD

For about three months before this breathwork session I had been dealing with a lack of the sense of belonging. I was not good enough—why had I ever thought I could be a healer or a teacher?

The morning of the breathwork, I felt cramping in my abdomen. It was not a flu-like cramping; it was more like menstrual cramping. I have been postmenopausal for a number of years, so that was curious.

Breathwork experience: I saw what appeared to be a beautiful waterfall and felt that it was there for me to slide down. Then I saw the baby I lost on Father's Day in 1974—it was a fetus. The memory returned of the clot lost in the toilet and of flushing before realizing what it was. I realized then that the water falling was really the water flushing.

The message from the baby was, "I'm okay and you need to be okay. Deliver me the right way and let me go." It was an honoring of the baby and of the baby's passing. I then delivered the baby and said goodbye. The baby said, "Goodbye, and this will help you with your sense of belonging." I cried, grieving the loss of the baby, feeling the pain of that and then the pain of the world—so much pain.

The realization came that I do belong here on this planet and that my sacred purpose is to continue on my healing path and hold space for others to do the same. My baby came back to say, "You do belong and this is your sacred purpose—it was not my time then, but it is our time now." Then I saw fields of energetic light flowing at me.

My wonderful group of SHIP-mates helped me through a soul retrieval. During that process I was given a teddy bear to hold. I found the little girl inside who had been abandoned, and realized that I had not abandoned the baby I lost; rather, that baby was sent as a guide for me. That baby's sacred purpose was to give me my sense of belonging and to confirm my sacred purpose—to be a teacher and a healer. I now have Baby Bear as one of my guides, and whenever I am feeling unsure or frightened, I can go to Baby Bear. (Plate 24 of the color insert is a picture of me with some expressive artwork I created following a breathwork session.)

HOLLY FREY (DANCING BEAR),
WISCONSIN

DIVINE SYNCHRONICITY

I could not submit this writing of my healing experience with Shamanic Breathwork without first explaining how I came to be at Venus Rising. I was in a state of severe depression, driving down the road with my car packed with my belongings and no destination in mind. I knew that Brad and Star Wolf had a retreat center in North Carolina, but had no idea exactly where. A friend asked me to look at a piece of land she was thinking of purchasing near Sylva, North Carolina. I turned onto Bradley Branch road, missed my turn, and instead turned into Venus Rising. There was Brad walking down the road. This was a gift from my higher power and started me on the journey of Shamanic Breathwork that saved my life. It began a support system of loving people I would need very profoundly in the coming years.

The foundation of my healing was Star Wolf and Brad's teachings on codependency. Emotional blocks had to be removed to fully comprehend the hold this disease had on my functioning. In all of my experience as a student and client of psychotherapy over the years, nothing has so fully penetrated those blocks as Shamanic Breathwork. Being intelligent was no assurance of comprehension. It took an energetic, emotional, and spiritual release in my body (and consequently, in my psyche) to transform the package that is "me." I no longer wake in the morning with suicidal thoughts or go to bed at night hoping not to wake in the morning. Now I can say that I enjoy life and am spiritually content.

My journey in self-discovery enabled me to be the primary caretaker for my daughter for eighteen months during her battle with cancer, and to heal some issues between us before her death. I don't believe I could have stayed on this pilgrimage with her had it not been for Shamanic Breathwork, and the support of Brad and Star Wolf and my friends at Venus Rising.

KAREN SMITH (JEWEL OF TRUTH),
NORTH CAROLINA

A WAY OUT OF THE DARKNESS

My name is Yvonne Walker and I would like to share how the Shamanic Breathwork process and Linda Star Wolf have been blessings in my life. I met Star Wolf in 2007 at a workshop and book signing in Goshen, Ohio. A good friend had called and asked me to attend the meeting with her. At first I said no, but after hanging up, a voice spoke to me and told me I should go. I called my friend back and told her I would. We arrived late because we were unfamiliar with the area. The room was full of people and the energy felt great. We found a seat and immediately got involved with the workshop. Star Wolf spoke of her new book and led us on a shamanic journey. This was my first experience with her work and I was intrigued, to say the least. After it was over, we were asked to share our experience.

On February 5, 2006, which also happened to be Super Bowl Sunday, my son, Abdullah J. Walker, was murdered in Clifton, Ohio, where we lived. He was eighteen. At the time, I was struggling with drugs and alcohol. I had wanted to stop, but the devastation of losing my son led me to continue my substance abuse. The way I saw it, my life was over. I did not want to go on, and I hoped that drugs would take my life.

I shared this with the group and Star Wolf reached out to me. She gave me a card, signed my book, and wrote, "Call me" on the card. Eventually I called her and she told me about the SHIP program, and that she wanted me to be a part of it. First, however, she wanted me to get clean. She introduced me to Narcotics Anonymous and encouraged me to get a sponsor. I agreed, and as a result, Venus Rising offered me a scholarship and allowed me to be a part of this wonderful training process.

Before I completed my last SHIP training workshop, another of my sons was killed on September 17, 2008. He was eighteen also. I was devastated and had no money, but I called Venus Rising and my SHIP-mates covered the expenses of my last training workshop. I returned home feeling much better about my life, and had it not been for Star

Wolf, Brad, and the program, I do not think I could have made it. They truly saved my life.

Star Wolf is an extraordinary woman with a heart of gold. Having read her previous works and been a Shamanic Breathwork initiate, I know that this book will be an inspiration to whomever finds it.

WITH LOVE AND GRATITUDE, PEACE.
YVONNE WALKER,
OHIO

CUTTING THE CORD

I came to Isis Cove in February of 2008 for the first segment of SHIP, having first experienced the Shamanic Breathwork process the previous December. Events in my marriage were mirroring childhood experiences that had been dangerous and out of control. I felt my life was in danger in the marriage and had moved out, but I was in such a state of collapse from my codependent behavior that I had no energy or self-esteem to function at even the most basic level. The two breathwork and processing sessions in December had brought me over the hump of a breakdown and marital split. I knew somewhere deep inside of me that I really needed to continue what I had started, and even though I am not usually one to give myself permission to do the big things I want to do, I gave myself permission to do SHIP.

The first coming together of our particular group was for the Five Cycles of Shamanic Consciousness initiation. The teachings were liberating. The concept of the spiral path as a blend of the straight and narrow with the circular repetitive alternative gave me understanding of progressive repetition—coming around to similar places at a higher level of understanding and awareness—a path that goes somewhere but is in tune with the cycles involved in the progress. By the end of that first week I had dropped my negativity and had found that each of the participants in my group had enormous amounts of wisdom and spirit that I admired. I could not wait to come back in June to see them again.

On returning home I faced turbulent challenges at work, and my supposedly recovering addict husband was not, in fact, recovering. Therefore, I was doing both of our jobs in the company and covering for him with stories. This was a familiar pattern that I did not want to continue. New events began to transpire. I started *knowing* things of which I had no outside information or reason to know. The confirmations came later.

I went back in June for my second round—the Family of Origin and Dancing with the Shadow initiations with my SHIP group. I stayed on, and after a week of individual work with my husband, started apprenticing the first phase of the new SHIP. During the twenty-eight days I was there, I breathed five times and did a sweat lodge and a ritual piece in which I owned my natural psychic gifts. I went deep into my personal process and found nuggets of gold to bring back. Many stored memories, energies, and emotions came forth during that month. It was an amazing time.

The first few minutes back with my husband in early July were in such contrast to my experience over the previous month that I looked at him in the garage as we were bringing my luggage in and said, "I'm not sure this is going to work." I stuck it out through more of his rage and self-destructive behavior.

During my next SHIP I rarely thought of my husband, for the first time in our overly codependent marriage. *I* became my focus. Some news of him came on my last day there, and I realized how little I had thought of him, especially considering he had just had surgery. I was breaking free and becoming my own person again, and it felt good. I realized then that all of my misguided codependent beliefs that I thought had the power to keep him alive were a fairy tale. My staying with him had the potential to kill us both. I chose to move out and divorce him.

I continued my spiritual work with more apprenticeships and initiations. I was being acknowledged for what was actually showing up and lovingly guided, when needed, to a more life-affirming choice. I had always been forced to fit within the confines of other people's ideas for me, and I finally had permission to be outside the box. I was experiencing much anger and was able to safely move it out of my body on the breathwork floor. We did a cord-cutting release ceremony the last day of the workshop, and the importance of my relationship with myself as primary became cellular for me that day.

I have been ordained as a shamanic minister, and in January will complete the third phase of apprenticing to become a breathwork practitioner. My journey is just beginning and I can see how every event that I went through was exactly what I needed to do and was able to do at the time. I now have much more awareness and self-esteem, and know that I can never again allow myself to disappear for the sake of another, or for a relationship that serves no one. I can't do it, not because of something absorbed cognitively, but because of something I have lived and experienced at my most basic cellular level. This is true healing.

STAR DUST,
NORTH CAROLINA

LUCTOR ET EMERGO

The alarm clocks (yes, not just one) rang at 2:30 AM. Though it was still pitch dark, I was glad not to have to worry about driving to Manchester Airport in sleet or snow, as had been the case in February. By now it was June and I was heading out for the second of three weeks of SHIP, short for Shamanic Healing Initiatory Process. I looked forward to seeing my other eight SHIP-mates, the eight apprentices, and the permanent staff members: Star Wolf, Brad, and Ruby.

Gratefully, I exchanged my fleece sweaters for cotton summer clothes. After the long winter in Vermont I was more than ready for a drastic change in temperature. Upon my arrival in Sylva, North Carolina, I was not disappointed. It was like stepping into the tropics! With flowers everywhere, Isis Cove looked even more enchanting than it had the first time—a true fairy's haven. And—to my relief—no black flies or mosquitoes in sight, except some at dusk.

What will happen this time? I wondered. The first week had dealt with the element of water—the first of the Five Cycles of Shamanic Consciousness. While the process is different for each person, in my case it literally had become a watery week. The possibility of my sister Doe's dying that very week had triggered my grief, and once the faucet turned on, my tears had begun to flow abundantly over issues from long ago.

For the second week, the group would go through the elements of earth and fire, dealing with our family of origin and with the shadow. Frankly, I had felt great resistance to getting into family-of-origin stuff once again; I thought I had done enough of that while training to become a family therapist and a Rubenfeld Synergist. Was I not getting much too old for this? But then, the shamanic approach was so compelling, and this time around my orientation extended far beyond the practical goal of gaining a profession. At this stage of my life's journey, I had become mostly interested in spiritual growth and in reaching a state of wholeness so I could embrace true oneness. During the twenty-one day process at the Oneness University in India (January 2007), I had become aware that my early conditioning and experiences were standing in the way of the experience of oneness with everything. I knew that only more inner work could achieve that end. My ego had a good opportunity to learn more humility, especially since many of my SHIP-mates were much younger and had not been in the therapeutic profession.

As soon as I met my fellow travelers again, all my doubts disappeared. It was clear we had come home, ready to settle in for another week of intense sharing and sweet camaraderie. As a side benefit, no matter how much I love spending the bulk of my time alone or with my loving husband, it is a great treat to have a whole week of girl-time, often ending in belly-aching laughter in our bedrooms. One of my roommates asked me to promise I would not be serious. Not often do I receive such a wonderful request! After many years of pretty heavy-duty adulthood, my inner class clown could come out again—and she was ready to rock!

With some experience behind me in doing breathwork sessions, I easily got into the mainstays of the week's work. Each participant would breathe twice, as had been the case during the first week. Although both breathworks were profound, the second process clearly reached beyond my personal issues into a more global theme, and co-leader Brad Collins requested that I record it for the common good, thus this write-up. For my own benefit, I would like to begin the story with the first breathwork.

As before, the breathing and music naturally led me to much body movement. Aside from feeling a keen awareness of the sensations of the movements, not much happened until I felt someone push gently on my tummy. This began a different process where the music faded into the background, and my body sensations seemed to be less prompted by the rhythm of the music. A more autonomous process urged itself to the fore. As the apprentice continued to work with me, it seemed that I was getting into a birth process. Though part of me was the adult observing this miraculous event, once I came through the birth canal and into full birth it felt real enough, and I knew I had been born again. I felt relief and freedom and a sense of having been launched into a new place. However, soon my restless nature reasserted itself and the big question arose: "What now?" I realized it was up to me to find out what I wanted, and I drew a total blank. I realized my codependent habit of leaving decisions up to others. However, in this new place of the unknown I had to start from scratch, and that seemed impossible. Why was that so hard?

When my mind went back to earliest childhood, a huge cloud came over me, and I recognized this as my experience in Holland during World War II. It seemed to overshadow any of my small personal wants. My parents had much to worry about; mainly, how to insure the safety and survival of a family of six, given the bombings and scarcity of food. I felt a new sense of admiration and understanding for them, as well as great sadness for all babies born into the brutishness of war, their delicate psyches overwhelmed and numbed to the loss of their own emotional vitality, and the loss of basic trust that the world is a safe place in which to live.

After these realizations I returned to the question of, "What do I want now?" This made me do nothing but just listen to the music that, at the time, happened to be beautiful singing in a language I did not know. At some point my co-journeyer placed the big stuffed lion, which I had chosen before the session, on my belly. The lion, for me, represented the Egyptian goddess Sekhmet, one of my power figures. However, to my surprise, Sekhmet shape-shifted into a male lion that I recognized as the Dutch lion. How could I not have made the connection before?

Instantly I felt transported to my native Holland, whose national animal totem is a lion. The words that accompany the Dutch lion on the national heraldic weapon are, *Luctor et emergo;* "I struggle, and I emerge." The lion is always pictured standing on his hind legs, half-submerged in water. While seeing that image, I felt a flood of positive feelings rushing into me. I saw the enormous strength of the Dutch in fighting off numerous invasions by water throughout its history as an independent nation. How very amazing that the country had managed to throw out the Romans, Spaniards, English, French, and Germans, and maintain its freedom and identity! My inner world became very colorful as the red, white, and blue of the Dutch flag appeared, together with its orange banner.

Later in the day, while processing the session, I realized I had done a soul retrieval, retrieving a part of me that had to do with love and positive regard for my mother country. As suggested by our co-leader, Star Wolf, I also understood that having spent my formative years in victimhood had resulted in my not feeling strongly attracted to my own country. There is not much strength in being overrun and kept down by an enemy! But in my breathwork, seeing my people victorious over numerous invasions and occupations, rather than as victims, set the record straight. It was a powerful piece of healing on my journey toward wholeness.

The theme of the second breathwork session had already announced itself to me the day before, during a guided meditation. This inner journey had led to a house in which we were to go down into the basement.

In my case, I did not end up in the basement but in a small, outdoor, walled terrace just outside the house where I found a dead man lying in a coffin. I knew it was some relative I had never met, possibly a symbol of my ancestors.

The following night I dreamed that I had given birth to a baby who, soon afterward, began to talk. I turned to my husband, Bram, and shared my surprise that the baby could already talk. The baby asked for some cream. I went to get some cream, but when I returned to the room, the baby wasn't there; instead I saw a former college classmate who, in real life, died of breast cancer. She was sitting quietly in a chair holding a cup of coffee. I assumed the cream was for her coffee.

Upon awakening that morning, I knew I was primed to travel to the land of the dead as a destination in my Shamanic Breathwork. Star Wolf suggested I take Sekhmet along to help remove obstacles that might get in my way, as well as the Egyptian god, Thoth, who would carry light so I could see. After the music started it didn't take long for me to get into what I perceived to be the land of the dead. I walked through a dark cavern and heard the screaming of anguished people (prompted by the other breathers, many of whom were getting very loud). It sounded as if I had landed in a hell. I knew I was just visiting as a bystander and not there to stay, but I did not know how to get out of that dark place. I asked to be lifted up into some heavenly realm, but nobody came to help me. I felt a deep yearning, but I finally gave up and saw that it was not up to me to direct this scenario. Next I saw Isis standing on earth, holding open her winged arms. She looked welcoming, and next thing I knew I felt my arms becoming like wings, letting me fly up into the sky. For some time I enjoyed flying around like a bird.

Next, I became aware of a wooden panel with paintings of dancing skeletons. I recognized this panel as the inner wall of a covered bridge in Lucerne, Switzerland. I went up to the panel and invited the skeletons—all male—to dance off the panel and come with me into the river below the bridge. For a brief moment I felt infused with a deep sadness and knowledge that Christianity was dead. I felt this in my own body, but I reached above me, drawing down new life energy from Isis and the Egyptian mysteries. I felt that I was being infused with new energy and proceeded to baptize the figures who had become fleshed out, beautiful young men in the water. I dunked them under, one by one, and then led them out of the river to a green meadow covered with colorful flowers. I then flicked my hands over them and sprayed them with golden energy that came streaming from my hands. A golden dome appeared in the sky, and then I heard the drumming in the breathwork room letting us know the end of the session was here. Perfect timing!

I felt very honored that such a beautiful, restorative experience had been bestowed on me. Though much of this may come out of my own psyche, I had the sense that I had tapped into an energy and a reality that went beyond my own personal sphere. My favorite subject in my four years of history studies at Leyden University had been the Middle Ages. However, when I became interested in spirituality at a later age, I could not feel any emotional attraction to Christ or Christianity; I turned to Buddhism instead. Though I tried to reconnect several times with my Christian roots, it never worked—it never had enough energy for me. In my experience, Christianity has indeed died. What happened in the breathwork gives me hope and affirmation that the death of Christianity, as it is, needs to happen so that true oneness will have a chance to come through.

I also note that, in the guided meditation as well as in the breathwork itself, the dead people were men and that the friend who appeared in my dream was, in her real life, somewhat of a flirt. And there I went, descending from the sky, "inviting" the dead men skeletons to dance with me, off their wooden panels, into the water where they were reborn and baptized (water is the element of the second chakra). On one level I see this as symbolic of the death of the patriarchy and rebirth into a new era in which the feminine principle of love and connectedness will reign, and we all can become more fully human. I also see that, on a personal level, I am dying to my own dominant animus, to be reborn and baptized into my anima. I think it is time to start belly dancing!

BINEKE OORT,
VERMONT

SHAMANIC BREATHWORK
ROCKED HER WORLD

In 2006 I went to the first Wise Wolf Woman Council in Isis Cove at the behest of friends. I was inclined to discount what I thought would be a *woo woo*, *New Age* event. My intention was to go, hang with my friends, and participate in the activities if I was so moved; otherwise, I would enjoy being in the beautiful mountains of western North Carolina.

One of the activities I decided to try was Shamanic Breathwork. I really had no idea what it was about, but I thought it sounded interesting. Little did I know . . .

To say that it was a powerful experience does not begin to describe it. Put simply, I was so rocked by the experience and result that I decided I needed to seek more experiences and learn the foundation of this work, why it works, why it is so powerful, and how it can transform lives.

I do not intend to mislead by saying that my life changed overnight, but starting with that first time, in which I unloaded a ton of emotional baggage, and the feeling of sheer joy afterward, I began to utilize this dynamic process as part of my ongoing search and desire to change my outlook and approach to my life. Indeed, my life has changed and is changing by doing this work.

I completed the Shamanic Healing Initiation Process (SHIP) and have become an ordained shamanic minister. This process has helped me to see my purpose more clearly, and to see what my next steps will be for my life. It has also allowed me to witness beautiful and profound transformations in others.

I have said more than once that if all people practiced Shamanic Breathwork, there could be no more war. Sure, I know this is simplistic. But I also know that if everyone understood that there is an organic outlet for rage, fear, frustration, and deep hurt that resolves these internal issues all of us have, no one would want, or need, to take frustrations out on others. We would learn to coexist peacefully within our world community of all God's creations, rather than try to destroy each other, and we would learn to protect and restore this beautiful earth, where we were blessed to be born. Spread the word—Shamanic Breathwork is the way to heal the planet.

BONNIE RUBENSTEIN (BONNIE WISE WOLF),
WASHINGTON, DC

JOURNEY TO THE HEART OF COMMUNITY/INTEGRATION OF SHADOW AND LIGHT

My conscious spiritual journey began when I was searching for answers about my chronic, undiagnosed body pain that was having a drastic impact on my quality of life. When I was introduced to Shamanic Breathwork with Linda Star Wolf and Brad Collins, I knew that I had found the key to a meaningful life, with or without chronic pain.

The SHIP program was the beginning of a journey to my heart that has uncovered, recovered, and discovered my soul's calling of developing an intentional, heart-based community. When I was introduced to Venus Rising and Shamanic Breathwork, I was facilitating healing circles and had a private practice as well. I had visions of a community, but did not know what that meant until I began working with Venus Rising. The teachings and circle work of the Shamanic Breathwork process gave my spiritual practice a foundation of living life through the conscious heart, a higher heart (Spirit), and the human heart. Through Shamanic Breathwork I have been able to move through trapped energy in my body, which I was sometimes aware of and sometimes not, but I learned that my soul knew what it was time for, and I learned to trust in its knowing.

I discovered shadow parts of myself, such as the embodiment of the black widow spider, that at first shocked and shamed me into thinking that I possessed the ability to "dispense of my mate." During the teachings and process I came to realize that I have the ability to "cast a web" (develop intentional community), and that I do have the ability to dispense of those things that are no longer needed, when necessary for my personal spiritual growth. Now that I know that this is a part of me, I can keep it from acting in an unconscious, destructive way.

Prior to being introduced to Shamanic Breathwork I was on a path of loving the light and shunning the dark. Now I know that it is important for me to embrace all and to live my life in balance—not to live so far "above" the darkness that I couldn't, and wouldn't, be aware of it, but to live on earth as a vessel between heaven and earth. Living "out of my body" served me well when growing up with realities that were too harsh to accept, but now I would rather live in, and experience the juiciness of life: "The light, the dark, no difference," as Star Wolf would always say.

SOPHIA SAVORY (WOLFANGEL),
OREGON

11
Preparations and Instructions for Breathing Alone

. . . .

At some level, none of us ever enters into a spiritual journey alone; we are always supported by our spirit guides, helpers, and higher powers. While working with a Mayan teacher and friend of mine, I kept noticing that he always used the word "we" instead of "I" or "me." When I asked him the reason for this, he said that most human beings are too arrogant and imagine that they are doing everything on their own, without any guidance or help from the spirit world. He believed that none of us would be here or make it through one day without divine assistance from those who watch over and love us. So when he said, "We go here, or we are going to do that," he was referring not only to himself, but to those guides who lovingly walk with him every day upon his earth walk. His humilty about not doing his earth walk alone touched me deeply, and he inspired me to remember upon rising each morning to thank all the helpers—in both the visible *and* invisible realms—for their love and guidance for my own earth walk.

Having acknowledged that we are never alone in the spirit world, it is still up to all of us, as spiritual beings having a very human experience, to take responsibility for ourselves; and if we are going on a journey of any kind, to make the appropriate preparation for our travels. The following information will assist you in preparing for your Shamanic Breathwork journey and support you in having a meaningful, transformative experience. I hope you will add your story and journey to hundreds I have collected over the years, and share them with the Shamanic Breathwork community that awaits you.

As is true for any other kind of healing modality, there are some things to note at the outset in order to insure the best possible outcome for the work. The most important component of any Shamanic Breathwork journey and session is that of creating a safe and sacred space in which the journeyer can enter into an altered state of consciousness. Unless one is feeling relaxed and confident enough to enter into the process, it simply won't work. Any serious energy worker and practitioner knows that it is very important to educate the participant about the process being engaged in, and to explain and set the boundaries that create the sacred container, or vessel, for the experience. An individual who has been well prepared and given appropriate instructions is then capable of deciding how to employ the tools that have been given for use upon the journey.

Another very important aspect of the Shamanic Breathwork journey is for the journeyer to always remember that she remains in charge of her process. This is true whether in a group setting or breathing alone at home. Unlike the experience of an altered state created by substance use, if something is not feeling appropriate, the journeyer can simply, at any time, stop the circular breathing, sit up, and follow the directions to return to normal outer awareness. Following these instructions will bring about a return to the original state of consciousness within minutes; at most, within an hour.

It is not advisable to attempt a breathwork session of any kind under the influence of alcohol or recreational drugs. Anyone carrying a psychiatric diagnosis should find a Shamanic Breathwork facilitator to serve as a guide, rather than breathing alone, and check with your doctor or a trusted health practitioner. We have worked with many individuals who have been diagnosed as depressed, or who have anxiety disorders or other psychiatric problems. There has seldom been a problem for anyone around the breathwork process, especially when working with an experienced facilitator.

In fact, any difficulty around the Shamanic Breathwork journey pales in comparison to what I often witnessed while working in mainstream counseling at mental health and treatment centers, where I frequently witnessed problems in conjunction with the prescription of medications. Obviously we would not offer Shamanic Breathwork to anyone who is seriously mentally ill or psychotic. Nor would we encourage anyone who has had a recent injury, surgery, or serious health complication to do Shamanic Breathwork, either as part of a group or alone. We also suggest that pregnant women not do Shamanic Breathwork. We have made a few exceptions to these rules for individuals who are experienced in doing deep inner work and journeying, provided they do the breathwork with a skilled facilitator.

It is very important to note that over the past twenty years our certified breathwork trainers and I have facilitated hundreds of people on various kinds of breathwork journeys without any serious complications ensuing. We always err on the side of safety for those who come to us for transformation and assistance in healing their lives, and at the same time, we trust that whoever shows up has a divine appointment and is here for a reason.

At a treatment center for severe anorexics I facilitated Shamanic Breathwork for a roomful of individuals with eating disorders. I have facilitated breathwork for people in hospice, people with pacemakers, people who have undergone (triple) bypass operations, and individuals with cancer and other health disorders. Again, these are individuals who should not breathe alone or with an inexperienced facilitator.

It is important to always check out the background credentials and experience of an intended facilitator when doing energy work. Venus Rising's Shamanic Ministers Global Network has a code of ethics that must be taken seriously by anyone we ordain and certify. Any failure to comply with these standards will result in ordination and certification from our organization being revoked.

Another very important component of the Shamanic Breathwork journey is to be able to integrate the experience into one's everyday life. There are many ways to integrate the journey. One of the best, of course, is to do the work in groups and participate in the circle's sharing during the workshop and afterward. If you are going to journey by yourself, it is strongly suggested that you have a soul friend, mentor, or counselor whom you can turn to and with whom you can share your journey. Being listened to is an important part of any process that involves change. Other methods for integration have been discussed in depth in chapter 4. These methods include scribing, art processes, and garnering support from other kindred spirits when the journey is over.

I used to always advise others not to do breathwork alone, but over the years many individuals have told me they have put on music and done some shamanic breathing on their own with great results. This has caused me to rethink some of the early parameters I set around Shamanic Breathwork, and to truly trust the shaman within us all. I have undergone several hundred of my own journeys and most of them have been with a co-journeyer—that is how I prefer it. However, I have often been known to put on some evocative music in order to do breathwork trance dance and energy release work, or to facilitate different art processes.

One of my teachers told me long ago that we all have an inner healer guiding the process, and as long as we are in connection with that spirit within, we will not journey further than we should. Thus far in my personal and professional life I have found this to be true. Shamanic Breathwork is one of the safest and most effective methods for imparting transformation that I have ever experienced or facilitated. It is the primary tool that I continue to use in my own life to expand my consciousness and heal the issues that surface.

※

The following protocol is suggested for a successful solo Shamanic Breathwork journey, in order to gain the most benefit without a human co-journeyer, or facilitator, by your side. A little bit of preparation for your journey will go a long way to ensure that you have the best experience possible.

If you are going to journey alone, it is strongly suggested that you consider setting up, in advance, a time to share and process your journey soon after your breathing is done. This should be with a soul friend, teacher, counselor, or sponsor. Speaking about your journey with another can be very reassuring, healing, and integrating. Be sure the person with whom you share has the capacity to hold space for you with the sophistication needed to understand your process. You certainly do not wish to be misunderstood or invalidated when you are feeling vulnerable and open. Let the person you have chosen know in advance what your boundaries are, and what you will need in the way of feedback and space holding. You may even want to give them this book ahead of time, and ask them to read this chapter and chapter 4 on the Shamanic Breathwork experience.

The intentional setting of a safe and sacred space is necessary in order for the journeyer to be able to relax and let go into the experience. Your breathing space should be private, quiet, and comfortable, with phones and other outside distractions and noises eliminated. It is important to create a sense of the sacred and to offer up your heartfelt intentions and invocations—or simply a prayer of surrender to spirit or a higher power. This is the time to call upon any spirit guides or other helpers to escort and assist you during your Shamanic Breathwork session.

You can follow the same directions that are given for a group breathwork session. Light a candle, lower the lights, and smudge the area and yourself. The CD provided with this book should be at hand and ready to play.* Find a comfortable place to lie down on a mat with a blanket

---

*The CD included with this book also has a guided spiral meditation that follows the Shamanic Breathwork session. You may wish to listen to the guided meditation immediately following the breathwork, or you can save it for another time. The spiral meditation can stand alone as a powerful way to access your inner wisdom, or shaman.

and pillows if necessary. An eye mask is recommended, and it is also advised that you have a journal ready for afterward, when you will want to record your experience in words.

To create a relaxed mindset and an atmosphere of openness to the experience, a relaxation meditation or guided imagery sets the tone before beginning the session. Begin by making yourself comfortable and regulating your breathing to slow, deep, and even breaths. Concentrate on relaxing your toes; visualize relaxing the muscles. Next, relax the feet, ankles, and calf muscles, and continue this mind/body meditation until both are free from any tension created by the day's events and life's circumstances.

If you have a drum, you may want to begin your session with a few minutes of soft drumming and align your heartbeat with the beat of the drum. This is not necessary if you do not have access to a drum, but it is a plus if you do have one. After drumming you may turn on the journeying music, place your eye mask on, then just lie back upon your mat and begin to breathe in and out to the music (in the prescribed, rhythmic manner). Breathe until you are surprised, allowing the images, sensations, emotions, and releases to occur without trying to control them (referring back again as necessary to instructions on a basic group session given in chapter 4).

The music will guide you through the seven major energy fields, or chakras, over the course of about an hour. Allow your body to move upon your mat in any way that you are guided. If you feel the need to open your eyes to orient yourself at any time during your breathwork session, do so briefly and return to your journey. It is best to breathe in a space that has been cleared ahead of time or does not have furniture too close to your journeying space, so that you will feel free to move around if your body wants to do so.

The music, along with your intentional breathing, surrendered heart, spirit guides, and inner shaman will facilitate a sacred shamanic inner journey. Toward the end of the session, the music will begin to slow and move into a higher vibrational frequency. During this time you will naturally begin to feel more open and expansive, and will wind down any cathartic processes. As the session ends there will be a song of return that will naturally ground you in your body and heart chakra. Slowly begin to return to your outer reality and your normal breathing and awareness.

When you feel that you are "back," you may sit up and quietly write in your journal, or create an art drawing, collage, mandala, or another piece of artistic expression to ground your experience. You may wish to have a bottle of water, a few nuts, or a fruit snack close by to enjoy. It is best not to become overly energetic until you have grounded yourself in this manner, as it is easy to underestimate the altered state in which you may still find yourself.

You can also ground yourself by listening to relaxing music and eating a meal. It is normal to feel a lot of emotions at the end of your session, especially if you have revisited sensitive areas of your life. Don't be afraid to feel your feelings. Feelings are not facts; they are just pent-up emotional reactions and are best released, rather than repressed. Many more individuals have been hurt by their repressed and unexpressed emotions than by taking responsibility for releasing them in a healthy manner.

Therapists often teach their clients how to do anger work at home by beating on pillows to let off steam. Spiritual teachers and counselors often suggest using guided meditations to help clients connect with grief, anger, or other negative emotions and past experiences in order to transform them. There are, of course, many guided meditations that also teach how to connect with the joy, magic, and beauty that resides in all of us.

If this is the time you have set up to speak to someone about your journey, proceed in calling or meeting with that person. You will want to share your journaling and art piece as well. If you are not going to process with another, take the time to review your journaling and your art piece, and perhaps take a quiet walk or warm bath. Be sure to stay hydrated and get plenty of rest before returning to your regular schedule and outer world. (As well, follow the guidelines in chapter 12 for embodying shamanic consciousness to ground yourself and to keep the process alive in your everyday life.)

Over the next few days or weeks, keep the process alive by journaling and paying close attention to how your breathwork experience may be showing up in synchronistic ways around you in the world. Keep your artwork hung within view and your journaling handy, as these expressions of your journey may reveal more of the process as you continue to dwell on their meaning.

May your inner shaman guide you to your heart's true desire and assist you on your path of transformation and manifestation of your dreams in this world.

12

Embodying Shamanic Consciousness in Everyday Living

· ·

The following are shamanic-psychospiritual tools to assist individuals in keeping their process alive and grounded after the Shamanic Breathwork journey. Unless we are able to embody, on a daily basis, the shifts that we have made during a breathwork journey, they become irrelevant. There is a Native American saying that makes this point by asking, "Does what you do grow corn?"

VENUS RISING GUIDELINES FOR REENTRY AFTER SHAMANIC BREATHWORK

After entering an altered state or going deep into process, one should practice these practical guidelines designed specifically for individuals who have participated in Venus Rising workshops or Shamanic Breathwork journeys. They are helpful instructions for returning from altered states work and integrating the right and left sides of the brain.

- ᴐ Be gentle with yourself.
- ᴐ Be kind to others. Do not expect them to have a clue about what you have just experienced.

- ⊃ Nurture in nature—walking is good for you.
- ⊃ Rest, relax, and get a good night's sleep (or two).
- ⊃ Drink plenty of liquids—water is the best!
- ⊃ Eat grounding, nourishing foods—not junk food or fast food. Watch out for sugar and caffeine cravings. Try fresh fruit and herb teas instead.
- ⊃ Do not fast or skips meals for a while.
- ⊃ Take time to journal, do artwork, dream, and attend to your inner life.
- ⊃ Meditate daily, even if it's just for ten minutes (learn to listen to your inner voice).
- ⊃ Dance, dance, dance!
- ⊃ Yoga and other forms of movement are wonderful.
- ⊃ Connect with kindred spirits in person, by phone, or maybe even by group e-mail.
- ⊃ Do take some time for solitude or reflection, but please do not isolate!
- ⊃ Follow up with aftercare, if necessary, by making an appointment with your therapist, spiritual teacher, or soul guide. Remember, you do not have to go it alone if you need support along the way in dealing with old patterns, addictions, or issues that resurface.
- ⊃ Attend any regular groups, circles, or meetings you normally attend, such as Twelve-Step meetings, counseling groups, talking stick circles, drumming circles and so on.
- ⊃ Get a massage, Reiki session, or other bodywork.
- ⊃ Build an altar to connect more fully with your higher power and spiritual allies.
- ⊃ Attend to skin hunger by cuddling with a two- or four-legged being, or both! Animal companions are great to hang out with.
- ⊃ Watch a funny movie or a romantic comedy.
- ⊃ Listen to some easy listening music—nothing too cosmic or spacey for a few days.
- ⊃ Don't take yourself too seriously.

- Don't become complacent.
- Do not forget what you learned while you were here—keep nurturing the seeds of consciousness one day at a time.
- Read a good book to keep your mind alert.
- Don't get a divorce (just yet); don't get married (just yet); don't quit your job (just yet); don't adopt a pet (just yet); don't change your hair color or get a Mohawk hairdo (just yet); and don't give all your possessions away and join an ashram in India (just yet).

In other words, let things settle down and have time to integrate into your life before you make any major changes. If something is truly valid for you, it will still ring true in thirty days if you are taking the steps to integrate the changes into your life, rather than just reacting to troublesome situations.

If you take prescription medication and decide to quit, please consult with a doctor before stopping. It is suggested that you refrain from alcohol and other mind-altering drugs (other than your prescribed meds) for at least twenty-four hours after a workshop. Try not to overschedule your time for a day or two after the event. Look for ways to practice what you have learned in your everyday life (study the Spiral Path of Alchemical Transformation and the Five Cycles of Shamanic Consciousness).

Everyone at Venus Rising has walked the path of transformation for many moons, and we are no strangers to these symbolic shamanic death and rebirth experiences. That is why we call the process "awakening the shaman within." We know firsthand the healing power of these initiations that can shift individuals from the ego's agenda to the soul's purpose. It takes time, trust, and patience to work through all Five Cycles of Shamanic Consciousness. As shamanic soul guides, we are committed to assisting others on both their human and spiritual journeys, in order to embody their wholeness right here on our beautiful Mother Earth.

Remember, life does not happen in a straight line; rather, it spirals out from our vibral core. If we are truly embracing the adventure we call our lives, then we will all travel through many ups and downs along the way to higher love and wisdom. So travel the spiral path trusting in the process, your higher power, your soul companions, and your own precious spirit. We believe in you and hold the vision of your true self until you can fully embrace that vision for yourself.

THE CODE OF ETHICS FOR THE AQUARIAN SHAMAN: A NEW PARADIGM

This is a new paradigm code of ethics for anyone who identifies with living, serving, and working on a path of higher consciousness. All of the shamanic ministers and Shamanic Breathwork facilitators certified through Venus Rising agree to abide by the code of ethics listed below.

- Be honest, work on yourself, live your truth, don't use others, make mistakes, make amends, listen to feedback, and move past defensiveness.
- Become a spiritual warrior.
- Have a heart and a mind—use them both.
- Be open to support from your spirit guides.
- Live inside your body—be juicy.
- Take your own advice—live and let live.
- Take things as they come—one day at a time . . . and forgive yourself when you do not.
- Be mindful and spontaneous at the same time.
- Move past one-sidedness.
- See the beauty and perfection in *everything*!
- Be open to change and *let go*! Be open to joyfulness.
- Believe in yourself, in others, and in synchronicity and grace.
- Let gratitude fill you up, and let it flow to others.
- Show the same patience to others that the universe has shown to you.

- Be flexible and tolerant; include yourself.
- Become a shadow dancer—the light, the dark, no difference.
- Never take advantage of others—remember the law of karma.
- Seek to empower those you serve.
- Avoid comparing yourself and your gifts with others.
- Let go of competition and scarcity consciousness—believe in abundance.
- Hold the vision for those who seek your guidance. Offer them loving kindness.
- Do not take others hostage to your ideas of who they should be.
- Do not enable others to stay as they are.
- Let there always be an equal exchange of energy between you and those you serve, so as not to create confusion or a "less than" relationship.
- Feel your loving feelings and body responses for others.
- Have loving boundaries. Never shame another for loving, sexual, and nonsexual feelings.
- Create a big, safe container in which these bright, beautiful souls may cook so the fires of transformation can work their magic on us all.
- Remember, we are all traveling on the wheel of life back to where we came from, doing the best we can.
- So treat others as you want to be treated—with consideration, dignity, and respect, no matter who they are. We are *all* God's favorite child.

13
THIRTY SHAMANIC QUESTIONS FOR HUMANITY

*Dismantle Your Old Ego Agenda
and Recover Your Original Soul Purpose*

. . . .

The Thirty Shamanic Questions were birthed to help save the life of a dear friend who was suffering from such a severe depression that she had become suicidal. She was in a major life transition that threatened to overwhelm her sanity. I, her friend and teacher for many years, felt helpless in this situation. Feeling overwhelmed, I sat down, said a prayer asking for help, and turned to my computer. I spontaneously typed out these words: "Awaken the shaman within. Thirty shamanic questions to dismantle your old ego identity and recover your original soul purpose."

The words began to flow effortlessly through my consciousness, and in less than a couple of hours the Thirty Shamanic Questions were born. These questions are called shamanic because they are designed to serve as a guide to the process of letting go of old ego attachments (a symbolic death) and moving into a rebirth experience. A shaman is often called a wounded healer—one who has learned how to heal himself of the pain of life's experiences, and then shares the wisdom gained from those experiences with others.

I, too, am a wounded healer; I embrace the shamanic path of spiritual growth and healing. I, too, have struggled with numerous difficult issues and addictions on my life's journey. I have had many symbolic death and rebirth experiences, which I refer to as the "shamanic path of conscious awareness." This has prompted me to reach out and assist countless others along the way. Over the last three decades I have helped individuals from every walk of life navigate the uncharted territory from ego to soul's purpose.

The Thirty Shamanic Questions form a structure for the work I have been doing with others. They are intended to accelerate and support transformation. What makes this process special, and one of the reasons it works so well in comparison to other self-help processes, is that we are not meant to walk this path alone. The journey is shared with another, whom we refer to as the co-journeyer. It is similar to what happens when someone sponsors another person in a 12-step program of recovery. When two people make the commitment to do the questions together, in loving connection to one another, the magic truly begins.

My friend did not kill herself. She worked the questions and then passed them on to many others. That was four years ago. Since then she has made significant and soulful changes in her life; indeed, she wrote a follow-up commentary for this section of the book. The Thirty Shamanic Questions have spread like wildfire around this country and to several other countries, including Germany, Australia, and England. They have found their way to those who are ready to heal and become more of who they really are. I trust that if the Thirty Shamanic Questions have found their way into your hands and heart, it is not by accident; indeed, it may be the answer to a prayer.

STAYING AWAKE

It is very difficult to stay fully awake while your old ego attachments are dying and you are birthing your soul's divine purpose. These Thirty Shamanic Questions are intended to help you stay alert. Working one question a day for thirty days will change your life, and a new vision of who you really are will begin to unfold right before your eyes. This book is a guide to that unfolding process; it will help you to reclaim your lost soul parts and shape-shift your old reality, as you discover your sacred purpose and remember who you really are.

If you follow the format and instructions detailed in the following chapters, your old ego attachments will begin to dissolve and your soul's voice will begin to lead the way. Ego attachments are developed early in life as a protective mechanism that helps us to adapt to our surroundings. They help us survive during our childhood and get our needs met. The ego is not meant to be permanently in charge of our life's path and purpose, however. In order to be truly happy we must sooner or later begin to rely on something higher than our ego's interpretation of who we are. This ultimately leads to the symbolic death of old ego attachments.

This is a difficult shift. Even when we sincerely believe there is a sacred reason for us to be on the planet, that we have a unique role in God/Goddess' creation, doubt will surely raise its head when the ground beneath us starts to shake. There is a natural tendency to run for the shelter of what we know, even if it is not what we really *desire*. The unknown future can feel threatening and fears can all too easily sabotage hopes and dreams. Rather than embrace the void, we often opt for safety, or what we define as safety. The irony is that what may seem safe may actually be destroying us and hurting what we love and cherish most.

When we begin to make the shift from ego to soul we often encounter interference from those closest to us. It is understandable that those to whom we are most closely connected—partners in love, work, and play; our children and employers or employees—are resistant to this shift. We have created predictable patterns, healthy or not, that help others know what to expect in their connection to us. These connections may change considerably when someone begins to listen to the soul's longing.

It is important not to judge those who do not understand, and equally important not to allow their judgments to interfere with our making the decisions we need to make. We must remember that they still see us from their ego point of view and are, in fact, simply mirroring our own ego's perception of who we are. They have not had the time or opportunity to process and accept the change (the symbolic death). The discomfort will pass in time, and if there is an authentic connection these relationships will not only survive, they will thrive, because they will be more open and honest. During this time it is important to remember to *trust love*. All things that are not love will begin to fall away—and isn't that what you really desire?

Even after you make up your mind to "Let Your Soul Be Your Pilot," as singer-composer Sting wrote, there still will be a strong pull to revert back to the familiar, rather than move forward to the new. You will need support, soul friends, soul tools, and a faith and trust in something bigger than your ego's point of view in order to put down firm roots in new ground.

It saddens me to see people in the middle of major life changes "go back to sleep" and stay in addictive processes that create massive soul loss, not only for themselves but for those around them. While I know—and on some level trust—that it is all a part of their journey, it still disturbs me, especially when someone's life and well-being is threatened by a return to an old situation, addiction, or pattern. This disappointment has been a powerful motivator for me and has led me to work more diligently to discover better methods and tools for healing.

The Thirty Shamanic Questions are the result of that search. They provide a highly transformative process of healing and self-discovery that can cut through months, or even years, of talk therapy. As inner wisdom is accessed, the answers to seemingly impossible questions begin to take shape and become available to our everyday reality. Gaining access to inner knowledge is actually the easy part . . . staying connected to the revelations and insights takes more time and effort.

Answering these though-provoking questions with a kindred spirit, someone you can trust to hold space while you dive into the secrets of your soul, helps to keep the process alive and moving forward. In time, as the soul's voice becomes stronger and louder than the ego's fear, a deepening will occur, which some refer to as serenity. An unshakable faith—that there is indeed something in the universe that loves us deeply and has a divine plan for our lives—begins to grow. A deep knowing begins to grow that our lives are not a mistake, and this must surely mean that we are here on purpose.

As we work this process, the bigger picture begins to shape our daily reality. The ego calms down and finds its rightful place in service to the higher self of love and wisdom. May we each be graced by this larger reality in our daily lives as we walk forward toward the soul's destiny.

While working the thirty questions, it may be useful to be reading *Codependents' Guide to the Twelve Steps,* by Melody Beattie. A good goal would be to have this book read by the completion of the thirty questions. You may also like Beattie's daily reader, *The Language of Letting Go.* In addition, you may want to study and work the Shamanic Twelve Steps of Recovery, which are summarized in Appendix One in this book.

Unless you are willing to make the commitment to follow through for thirty days, please do not attempt to begin this process. It will be fruitless and a waste of time! However, if you are ready to begin, let your heart be glad, for you are embarking on a journey that will set your spirit free, one day at a time.

GETTING STARTED WITH THE THIRTY SHAMANIC QUESTIONS

The Thirty Shamanic Questions were originally designed to be given one day at a time for thirty consecutive days. A sacred agreement is entered into by two individuals whom I refer to as shamanic co-journeyers. The intent of the agreement is to provide the co-journeyer answering the thirty questions a sense of safety and being honored, which is provided by the co-journeyer holding space. The co-journeyer holding space is a "graduate" of the thirty questions, meaning this person has already successfully completed answering the Thirty Shamanic Questions.

The two co-journeyers agree to connect daily until the questions are finished. Occasionally it is not possible to finish within the thirty-day time frame; this is acceptable as long as there is a legitimate reason for the delay. This process is not intended to be dogmatic or rigid. It does, however, provide efficient, disciplined, daily support to the process of major life transformation. Unless there is a heartfelt commitment, the process will not bear fruit.

When I worked the questions with one friend, one of the intrepid souls I referred to in the dedication of this book, we ended up doing part of it via e-mail while she was traveling in England. While she was receiving these questions from me she was simultaneously working them with two other people—one in Iowa, and one in North Carolina. Another time I worked the questions while on vacation at Disney World, with a co-journeyer who lived in Maui. We used a combination of phone conversations, voice mail, and e-mail to complete the process.

It is important to be truly committed to the Thirty Shamanic Questions process whether you are giving or receiving the questions. As with most things in life, you will receive back only as much as you put into the process. There are many innovative ways that people have found to work together. Several therapists have begun using the questions with clients, giving them several to answer, one day at a time, until the next prearranged appointment. A few people have passed the question they have answered the previous day onto someone else, who was a day behind them in answering the questions.

People have made this journey in all kinds of combinations, such as friend to friend, spouse to spouse, parent to child, sibling to sibling, employee to employer. There are therapists who have been open-minded enough to receive the questions from their clients. I know of one journeyer who worked the questions with two friends simultaneously—a married couple—via three-way telephone conferencing. There have even been discussions about starting weekly meetings to discuss the Thirty Shamanic Questions.

The Thirty Shamanic Questions not only appeal to, but also "work" for people of all ages and from all walks of life, from early twenties to late seventies. Among them are Christians, Jews, and Buddhists, as well as worshipers of the Goddess, nature, and New Age beliefs. Some people are agnostic; others feel a direct connection to their higher power. Several have been involved with 12-step recovery programs, such as Alcoholics Anonymous, Al-Anon, or Co-Dependents Anonymous. Several had previously worked with a counselor or therapist on personal issues. For some it is their first time engaging in any kind of shamanic-psychospiritual process.

The reports of lives that have been changed, healings that have taken place, and love that has been shared among so many individuals who have had the courage "to change the things they can" touches my heart beyond words!

This book now offers the journey to a larger audience. In so doing I would like to humbly offer some suggestions as to how this process might work best for all concerned.

HOW TO BEGIN

Many of you will make the journey through the Thirty Shamanic Questions with a friend who agrees to co-journey with you. Chances are that neither of you will have worked the questions with a "graduate" of this process. I strongly recommend that the two of you do one question, one day at a time, and do not look ahead. Part of the magic of this process is to allow yourself to be surprised by the questions and to answer them from your current perspective.

The steps of your journey are:

> Make and review your commitment to co-journey with each other as you each work the thirty questions one day at a time, and set a time to speak to each other the next day.

- As you and your co-journeyer begin your time together, take a few minutes to create a sacred, safe space, letting everything else drop away. You may want to meditate, offer a prayer, or choose some other ritual to use together every day.

- Next, read the first question aloud and write it down. You may decide to alternate who reads the question to whom. You will both write the question in your journals, and at some point before you speak the following day, take time to reflect and write your answer to that day's question.

- The following day each co-journeyer will share his or her answer to the previous day's question. Then say and write down the next day's question. Each day, before parting, you and your co-journeyer should set the time for reconnecting the following day.

- This same process will continue for thirty days or however long the process ends up taking. Try to stick to your original commitment as much as possible. The rewards will be well worth it in the end.

ADDITIONAL SUGGESTIONS

- Remember that you are not your co-journeyer's therapist. You are sharing a journey and are holding space for each other in a deeper way than you may ever have done before. How much time you want to spend with each other on a daily basis should be discussed before starting. Some people make it short and sweet (maybe ten to fifteen minutes), while others take a little longer. You can certainly renegotiate the time commitment along the way. Some people prefer to talk at the same time each day; others are more flexible and make their arrangements on a more spontaneous basis.

- I recommend buying an attractive journal with plenty of paper for answering your questions. You may find that if you co-journey again with a different person, new information will arise that you may wish to add to your initial journal.

ɔ I like to begin my day by meditating for a few moments on a daily reading of some kind. My favorite inspirational book for this process was previously mentioned: *The Language of Letting Go,* by Melody Beattie. I believe you will find this book helpful in answering the Thirty Shamanic Questions, whether you believe you have codependent behavior or not.

ɔ Give yourself the gift of a few minutes of uninterrupted peace and quiet time each day to reflect upon your answer to the daily question.

ɔ When you complete the process, celebrate with your co-journeyer. Perhaps you will want to give each other a small gift—a token of some kind to symbolize the journey you have made together.

ɔ Pass it on!

ɔ Last, I would love to hear about your journey. If you would like to share the journey you have taken through the Thirty Shamanic Questions, you can do so by contacting me at my blog: http://aquarianshaman.lindastarwolf.com.

OTHER WAYS TO WORK THE QUESTIONS

ɔ If you prefer to work these questions with a seasoned journeyer, you may contact a graduate of the process through the Venus Rising Institute of the Shamanic Healing Arts. E-mail us at venusrising@shamanicbreathwork.org, or call (828) 631–2305.

ɔ You can take this book to your counselor or therapist and ask if that person would be willing to assist you through the process.

ɔ You can start a Thirty Shamanic Questions study group. Go to the Venus Rising website for directions on setting up a group.

SPECIAL NOTE TO SHAMANIC JOURNEYERS

This journey is not meant to be taken alone. The spirit of unconditional love and acceptance that we access by working this process with another person can be one of the greatest healing experiences we will ever encounter in this lifetime.

The Thirty Shamanic Questions

> 1. Are you willing to commit to this process for thirty days to uncover, recover, discover, and remember why you are here? If so, write your commitment down on paper. Then write why you are willing to commit to this process.

I have held my destiny in my two hands and I am the shape I have made. I have suffered and loved. I have walked through fire and did not burn. I've been blown by wind and did not fall. I've walked the long road and kept to my journey, though I met no other traveler. I have lost and found myself in every rock, field, and tree. I know what I am and what I imagine. I know shadow and light, and I have never been satisfied with shelter and bread when the great was left unattained. This I have done to enter death and turn from nothing toward life. I shall pass into heaven, even I shall pass like eternity, quietly in the fire and the flesh.

NORMANDI ELLIS, *AWAKENING OSIRIS*

Making a commitment is a matter of the heart. It takes courage, strength, persistence, and willingness to follow through on your word. To make it only part of the way, or to turn around and try to go back, or to just quit is not only self-defeating behavior, but disloyal to your own soul's journey. If your heart is not fully in your commitment (no matter how good your initial intentions are), most likely you will not be able to achieve or complete this process or any other. That is why this first question needs some reflection and needs to be pondered deeply.

The hidden question is, "Am I ready to change?" If you have arrived at this place in your life, chances are you have come to a dead end with some situation, person, place, or thing. There may be a feeling of loss, confusion, anger, grief, or even excitement and eagerness to move from this place. This process is not for those who want to continue things the way they are. Rather, this is a process that calls to those who are seeking real change in their lives.

Imagine if Frodo from *Lord of the Rings,* or Dorothy from *The Wizard of Oz* had not been seriously committed to their respective paths. The endings of their stories would surely have been quite different. Both understandably wanted to go back to what once felt safe and familiar. Frodo longed for the shire; Dorothy often felt lost and wanted to go home. They both, however, kept moving along their chosen paths. Some deep inner calling helped them to remain true to themselves. Their inner commitment to what they truly loved and valued kept them moving steadily forward despite all obstacles and challenges.

Writing down your commitment and your reasons for entering into this process will help you to keep your promise not only to yourself, but also to your co-journeyer. If you are doing these questions for the first time with another first-timer, it will be very important to discuss this initial question in depth. It is important that you each share the same level of dedication to the Thirty Shamanic Questions process. If not, it is best not to begin. Wait until you are both ready, or find someone else who shares your readiness and level of commitment. It would be very disappointing for one co-journeyer to suddenly stop the journey while the other is fully committed and engaged.

Once the commitment has been made and shared you are ready to move on to the next question. Congratulations if you have successfully made the commitment to one another. The success of the process depends on it! Now you are well on your way to moving from your ego agenda to your true soul purpose. May you have abundant blessings on your way.

> **2. How important is it to you to know the truth about yourself—"the light, the dark, no difference?" To what lengths are you willing to go to discover this truth?**

Would it not be a sign of great ignorance, my daughters, if a person were asked who he was, and could not say, and had no idea who his father or his mother was, or from what country he came? Though that is great stupidity, our own is comparably greater if we make no attempt to discover what we are, and only know that we are living in these bodies, and have a vague idea, because we have heard it and because our faith tells us so, that we possess souls.

TERESA OF AVILA, INTERIOR CASTLE

Many of us believe we need to deny our darker feelings, which often originate from painful past experiences. While a positive outlook on life can be inspiring to self and others—and prayers of affirmation are often uplifting—they are only half of the equation. If the darker side of our human nature is denied and repressed into the shadow, we may be acting out of unconscious, self-destructive patterns in our daily affairs.

The purpose of this question is to deepen your commitment to knowing yourself more fully, and to evaluate your willingess to honestly investigate both your light and shadow aspects in order to discover your wholeness. The truth is that all of your experiences—the good, the bad, the beautiful, and the ugly—have all helped to make you who you are and to bring you to where you are today.

If you examine your journey with a fearless, nonjudgmental eye, you will see that there are many things about which you can feel proud. You will discover that many of the hurt and wounded parts of you have also been highly creative adaptations that your inner child's ego created along the way in order to manage fear, confusion, anxiety, and anger. Even though you have physically grown up, the child's decisions, which informed and help create your ego's defenses, are still in operation today. These ego defenses influence your current situation in so many ways. Whether or not you see that this is true, it is the reality, and brings us back full circle to your willingness to discover the whole truth about yourself—the light, the dark, no difference. If you feel yourself balk, do not fear. Many have done so before you when encountering this second question. Take a deep breath and remember your commitment in question number one, and why you entered this process in the first place.

> **3. What is the difference between the ego and the soul? How might they have differing agendas for your life?**

The Self is not the ego! Make this distinction right now. The Self dons the ego so it can identify with society and relate to the status quo—so it can fit well enough to do its sacred work. The ego is only your outer shell, the part of you that takes all the grief! Your ego is your soul's personality, the mask created so your soul can take on human form.

JACQUELYN SMALL, *BECOMING A PRACTICAL MYSTIC*

As discussed in question number two, the ego's agenda is mainly a protective device developed in childhood, with multiple walls and angles that form a self-defense mechanism. The ego has created a shadow where we deposit all the stuff we think is unacceptable about ourselves. These are the urges, thoughts, behaviors, and feelings that do not fit into the ego's ideal self. The ego then projects a persona of positive attributes and characteristics that we want or think we should have—or that our parents or significant early influences projected onto us.

Many, if not most, people go through their entire lives living almost strictly from ego identity. How they dress, the car they drive, the people they relate to, the kind of house and neighborhood they live in, the career they pursue, the amount of money they have in the bank, their relationships with their children and other family members are all preordained by ego needs. Many people look to the outer world as a barometer of success as dictated by the ego, which often leaves them feeling empty and alone.

The search for something more is a longing for the soul to speak and for the ego to listen to the soul's call. When the soul begins to shift into focus and the ego's dominance begins to subside, it often feels like being on a roller coaster; the world is being turned upside down. While at first this may include a fair amount of discomfort, the end results are certainly well worth the ride. (At this point it may be worthwhile to read testimony from some others who have gone before you on this path, to help you remember why you have been called to this process.)

Your soul's purpose is why you are here on earth. Soul purpose incorporates the ego's true needs, but not necessarily its wants. The soul wants to assist the ego with the important task of letting go of old dysfunctional patterns that are no longer useful, and to take its rightful place as your true guiding source. In other words, your soul wants to become your pilot, leading you on your way. The difference between ego dominance and soul dominance is profound. It is as different as night and day. Do not fear. That which is essential to your true being will not be lost in the process.

Welcome to the crossroads of change. Welcome to the journey of the soul.

> 4. What is your relationship with God/Goddess now? What was your religious upbringing or spiritual belief throughout your life? Have your beliefs changed, and if so, in what way?

Were one to characterize the life of religion in the broadest and most general terms possible, one might say that it consists of the belief that there is an unseen order, and that our supreme good lies in harmoniously adjusting ourselves hereto.

WILLIAM JAMES, *VARIETIES OF RELIGIOUS EXPERIENCES*

We all are affected by our relationship to the Divine, and our religious or spiritual beliefs and practices, or lack thereof. None of us have escaped the beliefs and practices of our significant caretakers and childhood culture. Some people never question the religious and spiritual beliefs they inherited from their families, while others openly rebel. Even if your parents or caretakers were atheist, agnostic, or indifferent to religion, you were still affected by their belief system.

Regardless of the belief system you grew up with, I know this truth. After thirty-two years of working as a soul guide for others, I have never encountered anyone who did not long for a connection to something greater than himself. Many are searching to find a unique spiritual path, while others follow a more traditional religion, but all long for some sort of connection to the Divine.

By reviewing the various twists and turns in your own relationship to the Divine, you can begin to be present with your current spiritual beliefs. You can then determine how aligned you are to your core beliefs. Spiritual beliefs play a large part in the decision-making process for most people, even if it's completely unconscious. For example, in my thirties, even though I thought I had given up belief in the devil, I realized that there was a very young part of me that still believed in a scary, horned, hateful cartoon character who was out to get me!

Some religions teach that it is wrong to question beliefs that are firmly entrenched in their system. This comes from a place of fear and is a construct of the ego. A deep spiritual and/or religious connection to the Divine occurs only through facing the more difficult spiritual questions and connecting with an inner resonating voice of assurance. In order to make lasting changes you must know what you believe and why. Be prepared to question these beliefs before you can authentically move forward to self-discovery.

5. What does humility mean to you? Discuss the difference between humility and humiliation.

> *. . . during the descent we also lose the way others see us.*
> *This is not always a bad thing in the long run, but it is*
> *humiliating and painful. The mask that we present to*
> *the world slips off and the face behind it becomes visible,*
> *with its expression of terror, greed, despair, dishonesty—*
> *whatever is usually kept in the cellar. The moment of*
> *surrendering the old image—of life, of the self—is most*
> *painful. At such a time we know that we must strike out*
> *on our own, but in our new solitude and shame sometimes*
> *we go under, for awhile, or forever. Nonetheless, the*
> *stripping away of the mask that links us to all that we are*
> *known to be and do is a necessary part of the descent, one*
> *that eventually allows a fresh start.*
>
> JOHN TARRANT, *THE LIGHT INSIDE THE DARK*

Although these two words look and sound similar, they are quite different in meaning. It is important to look back at the times you have felt humiliation in your life and examine your response to these painful situations.

Humiliation can actually be the first step toward acquiring humility. Humility is a state of grace that allows us to love and accept our human selves, as well as our more divine nature. When we truly accept our humanity we can more honestly access our strengths and weaknesses. These qualities can provide us with valuable information and support for personal growth. If we hold onto that humiliation and stay locked in shame, we will be unable to take a true inventory of ourselves.

An attitude of humility opens the door to asking for help from a greater power and from those around us. It reminds us that we are not supposed to do it all alone. The root word of both humility and humiliation is *humilis,* or low, which derived from the Latin word *humus,* or earth. Humility is a form of grounding and helps us to embody our wholeness.

> 6. Write out an in-depth description of what you would like your greater power and spiritual source to be. Be as free and open as you possibly can imagine, and don't limit your vision of what the Divine should be like.

If there is a fear of failing, the only safety consists in deliberately jumping.

CARL JUNG

What is keeping you from having a more intimate relationship with a greater or higher power? Perhaps as an adult you never developed your own spiritual beliefs and established an authentic connection to the spirit of the universe. With this question you are being offered the freedom to choose your heart's desire so that you can develop the trust you need to transform your life. Think out of the box. Be as creative and expanded as you can allow yourself to be at this time.

You might make a list of all the most positive, loving, and supportive qualities you can imagine, and assign these to your greater power. Some people may feel it is wrong to create God, so to speak, but that is exactly what each of us did in our own minds as children. By using the imagination of your higher mind you are more likely to come up with a divine presence you can be close to and trust to guide you on your path.

> 7. If you are willing to directly connect with the divine source of your deepest understanding, then write out a prayer of surrender. Ask your divine connection to guide your life from this moment forth, one day at a time.

We were now at Step Three. Many of us said to our Maker, as we understood it: Higher Power I offer myself to Thee—to build with me and to do with me as Thou wilt. Relieve me of the bondage of self, that I may better do Thy will. Take away my difficulties, that victory over them may bear witness to those I would help of Thy Power, Thy Love and Thy Way of life. May I do Thy will always!

THE BIG BOOK OF ALCOHOLICS ANONYMOUS

This prayer forms the foundation for the Thirty Shamanic Questions process. When you surrender your ego's agenda to your greater power and humbly turn toward your soul's purpose, there is an opening. Light begins to pour into your life from unseen sources to guide your steps. It is here that the soul begins to descend deeper into the body; inner peace may be felt for the first time on this journey. As you continue to surrender into relationship with your divine source you will become stronger with each passing day. Suddenly you will realize that you are never truly alone on your path.

> 8. Make a list of all the things you really like about yourself at this moment, and all the things you really dislike about yourself at this moment. Answer this question: Am I really willing to change the things I can change and accept the things I cannot change?

Rain on dry land is an extraordinary thing, is it not? It washes the leaves clean, the earth is refreshed. And

I think we all ought to wash our minds completely
clean, as the trees are washed by the rain, because they
are so heavily laden with the dust of many centuries,
the dust of what we call knowledge, experience. If you
and I would cleanse the mind every day, free it of
yesterday's reminiscences; each one of us would then have
a fresh mind, a mind capable of dealing with the many
problems of existence.

J. KRISHNAMURTI, *THINK ON THESE THINGS*

By being willing to know your self more fully through allowing your greater power to guide your soul, the ego begins to find its rightful place in your life. The ego finds its place in service to the soul's purpose.

With this question the ego is encouraged to survey and take an honest inventory of what it truly likes and dislikes about itself. There are some things that cannot be changed, and these the ego must humbly accept. There are other things the ego must accept responsibility for changing.

> 9. List the reasons why, in the past, you have not changed the things you dislike about yourself. Discuss feelings of powerlessness and unmanageability. Give examples.

Grant me the serenity to accept the things I cannot change,
The courage to change the things I can,
And the wisdom to know the difference.

THE SERENITY PRAYER

It may seem like a contradiction, but sometimes we must surrender to win. I first heard this when I was twenty-nine years old. I had just entered Alcoholics Anonymous and my first sponsor told me that in order to get sober I had to admit I was powerless over my drinking and my life was unmanageable. I remember anger and resistance rising up within me. I felt myself bristle as I protested. Yet, upon honest reflection, I had to admit that I had repeatedly tried to stop drinking, only to fail time and time again. I just could not understand it. All my life I had been accused of being stubborn and having a strong will. Why couldn't I use my will to quit drinking?

I did not understand it at that moment, but it was very important for me to become less reliant on my ego's self-will and more reliant on something greater than my little self. Shortly after I admitted my defeat by alcohol, accepting that my best efforts were not working, I was released from my obsessive/compulsive desire to drink, one day at a time. I have been sober for the past twenty-three years. By turning matters over to my greater power, I have been able to transform countless self-defeating behaviors and attitudes.

Being in control is highly overrated!

10. Who are the people who have hurt you most in your life (living or dead), and how do you feel about them today?

People are often unreasonable, illogical, and self-centered; forgive them anyway. If you are kind, people may accuse you of selfish, ulterior motives; be kind anyway. If you are successful you will win some false friends and true enemies; succeed anyway. If you are honest and frank, people may cheat you; be honest and frank anyway. What you spend years building, someone could destroy overnight; build anyway. If you find serenity and happiness, they may be jealous; be happy anyway. The good you do today, people will often forget tomorrow; do good anyway. Give the world the best you have, and it may never be enough; give the world the best you've got anyway. You see, in the final analysis, it

is between you and God; it was never between you and
them anyway.

MOTHER TERESA

If you are a human being you have been hurt.

Many of our deepest wounds happened in early childhood when our defenses were virtually nonexistent. We depended on others not just for love, but for our very survival. Often it was those we loved and depended upon who hurt us most in our young lives. Parents and other significant players are often unconscious of the wounds they inflict upon the psyches of young children.

In shamanic terms we refer to this as "soul loss." Part of the psyche becomes repressed, neglected, or disassociated, and therefore unavailable. When we can tell the truth about who has hurt us the most and honestly state how we feel about these individuals today, whether living or dead, the secrets that have kept us trapped begin to release their power over us.

The truth shall set us free.

> 11. How are you different from those people who wounded you? What characteristics and behavior do you share with them? How are they mirrors for your soul's journey?

A Native American grandfather was talking to his
grandson about how he felt.

He said, "I feel as if I have two wolves fighting in my
heart. One wolf is the vengeful, angry, violent one. The
other wolf is the loving, compassionate one."

The grandson asked him, "Which wolf will win the fight
in your heart?"

The grandfather answered, "The one I feed."

It can be very disconcerting to suddenly realize you have taken on some of the characteristics of those who have hurt you.

Children often inherit their parents' unhealed behaviors, addictions, and attitudes. Adults closely connected to a spouse, partner, boss, religious leader, or teacher may be influenced by the negative character traits of the other. Becoming identified with a perpetrator can give us the illusion of being in control and safe. In order to change we must be able to identify the undesirable attributes we have acquired along the way.

By recognizing that you have some of the same undesirable characteristics as those who have hurt you, you can begin to understand how they, too, may have taken on negativity from others. This opens the door for the heart to begin experiencing forgiveness.

We also need to give ourselves credit when we have not taken on negativity from others. For example, perhaps your parents were abusive but you refuse to be abusive to your children. In choosing a more positive path, you are doing a service to your self and creating a more positive model for your children.

12. Why is it important to stop seeing yourself as a victim and forgive the past? Take time now to do a prayer of forgiveness, including a ritual of writing down who, or what, you wish to forgive. Then burn the paper, scattering the ashes to the wind.

The strength to look clearly at your past and take back aspects of yourself that you've given away lies within you. All you have to do is close your eyes, go within, and ask. The power you need is there, but it will only come out when your desire to change your life is stronger than your desire to stay the same.

NEALE DONALD WALSCH,
CONVERSATIONS WITH GOD

Certainly children are victims when abused by others. Adults also may fall prey to perpetrators and feel victimized. However, victimization is a trap that keeps us stuck in patterns of the past. We can forgive the past by expressing our thoughts and feelings openly and honestly. The stuck patterns of victimization can then be released.

By forgiving the past you are not forgiving the act itself, but you are releasing yourself from the influence the negative energy surrounding the act has imposed upon your soul. Ritual is one of the most powerful spiritual tools we possess for transforming our suffering and releasing negativity. It can turn hurt and anger into true understanding and forgiveness, which translates into an act of power.

As a spiritual being you have the ability to release the physical trauma of the past and forgive those who have harmed you, thereby removing their power over you. No matter what has happened to you there is not one single blemish on your precious spirit.

13. How have you been dishonest with yourself and others?

What supports character, in turn, is integrity. Integrity is the inner sense of wholeness and strength that arises out of our honesty with ourselves; it is the ability to make the right connections and proper sacrifices, to find a life that is both moral and spontaneous. Character and integrity develop over time. They recognize the soul's pleasure in common life and also the equanimity that comes from a link with the source of things. This is why the actions of a person of character have weight. The Buddhist name for such a person is the Bodhisattva, one dedicated to inner knowledge for the effects it can bring about in healing the world.

JOHN TARRANT, *THE LIGHT INSIDE THE DARK*

Although this question may feel offensive to your ego's idealistic image of itself, it is important to take a closer look at the level of emotional self-honesty in your life and relationships.

In my early thirties I did some serious soul searching. I was able to see the truth beyond the image my ego held of itself. One example: I was still a smoker at the time. I was lying to myself daily about the ill effects smoking was having on my health. I did not want to face many things that were not working in my life. Suddenly a veil was lifted and I could no longer be in denial. It became clear that if I was not truly self-reflective, then I could not live fully in my truth. I was lying to myself and everyone around me.

This was very humbling. At first I felt ashamed, embarrassed, guilty, and confused. In becoming honest with myself I was beginning to take the necessary steps to face what was not working in my life. I started taking actions that would restore my soul to a path of integrity. Telling the truth can be liberating.

As my adopted Seneca Wolf Clan Grandmother Twylah Nitsch said to me, "The truth is the truth whether you say it or not."

14. What has been the payoff or protection for playing small and being less than who you really are?

It costs so much to be a full human being that there are very few who have the enlightment, or the courage to pay the price. . . . One has to abandon altogether the search for security, and reach out to the risk of living with both arms. One has to embrace the world like a lover. One has to accept pain as a condition of existence. One has to count doubt and darkness as the cost of knowing. One needs a will stubborn in conflict, but opt always to total acceptance of every consequence of living and dying.

MORRIS L. WEST, *THE SHOES OF THE FISHERMAN*

It is difficult to believe there is a payoff for being less than who we really are, but why else would we hold ourselves back?

One of the payoffs is a false sense of safety and security. It feels risky to be ourselves in the world. Each of us has a unique place and purpose on the planet. Fulfilling that purpose is not about trying to fit in, or having others like or approve of us. I found that as I stopped worrying about what others thought about me, I stopped judging myself. I began to realize that others did not judge me, but admired me. It was at this point that people started attending my workshops to learn how to really be themselves.

If you carry psychic wounds from your childhood from being seen but not accepted, you may still be in hiding. The only way to heal those wounds is to lovingly bring them into the light of day. Living a life where you are small, hidden, invisible, and less than who you really are may have been the right thing to do as a child, but no longer serves you as an adult. Each of us has a gift to offer to the world. It is our part to play in the human drama. If we never open up enough to discover and deliver our gifts to the world, we remain strangers upon this planet.

Being big and bold allows you to have a real effect on others and requires that you take responsibility for your actions. You will make a bigger splash when you dive into the pool of humanity.

15. Are you willing to forgive yourself and make amends when the time is right? If so, take time now to write a simple prayer of forgiveness for yourself. Write down what you wish to be forgiven for, and burn the paper, scattering the ashes to the wind.

I offer you this prayer for all the difficult relationships in our lives: God, grant me the serenity to accept the people I cannot change, the courage to change the person I can, and the wisdom to know, that person is me.

MARY MANIN MORRISSEY

Question number fifteen offers an opportunity to perform another powerful ritual to help release the guilt, fear, and shame of past misdeeds.

It is essential to forgive yourself. Instead of spiraling down the rabbit hole of self-loathing and judgment, it is better to accept that many of your past decisions and subsequent behavior originated from a fear-based ego response. Humbly assume responsibility for your wrong actions. Become willing to make amends when the timing is right. This takes courage, but it is one of the things you can change.

Write your prayer from the perspective of your soul. Speak lovingly to your misguided ego and give the past to the fire, the water, the earth, and the wind.

16. Ask yourself if you are willing to let go and let God/ Goddess direct your life as you move from ego wounds to soul purpose. This requires going within and listening to your greater power. Sit for at least fifteen minutes listening to your inner guidance. Then journal what you have heard.

The more faithfully you listen to the voice within you, the better you will hear what is sounding outside. And only he who listens can speak. Is this the starting point of the road toward the union of your two dreams—to be allowed in clarity of mind to mirror life and in purity of heart to mold it?

DAG HAMMARSKJOLD

Going within: Close your eyes, take a deep breath, and go within the silence of your own being.

See if you can shut out the outer world—even if for just ten or fifteen minutes. As your breath deepens, send a healing breath to your heart and allow it to open. Imagine that you are sitting comfortably in your heart waiting for your greater power to guide you on your path. The guidance may come into your awareness in a variety of ways; each person is different. There is no right or wrong way to receive a message from your divine source. It may come as words, colors, images, an intuitive thought, or just a quiet, inner knowing. After a few minutes, take out your journal and freely describe any sensations, thoughts, or messages you have received.

Practicing this process on a regular basis will bring surprising results over time.

> 17. Going within and listening with your heart, ask if there is anyone to whom you need to make amends in your life. If so, then make a list and write out why you need to make amends to each person.

You must embrace your past if you want to change your present. If you want to manifest your desires you must be accountable for everything that takes place in your world.

DEBBIE FORD,
THE DARK SIDE OF THE LIGHT CHASERS

Some people have been so lost in victimization that it is difficult for them to believe they have hurt others. They may not see a need to make amends to anyone else. Certainly most of us could be listed on our own amends list because of the many self-defeating behaviors we have inflicted upon ourselves or allowed others to inflict upon us. Others may feel so guilty and overwhelmed with the task of listing those they feel they have harmed that they do not know where to begin.

I have found the best way to create an amends list is to once again go within. Close your eyes, breathe deeply into your heart while remaining open, and silently send your prayers or questions out into the universe. Allow each person or scene to come naturally into consciousness.

Try not to judge or edit; just pay attention to what shows up. Trust the process. You might have your journal close by and from time to time, open your eyes and put that person's name down on your list. Take some time to journal more fully about what necessitates the amends you intend to make.

Willingness is the key to working this question, even if at first you find yourself justifying your behavior.

> 18. After discussing question number seventeen with your co-journeyer, determine if you need to send amends letters, make amends phone calls, and/or do a ritual for each person on your list. Make the amends simple, clear, clean, and honest. Don't do a lot of explaining or be too hard on yourself. Saying " I am sorry for . . ." is enough. (If you have not completed your list of amends, continue to do so and be finished by the time you finish the thirty questions.)

You are in partnership with God. We share an eternal covenant. My promise to you is to always give you what you ask. Your promise is to ask; to understand the process of the asking and the answering.

NEALE DONALD WALSCH,
CONVERSATIONS WITH GOD

It is often helpful to discuss with your co-journeyer what amends you feel called to make, and the nature of the amends.

Sometimes it is best to make direct contact via a face-to-face visit or a phone call. At other times that may not be appropriate, and a letter will suffice. It may be that you have lost contact with someone to whom you feel you need to make amends. The person may even be deceased. You can still make amends by writing a letter to the person and doing a ritual. Share it aloud with your co-journeyer. Offer your amends to the fire, and ask spirit, or source, to send it to that person, wherever he or she is.

In some situations a direct amends would do more harm than good. If you sincerely believe that to be the case, then it is best to use a ritual. In your ritual, state that when a future time is right you are willing to make a more direct amends. Make your amends clear and clean. Do not deny, rationalize, overly explain, or blame yourself too much. Be direct by saying, "I want to make amends for my behavior." Then state what it is you are making amends for in simple, straightforward terms. Try to let go of your attachment and expectation to outcome, whether favorable or unfavorable. The process will be freeing regardless of whether or not your amends and apologies are accepted. Those you have harmed deserve your amends, and so do you.

You may continue to work on your amends throughout this thirty-questions process. It may take some time to feel you have satisfactorily completed this part of the journey.

> ### 19. Do you realize the amends you make are really for yourself?

> *To accept shadow means . . . accepting the inherent ambiguities in life. We need to honor shadow, make it a part of us, not banish it, or heal it, or be dominated by it. An important result of shadow work, perhaps the most important, is the growing development of compassion, the opening of one's heart, the real and actual acceptance and love of others specifically for that piece of humanity's imperfection, which they carry. In what we don't accept about ourselves and others—what we individually or collectively deny, exile, or project—there lies the possibility to discover our fuller humanity.*
>
> JEREMIAH ABRAMS, *THE SHADOW IN AMERICA*

Carrying around guilt, resentment, shame, and anger hurts primarily you. When we find the courage to own our part, to acknowledge the actions that we do not feel good about, we are letting go of the ego's need to feel right and to protect us. Letting go of perfectionism and self-righteousness is vital to becoming whole. We are often pleasantly surprised when others respond by making amends back to us as well.

Be that the case or not, unburdening yourself through the process is essential to discovering a new freedom and moving forward.

> 20. Can you set others free to feel and do whatever they need? Can you trust that they have a greater power with a divine plan for their life? Discuss any codependent thoughts or feelings around this subject.

It may help you to realize that moving from the tribal mindset into individual power is inevitable. Most of us will arrive at some point in our lives when the world with which we are most familiar no longer works for us. For some people it happens more than once. We are meant to outgrow ourselves; indeed, we can no more avoid this development than we can stop the aging process. The only question is how gracefully—and healthily—we will handle the transition.

CAROLINE MYSS, PH.D.,
WHY PEOPLE DON'T HEAL AND HOW THEY CAN

Addiction comes in many forms.

Codependency is a debilitating, addictive process. From the outside it may look like being a loving, caring person, but excessive caretaking can descend into martyrdom. Most of us suffer from a certain degree of codependent behavior. One of the main symptoms is the belief that you know what is best for another; that it is your responsibility to fix, control, heal, or cure someone else. You are unconsciously projecting your process onto others "for their own good," or so you believe.

Those you care for may take advantage of the situation and allow you to enable them. They may rebel against you and become angry, defiant, and resistant to the changes you think they should be making. In either case, the relationship has become a reactive one, rather than being a mature exchange of ideas and feelings.

The answer to codependency recovery is to begin to redirect all of the energy you have been expending on changing others and focus it on yourself.

When I worked as an addiction counselor in treatment centers, I often found it much more difficult to teach codependent family members how to take care of themselves than it was to work with the patient suffering from alcoholism or drug dependency. When we love others it is difficult to believe we cannot control and fix them.

There is one who can do the job for us. If we trust that others have access to their own greater power, we will have no need to try and control them. It is enough to heal ourselves and hold the loving space for others to find their own answers.

Jacquelyn Small, my teacher and friend, once said, "Codependency is an honest mistake. It is the shadow side of love."

21. What does it mean to say, "I am responsible for only one person and that is me"?

Each of us must reinterpret his family experience from an evolutionary point of view, from a spiritual point of view, and discover who he really is. Once we do that, our control drama falls away and our real lives take off.

JAMES REDFIELD, *THE CELESTINE PROPHECY*

It is very healing to know we are really responsible for only ourselves.

Most of us have responsibilities to others. All parents know, or should know, that they are responsible for the well-being of their children. In all our relationships we make agreements and commitments that we are responsible for upholding. If we could not rely on each other's word, our relationships would be in constant chaos and would fall apart. This question addresses the problem of assuming responsibility for the actions of the adults in our lives over whom we have no control.

This question also leads us to accept that we are the only ones we can change. We do not know what God/Goddess's plan is for another. It is enough to look for our greater power's will for our own lives. Our job is to find the strength, one day at a time, to walk our talk and live a life of substance.

22. Do you believe that if you do what is right for you it will also be right for everyone else around you? Discuss any feelings of selfishness.

"Let me explain," Father Sanchez said. "When you have acquired enough energy, you are ready to consciously engage evolution, to start it flowing, to produce the coincidences that will lead you forward. You engage your evolution in a very specific way. First, as I said, you build sufficient energy, then you remember your basic life question—the one your parents gave you—because this question provides the overall context for your evolution. Next you center yourself on your path by discovering the immediate, smaller questions that currently confront you in life. These questions always pertain to your large question and define where you currently are in your lifelong quest.

Once you become conscious of the questions active in that moment, you always get some kind of intuitive direction of what to do, or where to go. You get a hunch about the next step. Always. The only time this will not

*occur is when you have the wrong question in mind. You
see, the problem in life isn't in receiving answers. The
problem is in identifying your current questions. Once you
get the questions right, the answers always come.*

JAMES REDFIELD, *THE CELESTINE PROPHECY*

We often try to do what is right for too many people. We try to please
everyone, only to find ourselves depleted and spread in too many directions. When this happens we are not being true to ourselves, and we
usually end up disappointing someone along the way. Taking the time,
space, and resources to care for your own well-being may feel selfish
at first. Self-care works like the instructions for the oxygen mask that
drops down over your seat in airplanes: "Please put on your own mask
first before assisting others."

It may feel wrong at first to do what is right for yourself, but ask
yourself these questions: "Would I want someone else to be false to herself in order to make me feel better? Do I truly believe I love myself or
others when I live a lie?"

Here is the truth. If you are not taking good care of yourself, then
you are most likely not doing a great job taking care of others.

> 23. Can you really be present for anyone or anything else if
> you are not present for yourself? Discuss.

*Life is a series of changes, yet many of us cling to familiar
people and things, disregarding our inner desire to grow as
individuals and in our relationships. Openness to change
can be risky—it can even lead to breakups—but without
it, a relationship will lose its vibrancy.*

BRENDA SCHAEFFER, *IS IT LOVE OR IS IT ADDICTION?*

Questions twenty through twenty-three are designed to keep the focus
on you. They ask you to "show up" in the present tense.

I truly believe most people live out-of-body and are longing for "near life" experiences. By working this process you begin to heal the past and come more fully into the present. Focusing healing energy into your life journey allows you to become available—in a good way—to those you love. You are able to offer your special gifts to the world around you.

Some people have fooled themselves into believing they are showing up for others, when really they are caught in codependent, self-sacrificing behaviors. If we are truly honest with ourselves we will realize that no matter how much we give to others, if we are not fully present for ourselves, then those around us are not seeing the best of what we have to offer. This means being honestly in touch with our thoughts and feelings on a daily basis.

24. **What does it mean to live in truth and to trust love, and why is this the only real answer to healing codependency?**

> *We may have difficulty seeing the game of cause and effect taking place because of the temporal space between the choice and when the consequence occurs. But the moment we made a choice, we created the consequence, too. Don't kid yourself. Those chickens are coming home to roost. It's simple but not easy to say the hard stuff in life. Just open your mouth and, without doing any more damage, tell the truth.*
>
> *Choosing to take responsibility for ourselves and for the consequences our choices create looks like hard work, but it really sets us free.*
>
> MELODY BEATTIE, *CHOICES: TAKING CONTROL OF YOUR LIFE AND MAKING IT MATTER*

To live in truth and trust love is an act of faith. It is a commitment to follow the path of the heart or soul rather than fear-based, ego programs of worry and control. As long as we are living outside of ourselves, trying to manage that which is not really ours to control, we are spinning our wheels in a codependent quagmire. The minute we stop trying to manipulate the world around us we are sending a message to the universe. We are making the choice to trust that something greater than ourselves is in charge.

I like to think that this "force" is the spirit of love. When we are being true to the essential self and following love's way we are no longer caught in the darkness of worry, anxiety, and control.

> 25. Go within and ask your higher self this question: "What would it look and feel like to be living my absolute truth in the world as co-creator with my divine source?" Listen and do not hold back in your journaling on this very important question.

> *My own life has been a magnificent treasure hunt, a sacred journey of alchemical healing, although I wasn't aware of its greater purpose during the earlier stages of the trip. I've moved from clue to clue, searching my experience for glints of brilliance, tinges of magic, the wonders of impossibility. Each clue has been a treasure in its own right, with special intrinsic value, and each has helped me to establish my direction.*
>
> NICKI SCULLY, *ALCHEMICAL HEALING*

Looking within to discover who we really are may not be new to some of us. Yet we all have room to grow.

Life travels in a spiral, not a straight line. As we cycle and recycle through our past, we can see what is of use to us and we can discard the rest. As we die to the old there is an in-between place that may feel like a void. Do not rush to fill it too quickly. This is a time of gestation for what is to come.

The ego may panic and try to recreate itself. The soul has the power to calm the ego's insecurities by beginning to envision the self that is yet to come. As we become more spiritually mature and replace ego's control with soul's bigger picture, we begin to get a glimpse of our future self.

Write in your journal about this future self. Use the power of your wonderful imagination. Dream big and become the cocreator of who you truly are.

> 26. Take time to reflect on how far you have come with these questions. Take an honest inventory of what needs continued work. In other words, what's next?

Our deepest fear is not that we are inadequate. Our deepest fear is that we are powerful beyond measure. It is our light, not our darkness, that most frightens us. We ask ourselves, Who am I to be brilliant, gorgeous, talented, fabulous? Actually who are you not to be? You are a child of God. Your playing small doesn't serve the world. There's nothing enlightened about shrinking so that other people won't feel insecure around you. You were born to manifest the glory of God that is within you. It's not just in some of us; it's in everyone. And as we let our own light shine, we unconsciously give other people the permission to do the same. As we're liberated from our own fear, our presence automatically liberates others.

MARIANNE WILLIAMSON, *A RETURN TO LOVE*

At this point it is important to reflect on the progress you have made thus far. Notice how different you feel from when you first began the process.

At the same time it is also important to realize that life is indeed a journey, not a destination. If you have elected to be on a path of direct experience, the path of the heart, you are going to continue to grow spiritually. To continue to grow spiritually means to keep learning more and more about yourself. It means releasing the obstacles along the way that block you from a closer connection to sacred source.

This essentially means learning how to change the things you can and surrendering the rest to your greater power. We do this over and over again, hopefully with more consciousness and grace, dignity and love each time around.

The question, "What's next?" implies acceptance of your humanity. It implies a willingness to continue the ever-constant search for higher love and wisdom.

27. With humility, write out a prayer asking your greater power to help you live the life you were meant to live with grace. Also pray for the wisdom and willingness to work on yourself one day at a time; and to live a life of integrity, knowing that as long as we are breathing, our mission here on earth is not finished.

We do not grow absolutely, chronologically. We grow sometimes in one dimension, and not in another, unevenly. We grow partially. We are relative. We are mature in one realm, childish in another. The past, present, and future mingle and pull us backward, forward, or fix us in the present. We are made up of layers, cells, and constellations.

ANAÏS NIN

The tiny acorn contains within its shell the mighty oak tree. So it is with all things.

We are so much more than old tapes and little ego stories. Humility is accepting not only that over which we are powerless, but also the beauty, power, and gifts that are locked within our soul natures.

As we continue on the path of spiritual growth and expansion, more and more of our gifts will be revealed and manifested in the world. From the soul's perspective, as long as we are alive we have both inner and outer work to do.

> 28. Make a gratitude list. Write down everything you can think of for which you are grateful. Keep this list and add to it over time.

It is impossible to feel unhappy and grateful at the same time—so count your blessings each day and be happy. An attitude of gratitude will set your spirit free from worry.

TWYLAH NITSCH,
SENECA WOLF CLAN GRANDMOTHER

An attitude of gratitude has been a large part of my spiritual path for many years.

It is impossible to be depressed or get stuck for long when we count our blessings. No matter what issues or challenges we face, as soon as we remember the good in our lives we begin to feel our greater power's love lift our soul. An attitude of gratitude gives us the courage and strength to trust the process and to know that all things must pass.

As old things pass, new things are born.

> 29. Go within and ask, "What is my soul's purpose and who am I really?" Then journal your answer.

He spoke of very simple things—that it is right for a gull to fly, that freedom is the very nature of his being, that whatever stands against that freedom must be set aside, be it ritual or superstition or limitation in any form.

RICHARD BACH, *JONATHAN LIVINGSTON SEAGULL*

The self you were yesterday has given way to the self you have become today. The self you are today will also give way to a newer self. Much like the snake that sheds its skin, or the caterpillar that becomes a butterfly, you will continue to evolve over time.

Take time to listen to the newly emerged self as it shares a deeper connection to your soul's purpose. Realize that you are finally becoming who you were always meant to be.

Spread your wings and take flight!

> 30. Reach out to another who is still struggling to remember who he is and why he is here. Offer to do the Thirty Shamanic Questions with that person. If you do not have someone in mind, write down a prayer and ask your divine source to send someone to you who needs your love and support. Burn the paper and scatter the ashes to the winds. Trust love, and watch for synchronicities. Then journal about how the Thirty Shamanic Questions process has been for you, and share it with your co-journeyer.

This little light of mine . . . I'm going to let it shine
This little light of mine . . . I'm going to let it shine
This little light of mine . . . I'm going to let it shine
Let it shine . . . let it shine . . . let it shine.

SUNG TO STAR WOLF WHEN SHE WAS
A LITTLE GIRL BY HER MAMMY CALLIE JONES

Wait . . . fly . . . but do not fly away!

Your time on earth is not finished yet. You have more lessons to learn and many learned lessons to share. In the shamanic tradition the shaman is the wounded healer, the one who has found the way to heal herself and share that gift with the community. It is your turn to share what you have learned.

We live in a time when the ego rules. Soul expression is greatly needed in our lives and on this planet. I know your life is busy and full of important things to do and be. Isn't everyone's?

If these Thirty Shamanic Questions have made a difference in your life, then say a prayer and ask the divine source to send someone your way who is also ready to remember who he really is. Pass it on to at least one person who is still struggling to die and be reborn to his or her soul purpose.

Be the bright shining light you came to be!

A NOTE FROM KATHY MORRISON

It has been several years now since these Thirty Shamanic Questions were lovingly created as yet another tool to pull me out of a lifelong depression. This depression was consuming me and keeping me in a prison of my own making—serving what seemed to be a life sentence. I'd been in recovery from addiction to alcohol and drugs for approximately ten years. However, the addiction that was currently sucking me of my life-force energy was codependency. Codependency is sometimes referred to as a "soul sickness," and is the "root of all addictions."

It became apparent that I had been putting small bandages on huge wounds for a very long time. I had been trying to put me back together before taking me completely apart. I was afraid to change and afraid of what would happen if I didn't change. I longed for something else because I was sick and tired of being sick and tired. Yet I was depleted of the energy to search.

The process of the Thirty Shamanic Questions has helped me meet and challenge these dilemmas in my life *head on*! I had to find the strength and courage within to step back from my job, my family, and my life as it was, and commit to the process of uncovering, recovering, and discovering who I really am. I needed to quit putting other people's needs before my own and begin the process of healing from the inside out.

Ruby, my co-journeyer in this thirty-day process, wrote the following and asked me to read it on a daily basis: *My ego is protecting me against hope. My ego believes that hope will kill me. My soul wants me to hope. My soul knows that hope will keep me alive.*

I have felt hopeless most of my life. My ego has wanted me to remain stuck and not move forward. I had smothered the voice of my soul and would not let it speak. As a result of this work, I *slowly* began to trust, and now this voice keeps me going forward one day at a time. Each day I ask myself, "What does my soul want today?"

I took a medical leave of absence from my job of twenty-plus years and decided that I had to put me and my recovery first. This has not been easy; my choice has alienated me from some of the people I love the most. I am hopeful that my willingness to work this process will give others in my life the permission to do whatever they need to do to move forward in their own lives.

I am committed to helping others awaken the shaman within. I am currently co-journeying with my thirtieth person, and the process has spread to many other people. It is an honor to hold space and bear witness for people working these Thirty Shamanic Questions to uncover, recover, discover, and remember who they are and why they are here. The purpose of my soul is being revealed to me as I continue my dismantling process. I believe that my soul purpose involves sharing my experiences of living with lifelong depression. This is a great gift to me and to others.

Blessings to each of you who steps forth and utilizes these Thirty Shamanic Questions to transform your life.

KATHY MORRISON (SUN DANCE)
NORTH CAROLINA

Now that you have completed the thirty questions, read and follow the Shamanic Twelve Steps of Recovery (found as Appendix One in this book), and continue to study Melody Beattie's *Codependents' Guide to the Twelve Steps* and *The Language of Letting Go* on a daily basis.

14
An Invitation to the Shaman Within

. . . .

I n the truest shamanic traditions, in the end is the beginning and in the beginning is the end—an ever-constant spiral of change. And so, we conclude this book with an invitation. Those of us who are embracing what we refer to as the Aquarian shaman's path are growing in number. In owning shamanic consciousness in everyday life, we are called to form the Aquarian Shamanic Council.

This is an invitation to all shamanic souls, ministers, teachers, visionaries, healers, facilitators, practitioners, and counselors who share the common bond of walking the heart/mind path as a peaceful warrior and spiritual midwife for the world. It is for those who are shapeshifters and walkers between the many worlds that bridge shamanic consciousness. We reach out not only to shamans from earth wisdom teachings and ancient traditional teachings but also to those who are continuing the conscious cocreative process by receiving downloads of higher love and wisdom—insights and practices from unseen sources. We invite the shaman within all of us to awaken and stand for healing and transformation in the world.

Creator gave us this precious life to explore what it means to be a real human being while manifesting our sacred purpose on Earth— remembering we come from the cosmos and are visitors on this planet for only a short while. We believe that the main purpose for being on this planet is to learn about our soul qualities, cultivate them within ourselves, and support those of others. These are the lessons of love, forgiveness, healing, compassion, and embodying divinity, while manifesting the idea of conscious cocreation.

To embody shamanic consciousness in our everyday living is the goal of all shamans—to appreciate and learn from the elders, the children, the animals, and all of nature. We look to the heavens and great star nations, and into the soul's wisdom to access all we have learned from our journey through time and space.

We are the star children learning to grow up and how to live on Earth. The longing many of us have felt for the mother ship to come and take us home is really an ancient memory of our lineage and ancestry. It is similar to longing for lost childhood, or for those we love who have passed over. It is not really about going *back home* but rather about *growing up* and becoming adult children of the gods. To grow up is to stand tall in truth, with love. Truth equals love, and the opposite of truth is lies, which are equivalent to evil or hate. You cannot have authentic, grounded, mature love without truth. Without truth, there is no trust; and without trust, we cannot surrender into the arms of love. Standing in truth is the first step toward becoming trustworthy and an agent for higher love and wisdom.

Walking in shamanic awareness is not necessarily about knowing the correct order for calling in the four directions, the exact number of stones to be placed in the medicine wheel, or the right way to behave in a purification, or sweat lodge. It is much more about learning how to heal oneself by knowing oneself—the light, the dark, no difference—and, through this awareness, awakening the inner shaman.

The inner shaman is interested in evolving spiritual traditions forward and away from dogma, yet respectfully honoring what has been. The shaman stands on a foundation of these teachings, yet continues to dream the dream forward in an upward spiral of spiritual wisdom. The modern day shamanic counselor blends mysticism and magic with compassion. In the Aquarian Age, it is time to revolutionize and shape-shift reality into higher consciousness.

We are all unique sparks of the Creator moving within a spiraling network of kindred spirits and fellow Aquarian shamans. We need to follow the spirit of the law, rather than the letter of the law. We can certainly learn many valuable teachings from our more traditional ancestors and from history. The elders teach and support us, and they deserve to be honored with respect. Their teachings are not meant to trap, suppress, or hinder the spiral of conscious spiritual evolution.

We believe the rigid adherence to dogma is based on fear, rather than love and truth. It originates from a time when there was a risk that the teachings would die and the world would be adrift without spiritual guidelines and support. The time has come to embrace the new and to stop looking outside of ourselves for what can come only from within. We are not suggesting that there is no need for teachers or healers; we need those as well. However, the time has come for each of us to step fully into our direct connection to the One—the Source of all creation—and acknowledge our true heritage. We, too, are divine and are the adult children of the great mystery.

When we know this truth deep within our hearts, no matter where we find ourselves in this vast universe we will know at last that we are finally, truly home.

The Shamanic Twelve Steps

This next piece is an excerpt from "God Comes through the Wound," an unpublished essay written in 2005 by Shamanic Breathwork facilitator Nita Gage, MA. I am including it here because it has proven to be a useful part of the Shamanic Breathwork healing process. The development of the Shamanic Twelve Steps of Recovery grew out of workshops that Star Wolf invited me to colead with her. She and I both had a deep commitment to addiction and codependency recovery. It was clear that shamanic work, and particularly Shamanic Breathwork, facilitated recovery. We encouraged people when they left the workshops to go back to their communities and find a 12-step group as an ongoing support system. We taught the importance of 12-step work in supporting their path of shamanic healing.

However, what we found was that while many people tried 12-step programs, they were not drawn to them, and did not feel it was what they needed. They kept coming back for more shamanic experiences, and enthusiastically participating in 12-step meetings held at the workshop. Nevertheless, when they went home, they remained dissatisfied with traditional 12-step meetings. We became curious about this phenomenon and wondered if people were just resistant, or whether there was something missing from traditional 12-step recovery programs. As facilitators of Shamanic Breathwork, we were all deeply supportive of individuals participating in traditional 12-step work, so it was important to understand why so many people resisted 12-step work after experiencing Shamanic Breathwork.

In time, after listening with open hearts and minds to what people told us, we came to understand. The Shamanic Breathwork process brings clarity and empowerment, along with recognition of one's wounds. Through the breathwork process, participants found their voices, their power, and their inner wisdom. The language of the twelve steps sounded to them like a language that would push them back into powerlessness, forcing them to keep looking for strength and wisdom outside of themselves. Although traditional 12-step programs have structure and small rituals, they did not provide the depth of ritual and ceremony that shamanic work provides. As a culture we have lost the ceremonial rituals that so effectively usher people through life in indigenous cultures.

As humans, we are hardwired for experiences that involve altered states of consciousness. It is in every one of our lineages, from every culture. We have all lost our tribes, whether we are Native American, African American, Latino, or European descended from Celtic tribes. The neglect of this essential part of our nature is one of the roots of addiction and misery. Not experiencing altered states of consciousness, and lacking regular access to our spiritual nature and the feeling of oneness, we feel starved. We long for that experience and will accept any substitute for that feeling of oneness. Once we reconnect to our natural and sober ability to access altered states of consciousness, the soul longs to keep it alive.

The integration of shamanic ritual and ceremony into 12-step work brings the work alive for many people. When we re-language the 12-step process with a clearer focus on finding the power and wisdom within ourselves, the 12-step program then becomes more relevant for many people. The incorporation of ritual and ceremony further ensures connection with inner spirit and wisdom. From studying the teachings of those who have gone before me, as well as the experiences of all those with whom I have worked, I heard a calling to rewrite the twelve steps. It started with my partner, Mary Lou Masko, reworking the steps to expand their reach beyond substance addiction to encompass all types of recovery. Based on what she had written, the refinement from a shamanic perspective birthed forward. With deepest respect for 12-step teachings, and through divine guidance, I rewrote the traditional twelve steps from a shamanic perspective. The Shamanic Twelve Steps have been powerful for many people in their journey of discovery and recovery.

SHAMANIC TWELVE STEPS FOR RECOVERY AND DISCOVERY—PREAMBLE

The shamanic recovery process is grounded in the traditions and principles of all 12-step fellowships. Our intention is to create a bridge that incorporates the roots of the 12-step philosophy and expands to embrace shamanic consciousness. It describes walking the shaman's path with daily awareness of our recovery on all levels, and discovering our own unique, lived expression of shamanic recovery. To recover from addiction we must be willing to open to the great mystery that we have experienced as a void.

We have tried to fill the void with all manner of substances and obsessive behavior. Knowing we are not alone, we find that what we thought was a frightening plunge into the void transforms, through surrender, to a dance with the mystery. Obsession alchemically transforms into passion, and the dance with our inner higher power becomes a union with the Divine. By facing and embracing the darkness we sought to avoid, we come home to ourselves.

This new shamanic recovery fellowship intends to deal with the whole spectrum of addictions and compulsions, and simultaneously access the inner healer/shaman.

SHAMANIC TWELVE STEPS
FOR RECOVERY AND DISCOVERY

1. We accept that we have given our power over to our addictive, compulsive, and codependent patterns of thought and behavior. In the attempt to fill the void, rather than embrace it, our lives have become unmanageable.

2. We have come to believe that a power—greater than anything we ever knew we could access within ourselves—can open us up to love and nurture us through our path of recovery and discovery.

3. Knowing that unconditional love is the healer, we have made a decision to surrender our will and our lives to the care of an inner greater power as we understand it.

4. We have made a loving and fearless inventory of ourselves.

5. We have shared our inventory with our greater power and another person without the need for self-recrimination, knowing that in naming our shadow we will open our hearts.

6. We are entirely ready to have our greater power remove all these obstacles and give up the need to be perfect.

7. We humbly asked our greater power to help us let go of all our distractions from the Divine that manifest in negative and self-destructive patterns of thought and behavior.

8. We have made a list of all the persons we have harmed while attempting to fill the void, and are willing to make amends to them all, forgiving them and ourselves.

9. We have made direct amends to those we have harmed, except when doing so would injure them or others. When making direct amends would cause harm, we make amends through a ritual or ceremony that honors the other and ourselves.

10. We continue to take personal inventory daily, as an act of reverence, committing to our personal growth. When we are wrong, we promptly admit it and lovingly accept responsibility for our mistakes. We also admit when our boundaries have been violated and

choose to fearlessly and lovingly tell the truth to free ourselves and others from the bondage of inauthentic living.

11. We grow through prayer and meditation to improve our conscious contact with our inner greater power, praying only for knowledge of our greater power's will for us and the love and strength to carry that out in our daily lives by acting from love, rather than from fear.

12. As a result of these steps we reach a greater understanding of our true selves and are able to carry the message of recovery and discovery in our daily lives. We may then live the passionate dance of cocreating our lives through the synthesis of our will with the will and wisdom of our inner divine spirit.

ADAPTED FROM THE TEACHING OF ALCOHOLICS
ANONYMOUS, CO-DEPENDENTS ANONYMOUS,
AND HUMANS ANONYMOUS

All it takes is a small number of seekers to start a meeting. All it takes is a deep and insatiable longing for the Divine. All it takes is to finally love yourself. The shaman is waiting inside of you to take you on the journey of your lifetime. The shamanic recovery and discovery process is your map to a greater power and to the shaman within.

Shamanic Breathwork Reiki

I n chapter 3, one of the workshop testimonials was from Barb (Three Hawks Dancing), in which she described the inspired moment when she volunteered to do Reiki on me. As a result, I realized the significance of Reiki in the Shamanic Breathwork healing process and worked with Barb to include it in our practice. Here, in her own words, she describes a bit more about this very important aspect of Shamanic Breathwork.

> *Linda Star Wolf birthed the Shamanic Breathwork Reiki*
> *symbols and activations during Reiki and breathwork*
> *sessions several years ago. I have found these symbols to*
> *be very effective and to carry a more powerful vibration*
> *than using the Usui Reiki symbols alone. The attunements*
> *are done during a Shamanic Breathwork session, which*
> *creates a very powerful initiation. There are three*
> *practitioner symbols and one master symbol with four*
> *levels of training.*

The first symbol activates the deep codes of DNA, our ancient memory about our future and purpose. It helps us to step off the mass consciousness path of linear thinking and moves us into a path of inner-dimensional travel. It activates the Five Cycles of Shamanic Consciousness and elemental forces that govern our existence. It is the beginning of the awakening, of remembering our divinity and our power.

The second symbol is a symbol of clarity, truth, and wisdom. This all-seeing, all-knowing, all-sensing symbol opens us up to our physic powers. No longer do we see ourselves or anyone else in the world as victims, because we see the bigger stories at play. We see psychic blueprints, the archetypes behind every act, situation, and creation.

The third symbol is a symbol of unity consciousness and merges us with greater love and wisdom. It merges our divinity—our heavenly energies—with our human life-force energies and existence. It brings the upper and lower chakras together and creates a sacred center space so that the healing powers of the heart may become fully activated. This sacred union teaches us compassion and understanding as we begin to understand who we are and understand our journeys, so that we can find self-love and acceptance. It creates a yearning to share this understanding with others. In this place of miracles, when we experience this consciousness vibrating through us, we have the power to heal ourselves of physical, mental, and emotional illness. During this activation we may actually feel a spiritual presence drop into our physical bodies. As we are activated, we are able to activate those energies in other people around us.

The fourth symbol is the master symbol. When the energy of this symbol is connected to our power center, to our navel, it becomes a connection and grounding cord to the earth, our sacred mother. There are power points, or grids, all over the world, and they are often referred to as vortexes, or navel points. They are considered to be places of great healing power, where energies are able to unite from both above and below. When our navel energy is hooked up with this symbol we experience a reconnection to our original source. It also connects us to the archetypal starship, the one at galactic center that is an overseer for humanity and holds the energetic grids for us.

When we walk with these downloads of energetic frequencies, our DNA is activated into remembering who we are and why we are here. By the time we receive this symbol we are ready to be in direct relationship with our original sacred purpose. This symbol allows us to receive direct, and almost instant information and feedback. This inner experience becomes a burning, aching desire and a fire in the belly, which creates the holy longing and gives us the passion, energy, stamina, and courage to work with the healing powers of alchemical transformation and the inner shaman. When the kundalini life force is activated in this way, it moves the life-force energy; we are moving with integrity, constantly and consistently each day, toward our sacred life purpose in the world.

Barb (Three Hawks Dancing)
Master Shamanic Breathwork Reiki teacher
for Venus Rising University

The Shamanic Ministers Global Network

The Shamanic Ministers Global Network (SMGN) is a worldwide association of shamanic ministers ordained through the Venus Rising Institute for Shamanic Healing Arts.

These ministers, trained through Venus Rising's university ordination programs, are taught to practice embodiment of the Code of Ethics for the Aquarian Shaman. All share the same commitment: supporting those we serve—members of our congregation, family, and friends—in embracing one basic concept central to the shamanic perspective. This concept is that the cycle of death and rebirth is a constant, and that our lives become incredibly enriched when we consciously embrace this awareness, rather than fight it. While individual shamanic ministers within this global network may use different tools to awaken shamanic awareness, all begin with this core understanding.

The shamanic ministers ordained through Venus Rising have all demonstrated a desire to heal themselves of their own fear of, and resistance to, the constant evolution of the spiral path and the Five Cycles of Shamanic Consciousness, and to assist others in the healing process. By completing SHIP, one can be ordained as a shamanic minister and become part of Venus Rising's Shamanic Ministers' Global Network. (A list of shamanic ministers can be accessed by visiting the Venus Rising website: www.shamanicbreathwork.org., which you can also access if you want to know more about the Global Network and are interested in becoming a shamanic minister.)

It is the belief of all involved in the Shamanic Ministers Global Network that holding a deeply personal and creative relationship with these processes of transformation will help create a better world here on planet Earth. Through right relationships with ourselves, our students, our congregations, our friends, our families, and Earth itself, all of us can become the change we wish to see in the world. Go in peace, dear shamanic soul journeyer, and always remember to live your truth, trust love, be grateful, and reach out to others lost in the darkness. Continue to become a cocreator with your divine source as you walk each day upon your sacred soul path. Live your life with passion, meaning, and purpose. Be a spiritual seeker and never, never, never turn back! Send your love into the future. The world is waiting for you.

GLOSSARY

· ·

addiction: Any self-defeating behavior that is obsessive and compulsive, wherein one experiences a loss of power and dysfunction. Compulsively doing the same thing in the same way, over and over, and expecting different results.

Akashic Records: The records of the soul's incarnation from lifetime to lifetime, including the soul's original intent and purpose; sometimes called the *Book of Life*.

alchemy: The speculative science of transmuting base metals into gold and achieving eternal life. In this context, the process that leads us from ego agenda to soul purpose.

altar: A sacred space created for the purpose of performing rituals and meditations for personal or group healing; can be dedicated to specific deities or spiritual forces.

altered state: A non-ordinary state of consciousness that supports access to one's higher self and other worlds; can provide insight into shadow, or unowned parts of self, as well as a deeper understanding of aspects of external reality.

amends: Taking responsible action to apologize for your part in any past hurtful, dysfunctional interactions with others. This may include writing a letter, making a phone call, meeting with someone in person, or performing a forgiveness ritual on your own or with a co-journeyer as a witness.

Aquarian shaman: One who knows that the shaman is within and lives in shamanic consciousness.

archetype: The psychic blueprint that lives in the realm of the soul and makes itself known to us in times of great change. Archetypes are also symbols that exist across cultural boundaries. Examples include the trickster, inner child, lover, and crone.

aura: The energetic, colorful, and vibrant field of energy, encoded with the Akashic Records, that surrounds the human body and all living things, including animals, trees, and rocks.

Babaji: Believed by many to be an immortal avatar of infinite love and wisdom with the ability to manifest in physical form at various times throughout history. One of his primary teachings is that the breath, along with an understanding of the elements, holds the key to immortality.

ceremony: The process of creating ritual space in order to connect to the Divine, either in celebration or as an arena for transformation, such as in the Shamanic Breathwork process.

chakra: Spinning vortexes of life-force energy that weave in and around all living things. Embedded within each chakra is the energetic imprint of all experiences in life.

circular path: The construct that all life travels in a continuous circle; dominant prior to the patriarchal, linear model. The imbalanced yin path.

codependency: An inauthentic, reflected expression of self. Any relationship in which we give away our power to any person, process, or thing.

co-journeyer: The person holding sacred space while the soul journeyer undergoes Shamanic Breathwork and/or answers the thirty shamanic questions.

consciousness: That which is recognized in our everyday waking state. The spiritual warrior seeks to continually bring insight and awareness into conscious reality.

cycles of change: The alchemical map of shamanic consciousness that describes movement through five elemental pathways of death and rebirth.

death/rebirth: Symbolic sequences of shamanic experience that lead from one level of consciousness to the next.

denial: An ego-defense mechanism involving the repression of our awareness of disagreeable situations and certain personality attributes. Denial remains in place until we find enough self love to accept that which we have previously denied.

drumming: In the Shamanic Breathwork process, using a steady drumbeat to mimic the heartbeat of Mother Earth and invoke an altered state prior to, or following, a shamanic journey session.

ego: The part of a human being that has, for survival purposes, adapted to cultural norms and to a projected ideal of who we should be and how we should behave. The ego is formed in early childhood as a result of interaction with family of origin and other significant caretakers.

elements: The four neter elements—water, earth, fire, air—as well as the fifth super-nature, or supernatural, element of spirit.

Emoto, Dr. Masaru: Japanese researcher and author of *Messages from Water.* Known for his research on the ways in which human speech, thought, and emotion affect water.

going within: Taking the time each day to just breathe and silently meditate; listening to your heart.

grounding: The process of incorporating altered states, otherworldly experiences, or spiritual experiences into our physical reality.

hieroglyphics: Creative symbols and language of the soul that are invested with meaning and purpose. The written language of ancient Egyptian priests.

Higher Power: The Divine as each individual understands it: God, Goddess, Great Mystery.

higher self/greater power: The aspect of self beyond our ego consciousness that sees the larger reality of our life experiences.

Holotropic Breathwork: A form of breathwork created by Stanislav Grof. One of the first techniques to use breath, music, and art to create an altered state for healing.

Integrative Breathwork: A form of breathwork created by Jacquelyn Small. Includes many Holotropic Breathwork techniques and added the integrative aspects of 12-step recovery, with an emphasis on group process.

Jung, Carl: Famous Swiss psychoanalyst and protégé of Sigmund Freud, sometimes called the grandfather of transpersonal psychology. He coined such phrases as archetype, shadow, sacred marriage, and collective unconscious.

linear path: This fading, patriarchal model states that life travels in a straight line, and has been dominant for the last three to four thousand years. The imbalanced yang path.

mandala: A Sanskrit word made popular in Western culture by Carl Jung, who used it to describe the quality of wholeness within the psyche. A mandala is also a transformative art work consisting of symbolic archetypal images.

medicine: As referred to by Native American people or other indigenous cultures, whatever is uniquely helpful or healing to each individual; for example, essential oils, breathwork, Reiki, nature walks, or gemstones.

persona: The ego's small self as projected to the outer world, masking the shadow from others. The persona houses the ego's agenda and is often motivated by fear.

rebirthing: The original form of breathwork created by Leonard Orr, inspired by Babaji, and spread widely by Sondra Ray.

recovery: The ongoing process of transforming addictive, compulsive behavior into a healthy, conscious lifestyle.

ritual: A sacred act that invokes spiritual intent and assistance for creation, healing, and change.

sacred marriage: The blending or unification of spirit, soul, and ego into a cohesive, harmonious state of consciousness.

shadow: The repressed, unconscious, disowned part of the psyche. The shadow must be uncovered and integrated in order to reach wholeness.

shaman: In various cultures a priest, priestess, healer, or medicine man or woman is referred to as a shaman. The shaman is the "wounded healer," one who has experienced and survived many ordeals, or "deaths," and returns to the community to share acquired healing wisdom with others.

Shamanic Breathwork: A form of breathwork founded by Linda Star Wolf that synthesizes ancient shamanic practices with current breathwork modalities and relies heavily upon group process techniques.

shamanic consciousness: Having the eyes to see and the ears to hear beyond the mundane outer appearance of any situation and into higher levels of love and wisdom. A state of consciousness within which one moves continually through processes of death and rebirth.

shamanic extraction: A technique involving the dissolution and/or removal of obstacles that are held in the energetic field and block the return of soul parts. It is often necessary to do an extraction before a soul return can happen.

Shamanic Reiki: A healing technique utilizing energetic symbols and vibrations transmitted to individuals during Shamanic Breathwork. Shamanic Reiki is also used to open individuals to their own capacity for transmitting healing to others.

SHIP (Shamanic Healing Initiatory Process): A series of specific workshops designed for personal healing and as a way for individuals to discover their role in the shamanic healing community.

smudging: The ceremonial burning of sacred herbs such as sage, sweet grass, copal, and cedar to purify or cleanse the auric field; a feather is often used to fan the smoke.

soul: The vehicle for our essential self as it travels from one state of consciousness to another. The soul is the mediator between our spiritual and human self and carries qualities of both.

soul purpose: The original, encoded, spiritual imprint or mission for the present lifetime.

soul journeyer: Someone who is willing to practice Shamanic Breathwork and/or undergo the soul-searching journey of the Thirty Shamanic Questions process in order to discover self-truth and find meaning and purpose in life.

soul return: The process of reclaiming lost soul parts, which are various aspects of self that have been lost through misuse, abuse, or trauma.

spiral path: A philosophical model explaining the orbiting evolution of our lives through our soul patterns in order to learn lessons resulting in spiritual growth. An ancient symbol representing the emerging synthesis of the linear and circular paths.

spirit: The pure, essential self that lives in a unified field of consciousness beyond time and space.

spirit guides: Energetic beings that can take many forms, such as ancestors, angels, totems, or historical figures; and that appear to us either in our imagination or in external reality in order to support our path on earth.

stalking: The process of the sacred witness seeking out those aspects of consciousness that need to be transmuted to higher levels of awareness. The stalking aspect of the psyche is sometimes called "the double," or spiritual warrior; its role is to seek out undeveloped, shadowy, and ill-formed aspects of personality.

surrender: The process of letting go of attachment to outcome, resulting in a sense of inner peace and well-being. Trusting the process.

symbols: The hieroglyphs of the soul. The creative images that emerge both spontaneously and intentionally during meditation or shamanic journeys.

synchronicity: A Jungian term for the noncausal connection between two or more various phenomena. Remarkable and/or meaningful coincidence.

synthesis: The energetic blending of various aspects of healing that results in the sum being greater than the parts; for example, the synthesis represented by the term "shamanic-psychospiritual."

Thirty Shamanic Questions: Shamanic-psychospiritual journey that assists individuals in living a more soul-centered life.

totem: Invisible helpers, including angels, ancestors, and animal or spirit guides, who can appear either in our imagination or in the outer world with the purpose of teaching us about their qualities and/or transferring their characteristics to us.

transformation: Moving from one level of consciousness to another through the process of death and rebirth. Comprehensive change.

trauma: Outer events that deeply affect the psyche and leave a cellular impression of wounding that blocks the experience of wholeness. Trauma creates energetic blocks that must be broken through and released.

unconscious: Everything not known by the ego mind; 85 to 90 percent of our psyche. The purpose of the shamanic process is to make the unconscious conscious.

yang: The masculine aspect of creation, or God, that is active, phallic, and directive; associated with light, or solar principles.

yin: The feminine aspect of creation, or Goddess, that is receptive, compassionate, and nurturing; associated with the void, or lunar principles.

BIBLIOGRAPHY

Abrams, Jeremiah. *The Shadow in America*. Novato, Calif.: Nataraj Publishing, 1994.

Abrams, Jeremiah, and Connie Zweig, eds. *Meeting The Shadow—Hidden Power of The Dark Side of Human Nature*. New York: Penguin Group, 1991.

Alcoholics Anonymous, The Big Book, Fourth Edition. n.l.: Alcoholics Anonymous World Services, Inc., 2002.

Andrews, Ted. *Animal Speak: The Spiritual & Magical Powers of Creatures Great and Small*. St. Paul, Minn.: Llewellyn Worldwide, LTD., 2002.

Bach, Richard. *Jonathan Livingston Seagull*. New York: Scribner, 2006.

Beattie, Melody. *Choices: Taking Control of Your Life and Making It Matter*. New York: HarperOne, 2003.

———. *Codependent No More*. Center City, Minn.: Hazelden Publishing, 1992.

———. *Codependents' Guide to the Twelve Steps*. New York: Simon & Schuster, 1990.

———. *The Language of Letting Go*. Center City, Minn.: Hazelden Publishing, 1990.

Braden, Gregg. *The Divine Matrix: Bridging Time, Space, Miracles, and Belief*. Carlsbad, Calif.: Hay House, Inc., 2007.

Butler-Bowdon, Tom. *50 Spiritual Classics: Timeless Wisdom from 50 Great Books on Inner Discovery, Enlightenment & Purpose*. London: Nicholas Brealey Publishing, 2005.

Castaneda, Carlos. *The Teachings of Don Juan*. London: Penguin, 1970.

Churchill, Pola. *Eternal Breath: A Biography of Leonard Orr Founder of Rebirthing Breathwork*. Bloomington, Ind.: Trafford Publishing, 2007.

Dellinger, Drew. *Love Letter to the Milky Way: A Book of Poems*. n.l.: Poets for Global Justice, 2002.

Ellis, Normandi. *Awakening Osiris: The Egyptian Book of the Dead*. n.l.: Phanes Press, 1997.

Ford, Debbie. *The Dark Side of the Light Chasers: Reclaiming Your Power, Creativity, Brilliance, and Dreams*. n.l.: Riverhead Trade, 1999.

Gawain, Shakti. *Creative Visualization: Use the Power of Your Imagination to Create What You Want in Your Life*. Novato, Calif.: New World Library, 2002.

Grof, Christina, and Stanislav Grof. *The Stormy Search for the Self: A Guide to Personal Growth through Transformational Crisis*. Los Angeles: Jeremy P. Tarcher, 1992.

Grof, Stanislav. *The Adventure of Self Discovery: Dimensions of Consciousness and New Perspectives in Psychotherapy and Inner Exploration*. Albany, N.Y.: State University of New York Press, 1987.

———. *Beyond the Brain: Birth, Death and Transcendence in Psychotherapy*. Albany, N.Y.: State University of New York Press, 1985.

Grof, Stanislav, and Hal Zina Bennett. *The Holotropic Mind: Three Levels of Human Consciousness and How They Shape Our Lives*. New York: Harper Collins, 1993.

Halifax, Joan. *Shaman: The Wounded Healer*. New York: Thames and Hudson, 1982.

Harner, Michael. *The Way of the Shaman*. New York: Bantam Books, 1982.

Harper, John Jay. *Tranceformers, Shamans of the 21st Century*. Riverdale, Ga.: Reality Press, 2006.

Ingerman, Sandra. *Shamanic Journeying: A Beginner's Guide*. Boulder: Sounds True, 2006.

———. *Soul Retrieval: Mending the Fragmented Self*. San Francisco: Harper Collins, 2006.

James, William. *Varieties of Religious Experience: A Study of Human Nature*. Cornwall, United Kingdom: Exposure Publishing, 2008.

Jung, Carl G. *Modern Man in Search of a Soul*. New York: Harcourt, 1955.

Jung, Carl G., Gerhard Adler, Michael Fordham, Herbert E. Read, eds. Richard F. C. Hull, trans. *Collected Works of C. G. Jung*. London: Routledge, 1973.

Levine, Peter A., and Ann Frederick. *Waking the Tiger: Healing Trauma.* New York: Random House Inc., 1997.

Lipton, Bruce H. *The Biology of Belief: Unleashing the Power of Consciousness, Matter & Miracles.* Carlsbad, Calif.: Hay House, 2005.

Loggins, Kenny and Julia. *The Unimaginable Life: Lessons Learned on the Path of Love,* book and CD. New York: Harper Paperback, 1998.

Meadows, Kenneth. *Shamanic Experience: A Practical Guide to Psychic Powers.* Rochester, Vt.: Bear & Company, 2003.

———. *Shamanic Spirit: A Practical Guide to Personal Fulfillment.* Rochester, Vt.: Bear & Company, 2003.

Millman, Dan. *The Laws of Spirit: A Tale of Transformation.* Novato, Calif.: H. J. Kramer/New World Press, 2001.

———. *Way of the Peaceful Warrior: A Book that Changes Lives.* Novato: H. J. Kramer/New World Library, 2000.

Mindell, Arnold. *The Shaman's Body: A New Shamanism for Transforming Health, Relationships, and Community.* San Francisco: Harper Collins, 1993.

Myss, Carolyn. *Why People Don't Heal and How They Can.* New York: Three Rivers Press, 1998.

Nitsch, Twylah. *Creature Teachers: A Guide to the Spirit Animals of the Native American Tradition.* n.l.: Continuum International Publishing Group, 1997.

Nitsch, Twylah, and Jamie Sams. *Other Council Fires Were Here Before Ours: A Classic Native American Creation Story.* New York: HarperCollins, 1991.

Orr, Leonard, and Sondra Ray. *Rebirthing in the New Age.* Berkeley, Calif.: Ten Speed Press, 1983.

Redfield, James. *The Celestine Prophecy: An Adventure.* New York: Bantam Books, 1994.

Richards, M. C. *The Crossing Point: Selected Talks and Writings.* Middletown, Conn.: Wesleyan Univ. Press, 1973.

Ruiz, Miguel. *The Four Agreements: A Practical Guide to Personal Freedom.* Carlsbad, Calif.: Hay House, 1997.

Sams, Jamie. *Sacred Path Cards.* San Francisco: Harper, 1990.

Sams, Jamie, and David Carson. *Medicine Cards.* New York: St. Martin's Press, 1999.

Schaeffer, Brenda. *Is It Love or Is It Addiction?* Center City, Minn.: Hazelden Publishing, 2009.

———. *Love's Way: The Union of Body, Ego, Soul, and Spirit.* Center City, Minn.: Hazelden Publishing, 2001.

Scully, Nicki. *Alchemical Healing: A Guide to Spiritual, Physical, and Transformational Medicine.* Rochester, Vt.: Bear & Company, 2003.

———. *Power Animal Meditations: Shamanic Journeys with Your Spirit Allies.* Rochester, Vt.: Bear & Company, 2001.

Scully, Nicki, and Linda Star Wolf. *Anubis Oracle: A Journey into the Shamanic Mysteries of Egypt.* Rochester, Vt.: Bear & Company, 2008.

———. *Shamanic Mysteries of Egypt: Awakening the Healing Power of the Heart.* Rochester, Vt.: Bear & Company, 2007.

Small, Jacquelyn. *Awakening in Time: The Journey from Codependence to Co-Creation.* New York: Bantam Books, 1991.

———. *Becoming Naturally Therapeutic.* New York: Bantam Books, 1990.

———. *Becoming a Practical Mystic.* Adyar, India: The Theosophical Publishing House, 1998.

———. *Embodying Spirit: Coming Alive with Meaning and Purpose.* Center City, Minn.: Hazelden Publishing, 1994.

———. *Improving Your Bedside Manner.* n.l.: The Eupsychian Press, 2008.

———. *The Sacred Purpose of Being Human.* Deerfield Beach, Fla.: Health Communications, 2006.

———. *Transformers: The Artists of Self-Creation.* New York: Bantam Books, 1992.

Sparks, Tav. *The Wide Open Door: The Twelve Steps, Spiritual Tradition, and the New Psychology.* Santa Cruz, Calif.: Hanford Mead Publishers, 1993.

Tarrant, John. *The Light Inside the Dark: Zen, Soul, and the Spiritual Life.* New York: Harper Paperback, 1999.

Teresa of Avila. *Interior Castle.* Mineola, N.Y.: Dover Publications, 2007.

Walsch, Neale Donald. *Conversations with God: An Uncommon Dialogue.* New York: Putnam Adult, 1996.

Wesselman, Hank. *Spiritwalker: Messages from the Future.* New York: Bantam, 1995.

———. *Medicinemaker: Mystic Encounters on the Shaman's Path.* New York: Bantam, 1998.

———. *Visionseeker: Shared Wisdom from the Place of Refuge.* Carlsbad, Calif.: Hay House, 2001.

West, Morris L. *The Shoes of the Fisherman.* n.l.: Toby Press, 2003

Williamson, Marianne. *A Return to Love: Reflections on the Principles of "A Course in Miracles."* New York: HarperCollins, 1992.

Index

ABOUT THE AUTHOR

Linda Star Wolf is a gifted intuitive, shamanic teacher, and ceremonial facilitator who weaves together threads of ancient and contemporary healing methods to address current needs. She is founder of Venus Rising Institute for Shamanic Healing Arts and Creator of the Shamanic Breathwork™ Process. Star Wolf holds a Doctorate of Ministry from AIWP (Association for the Integration of the Whole Person) University and is a nationally certified Addictions Counselor. As a Shamanic Minister, spiritual midwife, and guide for souls in the transformational process, Star Wolf has an extensive background both personally and professionally in the mental health and spirituality arena, with experience ranging from addictions work and 12-step recovery, to shamanic-psycho-spiritual work. It is her soul's passion and purpose to teach and serve as a loving guide to those who are ready to embody "Shamanic Consciousness in Everyday Life." She has led powerful transformational workshops—including the Shamanic Breathwork Process to journey beyond the self—in the United States and abroad for the last twenty years and has taught thousands of participants. She lives with her beloved husband Brad Collins, and a menagerie of four-leggeds in a conscious community, Isis Cove, located in the magical blue mountains of North Carolina. Star Wolf's main teaching is that we must become the change we wish to see in the world and we can heal the world by transforming ourselves.

ALSO BY LINDA STAR WOLF

The Anubis Oracle: A Journey into the Shamanic Mysteries of Egypt, 2008 (cowritten with Nicki Scully)

Shamanic Egyptian Astrology, 2010 (cowritten with Ruby Falconer)

Shamanic Mysteries of Egypt: Awakening the Healing Power of the Heart, 2007 (cowritten with Nicki Scully)

How to Use This CD

. . . .

This CD comes with two separate sessions. The first is entitled *The Spiral Journey* and is the one you will use when undergoing your actual breathwork journey. The second session, entitled *Spiral Breath,* consists of a guided meditation that you may want to do after your breathwork journey to further integrate your experience.

Note: The musical journey and guided meditation are designed to enable individuals to enter into the Shamanic Breathwork experience and other non-ordinary states of consciousness. They are not intended for easy listening, or to be used while driving or handling machinery.

To undergo the breathwork journey with the *The Spiral Journey* track:

- Find a quiet space inside where there are no distractions.
- *The Spiral Journey* should be ready to play and you should have a journal handy so you can write down your experience afterward.
- Call upon any spirit guides and helpers you may have, and offer up a sincere invocation that they assist you on the healing journey you are about to undertake.
- Smudge the area and yourself. Light a candle and lower the lights.
- If you have a drum, you may want to include some soft drumming at the outset of your experience.
- Lie down in a comfortable place on a mat with a blanket and pillow if you need them.
- Put on an eyemask if the room is too bright.
- Take some steady, deep breaths to relax, and then, beginning with your toes and moving upward along your body, focus on the different parts of your body, relaxing them in turn as you continue your deep breathing.

> Turn on the music and begin to breathe in and out to it. Breathe until you are surprised, allowing whatever comes up to occur and pass through you through your inhalations and exhalations. Do not suppress any emotions that come up—remember, this is a cathartic experience. If you need to move your body in response to what is coming up for you, then do so.

> The music will guide you through the seven chakras. Toward the end of your journey, you will naturally begin to wind down. As the session ends, there will be a song of return that will ground you in your body and your heart chakra.

> Slowly begin to return to your outer reality and when you are comfortable doing so, open your eyes and sit up slowly.

> At this point it is suggested that you further integrate your journey by writing in your journal, creating a piece of artwork, drinking water or eating a meal, listening to relaxing music, or taking a walk or a bath.

> Stay hydrated and well rested as you return to your regular schedule and your outer world.

> Continue to record in your journal any developments in your outer world that may reflect the inner healing work you have done.

The Spiral Journey and *Spiral Breath* tracks included on the CD that accompanies this book are selections from the two-CD set entitled *The Spiral* produced by Soulfood and Venus Rising, © 2000, and are used with the kind permission of SoulFood Music (www.soulfoodmusic.com).

The selections included are as follows:

The Spiral Journey—CD I (dreamy spiritual songs with a Native American flavor): Spiraling In; Neptune—Water—Pisces; Saturn—Earth—Capricorn; Pluto—Fire—Aries and Scorpio and Promethian Uranus; Venus Rising—Spirit (exerpt); Jupiter—Air—Aquarian energies of Uranus as Skygod (exerpt)

The Spiral Meditation—CD II (guided meditations narrated by Star Wolf, accompanied by entrancing music and nature sounds): Spiral Breath Meditation

To order the complete *The Spiral* two-CD set contact
Venus Rising Institute for Shamanic Healing Arts
www.shamanicbreathwork.org
or SoulFood Music
www.soulfoodmusic.com